*Tyranny and Political Culture
in Ancient Greece*

TYRANNY AND POLITICAL CULTURE IN ANCIENT GREECE

James F. McGlew

Cornell University Press

ITHACA AND LONDON

First published 1993 by Cornell University Press.

International Standard Book Number 0-8014-2787-8
Library of Congress Catalog Card Number 93-15653
Printed in the United States of America
Librarians: Library of Congress cataloging information
appears on the last page of the book.

♾ The paper in this book meets the minimum requirements
of the American National Standard for Information Sciences—
Permanence of Paper for Printed Library Materials, ANSI Z39.48-1984.

Contents

Acknowledgments

This book has taken a long time to write, and it would have taken even longer but for a generous grant from the American Council of Learned Societies and a fellowship at the Stanford Humanities Center, which allowed me a year free from teaching. I am indebted to the encouragement and suggestions of Toni Bowers, James Hogan, Daniel Hooley, Michael Jameson, Robert Kaster, Cynthia Patterson, Kurt Raaflaub, James Redfield, David Schenker, and Peter White. Thanks also to Bernhard Kendler, Teresa Jesionowski, Marian Shotwell, and to Cornell University Press's readers for their prompt and helpful comments, and to Roz Macken for her acuity and patience. Only a much better book than this would be sufficient thanks for the persistent efforts of M. B. Wallace to lend it respectability. Thanks of a different kind are due to my parents, to whom this book is dedicated.

J. F. McGlew

Tyranny and Political Culture
in Ancient Greece

Tyranny and History

It is so difficult—at least I find it so difficult—to understand people
who speak the truth.

Miss Bartlett in E. M. Forster, A Room with a View

This book began as a treatment of the image of the tyrant in
Greek authors of the fifth century B.C. and in democratic Athens.
That image was certainly complicated. When tyrants had disap-
peared from all but the remoter areas of the Greek world, tyranny
nonetheless remained an object of general fascination and horror.
The fifth century invested the tyrant with considerable ideological
force. The advocates and enemies of democracy made various uses
of him as a negative image of citizenship, while the more radical
sophists embraced him, for yet other purposes, as a positive image
of deliberately self-interested political action.[1] The book I intended
to write was to complement treatments of the rise and fall of tyranny
in the seventh, sixth, and early fifth centuries B.C., such as those produced a generation ago by Antony Andrewes and Helmut Berve.[2] I
did not think I needed to discuss the political or social characteristics
of archaic tyranny. It was enough to show that later images of the
tyrant continued and developed the self-representations of archaic

---

1. For the various elements of these views, see chaps. 1, 2, and 6.
2. Andrewes 1956 and Berve 1967. Major studies since their time include Pleket
1969, Mossé 1969, and Spahn 1977. Among treatments of the language of tyranny
in its earliest manifestations and the self-representations of tyrants, see Labarbe 1971
and Cobet 1981.

tyrants in response to the distinctive political and intellectual environment that emerged in fifth-century Greece.

What I have finally written bears little resemblance to that project. Instead of examining the post-tyrannical ideology of tyranny, I attempt to make sense of the Greeks' experience with autocrats and their reactions to that experience. This change represents a rethinking of tyranny and its political significance. I have come to doubt whether the distinction between the "real" and the "ideological" tyrant, which was the basis of my original project and most studies of tyranny, does justice either to the interpretations and uses of tyranny in the fifth century or to its appearance and collapse in archaic Greece. These doubts require a short explanation.

Scholars have had good reasons to distinguish carefully between real tyrants, who flourished in many Greek city-states beginning in the middle of the seventh century B.C., and their classical shadows. The very interest in tyranny in the post-tyrannical period, they argue, obscures its historical reality. H. W. Pleket expresses the common opinion: "The historian of the archaic period is, as regards the present subject, less handicapped by the scarcity of sources in general . . . than by the lack of contemporary sources. In this particular case the sources we have for a study of the Greek tyrants are to a high degree—if not completely—coloured by the undeniable aversion to the tyrant in later, more democratic times."[3] The problem allows for a single, if difficult, solution. Only by sifting with minute precision through the large bulk of lore that attached to tyrants and the biased assessments of those that followed them is it possible to discover the rational basis of their support. When looking for this basis, scholars have typically constructed their interpretations of tyranny to explain the tyrant's attractiveness as a ruler. This allows for positive assessments of tyranny's achievements that can also account for its political deficiencies. In some interpretations, tyrants have appeared as military innovators[4] or entrepreneurs who parlayed their economic preeminence into a new form of

3. Pleket 1969, 19–20.
4. For the connection between the hoplite and tyranny, see Andrewes (1956, 31–32), who seems to view tyranny, once it establishes its political existence, as a solution for diverse social crises. See also Forrest 1966, 88–122. For Corinth in particular, see Drews 1972, 129–44.

political power, or they have been stripped of historical agency and rendered as opportunists who profited from the social and political crises of early archaic Greece;[5] or, again, they are represented as religious and cultural reformers.[6]

Just as they have worked to distinguish archaic tyranny from its later representations, scholars have diligently separated the political, social, and economic reality of tyranny from the tyrants' own political ideology: the religious claims that tyrants made, their conspicuous public behavior, and the oracles, images, and poetry that were crafted for them.[7] For heuristic—albeit not metahistorical—purposes like those of pre-Althusserian Marxists,[8] tyranny has been split asymmetrically into infrastructure and superstructure. Its rise and existence are explained in terms of the political, social, and economic interests of individuals and social groups, while the language with which tyranny was presented and understood is treated as logically and perhaps chronologically secondary: as if that language did nothing more than rationalize the extraordinary power of the tyrant after the fact. Tyrants, we have come to believe, might have justified their power in a number of ways; the language and images they adopted were chosen because they were believed to maximize the profitability and duration of individual

5. So Ure 1922. The less radical view that tyrants were mere consequences of economic change is adopted by Roebuck (1972, 96–127) and apparently also by Sealey (1976, 38–65), for whom "to explain why Greek tyranny first arose in the seventh century is to explain why ostentatious splendor on a new scale became possible then, and the answer must clearly be sought in the growth of prosperity under oriental influence since late in the eighth century" (58).

6. The Peisistratids have been the focus of much reexamination along these lines; see especially Kolb 1977, 99–138; Connor 1987; Ober 1989, 65–68; and Shapiro 1989.

7. Louis Gernet's germinal essay, "Mariages de tyrans" (1968, originally published in 1954), represents an important exception. Recent work by Connor (1987) calls into question the separateness of the tyrant's private interests, and doubts that the cultural program of tyrants can be adequately understood as the mere "manipulation" of their subjects. So also Veyne (1988, 84–85), who argues that "the notion of ideology is a laudable and unsuccessful attempt to guard against the legend of the idea of a disinterested knowledge, at the limits of which there would exist a natural understanding, an autonomous faculty, different from the interests of practical life" and that "it would be better to admit that no knowledge is disinterested and that truths and interests are two different terms for the same thing."

8. For a more complicated image of ideology, see especially Althusser 1971.

3

rule. Only by bracketing the public posture and claims of tyrants as fictions do scholars believe they can avoid committing the historian's worst crime: to be tricked by the subject's own discourse. Thus, like Forster's Miss Bartlett, scholars have felt they can make much more sense of tyrants when they take their words as lies.

This bifurcation of tyranny into reality and ideology, now hardly new, still dominates our understanding of archaic Greece. Its influence can be seen in the virtual absence of studies of the political aspects of tyranny, that is, attempts to understand the rise and fall of tyranny as interactions between tyrants and their subjects. Instead, the political and rhetorical character of tyranny is typically presented as the consequence—natural, necessary, and hence insignificant—of the economic and cultural dynamics of archaic Greek society; most especially, tyranny is the by-product of complex tensions within the archaic aristocracy.[9] As a result, the gap between the reality and the language of tyranny continues to grow. The very tyrants who styled themselves as uniquely superior to their fellows find themselves relocated as the temporary and dispensable tools of forces they were unable to control or even to understand. Tyranny itself has dwindled to an unconstitutional and private form of subjugation that possessed no conceptual or institutional integrity. It came to exist in moments of political crisis exploited by individuals whose political language and self-representation had little to do with their common, but hardly universal, political achievement: displacing political power from an aristocratic elite (to which the tyrants belonged) and toward citizens.

For all its familiarity and apparent cogency, this traditional approach has no place in the present study. I have attempted rather to develop a new, less restrictive interpretive framework for tyranny that is based on a reexamination of its distinctly political aspects and that focuses closely on the relationship between the discourse and the political character of tyranny. I aim to take seriously the language that tyrants spoke and the reception their subjects gave them. This tyrannical discourse supports the view that despite the eco-

9. So Berve (1967) resists any explanation of tyranny as the consequence of struggles between social and economic classes in archaic Greece. His position has been developed most recently by Stahl (1987) and Stein-Hölkeskamp (1989).

nomic, cultural, and political domination of tyrants, tyranny arose through, and was sustained by, a complex interaction between tyrants and their subjects, and that interaction defined tyranny's sources, purpose, and limits. Tyranny, from this perspective, is political in the most elementary sense: a process of complicity, not simple ambition, transformed one citizen into a ruler and his fellows into his subjects.[10] Yet if the self-representation of tyrants articulates, rather than conceals, their power, that self-representation also circumscribes and limits it. Tyrants, by claiming (and being understood) to possess an unprecedented and unique right to autocratic individual rule, implicitly defined that rule as untransferable and unrepeatable. When their subjects learned about the extraordinary powers and privileges of tyrants, they also learned that these were terminal.

The tyrant's overthrow seems then to be the logical conclusion of his own self-representation, and the complicity of his subjects contains the seed of resistance against him. Yet this resistance did not constitute an absolute rejection of tyranny. Cities participated in the self-representation of tyrants less because they were blind or indifferent to its mendacity than because they perceived its coherence and decisiveness. Likewise, when they revolted, they did so not simply to destroy their master's power but to appropriate it for themselves and to possess and wield the distinctive freedom that his power elaborated. So, just as the city's initial complicity with its tyrant established a basis for resisting him, that resistance was the basis of an enduring complicity between the polis and tyranny.

This study begins with an examination of the self-representation of the early tyrants and the attacks made on them by their enemies, both of which are pervaded by the notions of hubris, divine necessity, and, most importantly and conspicuously, justice (*dikē*). From this early dialogue there soon issued a more complex interaction between tyrants and the poleis that were quickly learning to challenge them. This interaction is most evident in the emer-

10. Tyranny qualifies therefore as power in Foucault's (1977, 26–27) precise sense: it is "exercised rather than possessed; it is not the 'privilege,' acquired or preserved, of the dominant class, but the overall effect of its strategic position—an effect that is manifested and sometimes extended by the position of those who are dominated."

gence of a rich series of political images of autocratic power—the founder, lawgiver, liberator, and tyrannicide—which answer and criticize the tyrant's distinctive power and offer a real or symbolic replacement for it. All, like the tyrant's own self-representation, are images of power and resistance. In them is embedded the story of the life and death of single individuals, whose achievements were decisive for their city's political history; indeed these images function as narrative symbols of the distinctive (albeit unwitting) political contribution of tyranny: the sovereign polis. Tyrants were not unaware of the significance of these new, alternative images of autocratic power. And as their claims to be reformers of injustice became gradually less persuasive, tyrants joined their enemies at a costume ball of autocratic images: disguising themselves as founders or even as liberators, they sought to prolong their power by pretending to be anything but what they were.

The material that I employ to support my view of tyranny and its reception is not new: I draw from the Greeks' rich memories of their tyrants and their inventions and legends of lawgivers, founders, and the like. But the perspective I employ to make sense of this material is less traditional. I do not try to "decode" the Delphic oracles that variously support and castigate tyrants, the lore that grew up around tyrants, or the poetry directed against them, in the hope of locating social and economic causes and conditions motivating and enabling the tyrants and their enemies. Instead, I attempt to discover the power and constraints implicit in the language of tyrants: to reconstruct the expectations and options that discourse engendered, trace the history of its exploitation, and find the limits it imposed on those who used it. But while searching for the political power and historical logic inherent in these concepts, rather than the social and economic interests concealed behind them, I do not mean to reject the goals and methods of traditional critical analysis, but rather to avoid its pitfalls. Thucydides will continue to guide us in our quest to avoid the evils of credulity, to look for exaggeration, misrepresentation, and simple error, and to question the motives of our sources. But Thucydides' own use of a stringently critical methodology to puncture exaggerated claims about the past also serves to demonstrate that historical methods and conclusions can never be completely independent.[11] Critical methodologies are certainly not immune to uncritical application. A methodology that completely demythologizes tyranny is sure to reduce it to a nexus of social and economic interests. To identify those social, economic, and political supporters whom tyrants consciously or unwittingly served, without considering their posture, images, and language, is to doubt at the start whether tyranny possessed political principles or made real political contributions. Worse still, if we ignore or dismiss the discourse of tyrants and their opponents, we risk becoming entrapped by it; for tyranny played a crucial role in the development of the political ideas of interest, legitimacy, and representation, concepts that also are basic to the distinction between political reality and political ideology, with which conventional treatments of tyranny are concerned.

Yet it is obvious that the great mass of material about tyranny that comes to us from antiquity contains much that is false and misleading. In particular, the Greek popular history typically shaped the establishment of tyrannies into single coherent events bound up with the life and achievements of single individuals. The plain aorists Herodotus uses when he reports that Cypselus "attempted and held Corinth" (ἐπεχείρησέ τε καὶ ἔσχε Κόρινθον: 5.92ε1) confuse our efforts to recapture the founding of the Cypselid tyranny, much as the newborn Cypselus's sweet smile baffled the murderous Bacchiads. But if the popular history of the Corinthian tyranny distorted the memory of the Cypselids' rise, the distortion itself—that is, the remaking of the Cypselids' rise into a single event of monumental and mythic proportions—also articulates tyranny's political character. The point can be extended. Much of the lore surrounding the autocratic figures of the early archaic period— tyrants, founders, and lawgivers—belongs to the category that Thucydides rejected as "fabulous" (τὸ μυθῶδες: 1.22). But such material elaborates more than it obscures the political reality of such figures; in particular, it helps to show what drew to them the

11. It is true for Thucydides, as for modern historians, that the demythologizer's power springs in great part from his self-representation as disinterested. Yet that Thucydides was no enemy of speculation is clear from his own discussions of historical method (see 1.20–22).

romantic elaborations of legend. If therefore it is right to take the representation and reality of tyranny as inseparably bound, we cannot entirely discount materials not contemporary with tyrants, any more than we can ignore contemporary information that romanticizes their power.

To read the history of tyranny as a kind of story that follows a careful plot and gives precise roles to tyrants and their opponents, subjects, and supporters is not, I think, to falsify it. The historical empiricist tends to insist on the distinction between individual innovation and enterprise, on the one hand, and conceptual frameworks and historical logic, on the other. To such a critic, I will likely seem to transform individuals into causes and to read their actions as stage directions they found in a script. But I attempt to show that the individuals who appear prominently here—the Cypselids, Solon, the Peisistratids, Maeandrius of Samos, the Deinomenids, and the fifth-century Athenians—believed and wanted others to believe that they were following a script; that is, they variously appealed to, interpreted, and exploited a body of accepted truths and common images that were articulated in narrative frameworks associated with the quests and trials of particular individuals. Tyranny, from this viewpoint, very much deserves the storied reputation it has held since antiquity; for it was as a story that tyrants acquired power and that the cities subjected to them appropriated it. This is not to say that all tyrants or all cities that endured a period of tyranny behaved in precisely the same manner. But they developed similar strategies in response to common political problems: for tyrants, how to define and sustain personal possession of the city; for their cities, how to destroy tyranny without losing the extraordinarily subjective and personal power that characterized it.

The establishment and fall of tyrannies were neither intellectual exercises nor bloodless dramas. Indeed, the archaic Greek tyrants sometimes engaged in remarkable acts of brutality. By treating tyranny as a political phenomenon with a distinctive discursive character, I do not mean to deny or excuse its violence. But I reject the notion that tyranny (or any form of political power) exists exclusively by means of force. Rendering tyranny as primarily rhetorical does not diminish the significance of its brutality; indeed the violence of tyranny only then acquires meaning. It was incumbent on tyrants to articulate their distinctive claims to possess un-delegated and unrestricted authority in concrete terms, and their brutal treatment of their subjects did this uniquely well. The pri-ority of the tyrants' claims over their actions should explain the great attention I give to language and representation, media of power that both actively involved and victimized the tyrants' sub-jects.

But I do not primarily intend to attack conventional wisdom on archaic politics or the methodologies that sustain it. Instead I wish to address the connection between archaic tyranny and classical forms of political power. I focus on the tyrant as a progenitor of a political vocabulary that anticipates classical conceptions of sov-ereignty, and likewise on the actions, memories, and fictions by which the polis appropriates the tyrant's language and power. So in this book I argue that the collective sovereignty of post-tyrannical states was based not on the structure, function, or membership of their political institutions—for tyrants often made little changes in existing institutions, and the constitutional regimes that succeeded tyrannies learned little from them here. What they learned was to think of those who had political rights, whether the few in an oligarchy or the many in the democracy, as collectively sharing in the possession of the tyrant's unfettered personal power. Behind the change in the polis's function from mediating legal disputes in the early archaic period to protecting and representing its citizens' com-mon interests in classical Greece stands a shift in the perceived nature of power, not merely in its masters or its quantity.

From this perspective, tyranny confronts us with the funda-mental question of how classical poleis—in different but related ways—articulated sovereignty, discouraged the appropriation of political power by single individuals or factions, and persuaded their citizens that they were exercising power when they partici-pated in their institutions and when their political bodies deliber-ated. In effect, my aim is to argue, and to explore, a single paradox: that the freedom of the post-tyrannical polis continued the charac-teristic self-interest of the tyrant. This aim clearly assumes that the classical conceptions and images of sovereignty were the great political legacy of tyrants, and, still more important, that these images existed as the interpretive *memories*, not the simple *results*, of historical experiences of individual autocratic power. In this sense, I wish to revive a discourse that was crucial to the Greeks, who as early as Aeschylus's *Oresteia* identified a transformation from the submissive acceptance of autocratic and arbitrary forms of rule to collective and voluntary self-domination.[12] This is not to re-mythologize the early Greek polis and its struggle with tyrants, but rather to isolate and capture the elements of that struggle that made it a principal object of the political memory of later poleis. Hence the shape of the chapters that follow. In chapter 1, I explore the relationship between popular images of the tyrant and founder and the post-tyrannical city's own distinct sense of political sovereignty. I argue that the popular representations of the lives of such individuals reflect a considerable political investment in their memory. The stories of founders and tyrants spring from a politics of analogy: in the ambitions, achievements, failures, and deaths of such figures, the polis constructs and remembers its own political identity.

Chapter 2 addresses the self-representations of tyrants in the first generations of tyrannical power: the middle and second half of the seventh century. There was, I maintain, no convincing precedent for the extraordinary power exercised by the early tyrants and no political framework in which it may comfortably be located. In its rhetoric and reception, tyranny seems to have emerged through the manipulation of contemporary conceptions of *dikē* (justice), which functioned in the earliest accounts of the polis as the most pressing concern of civic action. Presenting themselves as (and apparently believing themselves to be) responding to breakdowns in justice, tyrants reshaped the early archaic polis's dominant concern with justice to build a foundation for individual autocratic power. As agents of divine retribution, they assumed extraordinary prerogatives to realize their designs and interests without answering to their cities in any conventional way. The basis of the tyrant's power, however, also limited its duration and suggested its end by an ancient *lex talionis*, which the tyrant could exploit but not control, and his corrective justice was itself understood to require correction, to which he himself characteristically fell victim.

In chapter 3, I highlight the remarkable figure of Solon, the most articulate enemy of tyranny and, as both political mediator

12. See most recently Meier 1980, 144–246.

and poet, the individual best able to devise an alternative to it. Solon understood and accepted tyrants' claims that injustice engendered tyranny. When named mediator in Athens, he was most concerned to give the Athenians the tools to combat injustice and prevent the need for an extrapolitical resolution: he opened the courts to anyone who saw injustice in the city, established an appeal to the popular courts, and placed strict limits on legal self-help. He corrected the political structure of Athens in such a way as to emphasize the opposition between sovereign laws and individual rule, and his new laws paradoxically disallowed even the tyrantlike powers that he himself was granted in order to institute them. Solon's solution was a failure: the Athenians ignored the laws that Solon gave them and soon allowed Peisistratus to establish a personal form of justice and a tyranny. In my view Solon failed because he undertook to resolve a problem that no individual could solve, for it demanded a collective solution. The polis did not need to avoid tyranny but to politicize it.

The character of that solution is described in chapter 4, which considers the reality and mythology of the fallen tyranny and the transition of autocratically consolidated political power from the tyrant to his city. In the Greek popular sense of history, the last tyrant of a dynasty was destined to pay for the crimes of his entire family. It is true that the Greek popular imagination represented this vengeance as popular, when only a minority of tyrants seem to have fallen to open revolts. But it is a rule without exception that tyrants could not simply resign their powers and return to citizen life. To explore the dimensions of this important rule, I examine the many personas that tyrants adopted in the later history of archaic tyranny. I argue that tyrants' attempts to reconfigure their power, which were at best temporary palliatives, revealed the extraordinary pressure to which they were gradually subjected. And, in this sense, the political realities of archaic and classical Greece confirm popular history. At the end of tyranny the roles of master and slave were effectively reversed as the tyrant's power was depersonalized and reintegrated and the polis came to function as the political entity in whose name citizens acted and to whom they were held accountable. In this reversal lay the origins of the classical notions of autonomy and liberty.

Chapter 5 is devoted to the *oikistēs* (founder), the figure on whom many of the Greeks' memories of colonization were centered. Founders, like tyrants, controlled their cities as if personal possessions; but their stories were less the products of history than invention. Instead of attempting to locate a kernel of historical truth in the plethora of tales that narrate the exploits of Greek founders, I undertake to locate and understand their narrative structures and imagery: the wandering *oikistēs* who escapes the stain of domestic crime or illegitimacy by leaving his home and traveling to the end of the known world, where he assumes tyrantlike powers to establish a new city. I argue that this image, propagated in different but related versions by various colonies, served to enforce and preserve concepts of collective independence and autonomy. The cults and legends that recalled the founder's achievements shaped his death into his new city's coming of age and formed the period of his individual rule as a single, remote, and unrepeatable event. And by remembering and honoring their founders' crimes and quests, colonies celebrated their autonomy from them and their own possession of the autocratic power that their founders held. Thus, in symbol and narrative, stories of founders captured images of collective sovereignty very much like those that came from the experience of tyranny.

As I have already noted, I do not consider the ideology of tyranny in the fifth century in isolation. Yet tyranny clearly does perform an ideological role after its collapse as a political form. This is especially true in classical Athens, where attacks against the democratic regime were defined as tyranny—a definition that, by implication, made the democracy synonymous with the polis itself. Yet tyranny functions in Athens in more important ways. In the last chapter, I undertake to make the distinctive logic of Greek tyranny specific in a close reading of the political language of the classical Athenian democracy. Examining the tyrant in his public manifestations, the fifth- and fourth-century Athenian legislation that made him illegal, and the tragedies of Aeschylus and Sophocles that replayed his demise, I attempt to show that the Periclean image of the free citizen who is a lover (ἐραστής) of his city, a virtual "tyrant citizen" who revives the language of tyranny in archaic Greece, rests on a distinctive and coherent image of citizenship. From this perspective, I turn finally to Plato's provocative attack on the democratic citizen in the *Republic*, which, while seeking to debunk the freedom (ἐλευθερία) of democracy as an invitation to tyranny, actually succeeds in emphasizing Plato's own dependence on the potential for reform that the tyrant's (and democratic citizen's) freedom articulates.

CHAPTER ONE

Tyrannus fulminatus:
Power and Praise

Quo quis loco fulmine ictus fuerit, eodem sepeliatur. Tyranni corpus extra fines abiciatur. Tyrannus in foro fulminatus est: quaeritur, an eodem loco sepeliatur.

Whoever is struck by lightning must be buried on the very spot. The body of the tyrant must be thrown outside the borders. A tyrant is struck by lightning in the forum: it is asked whether he should be buried in the same place.

Quintilian, *Declamatio* 274

Among the rhetorical exercises preserved under Quintilian's name is a declamation entitled *Tyrannus fulminatus*, "The Tyrant Struck by Lightning." The problem of the declamation is described above. The problem is typical of Roman rhetorical exercises in posing an imaginary situation to which contradictory conventions or laws can be applied with equal validity. The *Tyrannus fulminatus* draws on the popular conviction that lightning is an act of Jupiter with a definite message and purpose, and on the convention that the city must punish its tyrant by ejecting his body from the city. To argue effectively that the tyrant who is struck by lightning should be buried in the forum, a Roman schoolboy would insist that the

Abbreviations of ancient authors and works follow those adopted by *The Oxford Classical Dictionary*. All translations are the author's, unless otherwise indicated.

obligation to bury the victim of lightning where he falls carries the weight of a divine law, which the city would ignore only at great risk. Yet he could construct an equally compelling argument for the opposition position: to bury the tyrant in the forum, where even the most worthy (*optime meritus*: 274.9) could not be buried and where, in fact, only the city's greatest hero, its founder, was buried, would be tantamount to polluting the city.

In Quintilian's day, tyrants were fleshless creatures that came out only in the dim light of classrooms; and even there they were not taken very seriously. Petronius's Encolpius (*Sat.* 1) and Juvenal (7.150–51) dismissed the rhetorical struggles schoolboys fought against tyrants as trite and valueless—a judgment echoed by the more cautious Tacitus in his *Dialogus de oratoribus* (35.5). It was obvious to all that the political life of imperial Rome reduced the *Tyrannus fulminatus* to a logical quibble. But the Quintilian exercise preserves political characters and ideas that had been altogether crucial for the Romans in the last years of the Republic, when Romans variously struggled to understand, support, and resist autocratic power. Then Cicero, Rome's greatest rhetorical strategist, designed and argued elaborate declamations that brought tyrants and tyrannicides to the fore (*Att.* 9.4). This he did not just to amuse himself but to prepare for rhetorical warfare: it was against the idea and image of the *tyrannus* that Cicero measured Marc Antony in his *Philippics* (13.18).[1] Not only the exercise's image of the evil tyrant fits the political atmosphere of the late Republic; the founder—the one exception to the rule forbidding burial in the forum—is there by implication: the Romans burned Julius Caesar's body and buried his ashes near Romulus's tomb in the Roman Forum, a conspicuous public act that answered the dictator's own apparent interest in sharing the title and honors of Rome's legendary founder.[2]

Yet the Quintilian *Tyrannus fulminatus* does more than capture the Romans' historical struggles with individual rule; it replays and renews religious and political conceptions that were borrowed from the Greeks. *Fulminatus* captured in Latin the Greek *dioblētos*, "Zeus-struck," which describes the class of heroes whose deaths

1. See Béranger 1935, 85.
2. On Caesar's interest in Romulus, see Gelzer 1968, 318.

complete the record of their troubled lives and deeds with a mixture of honor and punishment.[3] Greek too are the human rewards and punishments that the Roman rhetorical exercise considers conferring on the *fulminatus*. In fact, burial in the agora (= forum) and expulsion outside the city's borders mark the extremes in the polis's memory of its most illustrious dead. The body that was expelled *extra fines* was understood as a curse on the city and a perpetual enemy of its citizens; to be buried in the agora, on the other hand, was to be honored as a civic hero of the first order. And, as the declaimers must have known, these were rewards and punishments with precise objects. Expulsion *extra fines* was the final vengeance exacted from the deceased tyrant,[4] while burial in the agora was an honor usually reserved for the city's greatest civic hero, its founder.[5] By treating tyrants and founders as deserving opposite fates, the Quintilian exercise implicitly recalled their roles as paradigms of political behavior in the Greek city-state: the tyrant, whose indifference to the constraints of political and personal morality both fascinated and horrified the Greek popular imagination, stood as a political opposite to the founder, whose achievements the city might remember as a lasting model of personal commitment to civic ideals. But more important, the exercise tacitly focuses on the city and its place in relation to its dead tyrants and founders. To answer the problem, the schoolboy constructed an imaginary city, which decided the rewards and punishments to which the declamation alludes and that profited or suffered as a result of its decision. In this sense, the hypothetical debate that the exercise was intended to engender rehearsed the polis's real place as the final judge over its citizens—even those who once dominated it and to whom it owed its very existence. So the Quintilian *Tyrannus fulminatus* through implication revives and sustains a complex relationship among three

3. See Rohde 1925, 581–82, and Garland 1985, 99–100. Zeus characteristically reserves his thunderbolts for those whose crimes (or achievements) challenge his power. To be sure, in Aristophanes' *Clouds* (397), the perjurer is said to deserve to be struck by lightning, but this does not trivialize the punishment; rather it elevates the crime above the level of ordinary misdemeanors.

4. Among tyrants whose remains were expelled when their tyrannies fell were the Cypselids of Corinth and Hieron of Syracuse (see chap. 4).

5. On the founder's burial, see below in this chapter and chap. 5 passim.

figures: the tyrant, whom the exercise represents as a curse on the city; the founder, whose distinctive honor of burial in the civic center the tyrant struck by lightning threatens to arrogate; and the city, which sits in judgment over the lives and achievements of both.

The Quintilian *Tyrannus fulminatus* not only flatters Greek political images by imitating them but, when imitating them, also considerably illuminates them. Following the lead of the *Tyrannus fulminatus,* I argue that the opposition between the tyrant and the founder pervades classical political culture and articulates the polis's self-representation as politically sovereign. This is hardly obvious. In stories of founders and tyrants the city appears as the victim of the tyrant's self-interest and the beneficiary of the founder's achievements. Yet in its citizens' individual and collective remembering of the final destinies of tyrants and founders, the city exercises political superiority over its formative early history and its own political models. This narrative control over the autocratic figures of the city's past will emerge as a measured response to the language of autocratic power and the threat of its return, a response—this is most important—that was in great part prepared by tyrants themselves. On the way to understanding this response and its relation to tyranny, I begin with the classical image and memory of founders, who, though creatures of political legend, possessed a significance for Greek political language that stands in inverse proportion to their doubtful historicity.

Stories of Founders

The Greeks had a great passion for legends about inventions and immensely enjoyed recounting the origins of various aspects of their common life, both material and cultural, as the works of single moments and the personal achievements of single individuals. This is particularly true of the invention of cities. Founders, whom the Greeks called *oikistai* or *archēgetai*, were credited with finding suitable sites for their cities, conducting large numbers of diverse colonists to them, and ensuring that they began their histories as true poleis—that is, that they preserved the religious traditions and cults

17

of the older cities from which they sprang.[6] The tale of the founder's achievements is now a virtually forgotten genre of oral literature, which must be reconstructed from fragments that found their way into works of history, geography, and mythography in the classical period and later. Stories of founders were, however, immensely popular in antiquity.[7] And it is most probable that their origin lies before the start of the archaic age: Homer preserves a trace of a foundation legend in the story of Tlepolemus's colonization of Rhodes (Il. 2.653–70). Over time, foundation legend developed into a genre whose authority was invoked and increased every time a new city was established. As Agesilaus and Alexander used Homer as a guide to heroic action and surrounded themselves with aspiring poets to grace their own deeds with the dignity that Homer gave Achilles and Odysseus, so too newly founded cities fed upon and in turn nourished the body and stature of foundation legend.

In this sense, foundation legends were invested with meaning as narrative models of city foundation and cannot be considered the simple products of an innocent desire to remember the past. They suppress more information than they preserve about colonization projects and the social crises and political decisions that gave rise to them. Moreover, to the frustration of historians since Thucydides, foundation lore identifies the early history of a city exclusively with the founder's personal quest; the establishment of the collective and political entity becomes the story of the founder's origins, his reasons for leaving, and his personal trials.

Distinctive patterns are conspicuous in these stories. As a rule, foundation legends remember single founders. Even when cities have alternative accounts of their origins with alternative founders,[8] particular narrative versions of a city's establishment typically focus on a single founder. A few legends make the identification of city

6. On the historical elements of foundation procedure and the oecist's place in it, see Graham 1983, 25–39; Leschhorn 1984; and Malkin 1987, 17–91.

7. See Pl. Hp. Ma. 285d on Spartan interest in legends of political origins. Polybius (34.1.3) notes the importance of such stories for a historian like Ephorus. Chapter 5 explores the analogy between the domestic and political spheres in Greek foundation myths.

8. Examples include Zancle, Rhegion (for the two, see Leschhorn 1984, 25), Gela (see Thuc. 6.4.3), Camarina in Sicily (see Thuc. 6.5.3), and perhaps Thasos, whose establishment seems to have involved two steps separated by a generation; see Pouilloux 1954, 1:22. Older cities more commonly had multiple founder figures; Athens had several.

foundation with a single individual into an explicit theme. Calli-
machus (*Aet.* 2.43.74–79) reported that the two leaders of the expedition to the Sicilian city of Zancle, Perieres and Crataemenes, each
wished to be honored as the new city's *oikistēs*. Delphi was invited to
decide between the two and determined that the city should honor
an anonymous founder instead of either Perieres or Crataemenes.
Roman foundation myth offers a less peaceful variation on this
theme with the contest between Romulus and Remus for the status
of *conditor* (founder) of Rome. The religious honors paid founders
confirm the exclusiveness of the founder's position in colonization
legend: no Greek colony is known to have honored two founders
equally.[9] The rule, one founder—one city, is followed even in the
farcical rendition of a colonization project offered by Aristophanes
in the *Birds*: although Euelpides and Peisetaerus jointly conceive of a
plan to quit Athens and together persuade the chorus of birds to
accept them as their leaders, Euelpides disappears in the course of
the play, leaving Peisetaerus to act as the new city's sole oecist.
Where there are conflicting traditions about the origins of a city and
its founder (the Rhodian story of Macar and the tales of the sons of
Codrus in Ionian colonization are examples), separate traditions
usually reflect competing political interests.[10]

The method of the founder's selection fits the magnitude and
uniqueness of his powers; as a rule, Delphi plays some role in
naming or confirming the founder, and foundation stories generally
abound in visits to Delphi and oracles.[11] This stress on the divine

9. Malkin (1987, 254) rightly stresses the limits of our evidence.

10. Miletus is an example. An oracle survives that makes Neleus the founder; on
this, see PW 2:301–2. Other accounts (e.g., Ephorus *FGH* 70 F 127) give the honor
to Sarpedon or Miletus, his lover. The latter surely reflects Athenian interests. See
also below.

11. On Delphi's role in colonization, see, most recently, Malkin (1987, 17–91),
who supplements PW 1:49–81 and Forrest 1957. Oracles are particularly prominent
in the principal foundation stories of early colonies. On Cyrene, see the foundation
decree incorporated within a surviving fourth-century Cyrenean law (5 ML); on
Croton, see PW 1:68–70; on Thasos, see Leschhorn 1984, 56–60; and on Ambracia,
see chap. 5. See also Fontenrose (1978, 143–44), who argues (to my mind unconvincingly) that Delphi's involvement in colonization and the great majority of
colonization oracles were much later inventions. It is true that Delphi is not mentioned in the oldest foundation legend, Homer's account of Tlepolemus's colonization of Rhodes (*Il.* 2.653–70), but Pindar seems to have felt a need to correct
Homer's omission in his account in *Ol.* 7.32: that Delphi must be involved was
taken as given already in his time.

support behind the oecist's actions is occasionally augmented when Apollo, rather than the founder himself or his home city, is given credit for the impulse of establishing a colony. The foundation decree "spontaneously prompted [αὐτομάτιξεν] Battus" to establish Cyrene.[12] Similarly, Myscellus, Croton's founder, is surprised by the oracle that sends him to his new home and is reluctant to believe it; he appears at Delphi in search of a solution for his childlessness, not for support in establishing a new city (Antiochus of Syracuse FGH 555 F 10), and he later quibbles with the site Delphi has selected for his new city (Hippys FGH 554 F 1). The founder's significance is hardly diminished when his actions are made involuntary; rather, Delphi's spontaneity confirms the founder in his role as Apollo's agent. But it is not only when Delphi speaks first that the founder acts for Apollo. Most of the surviving foundation oracles are commands in which the oecist (in fact or legend) finds a divine mandate to define his authority.

The religious dimensions of the oecist's selection in foundation legend suggest his political significance: foundation legends seem to have functioned virtually as manuals for the establishment of cities. This does not imply a blind devotion to the patterns evident in foundation legend. Greek cities, particularly after colonization became an important element of imperialist programs in the fifth century, occasionally selected more than one founder. The Spartans, for example, picked three to lead the expedition that settled Heracleia in Trachis in 426 (Thuc. 3.92), unwilling, apparently, to trust any single individual. So also the fifth-century Athenians named ten surveyors (γεονόμος) to be responsible for dividing land among the new settlers of Brea, perhaps the most important undertaking for the future political configuration of the colony. But while unwilling to allow control over their colony to be consolidated in the hands of a single founder, the Athenians seem still to have respected and valued traditional formulas concerning foundation; the decree establishing the colony formally names Democleides as Brea's autocratic oecist, whom the colony was surely expected to remember and honor as its founder.[13]

12. 5 (24) ML. On αὐτομάτιξεν, see also below p. 68.
13. For the decree and discussion, see 49 ML. Democleides is named [αὐτο]κρά-τορα at line 9; the ten γεονόμος (= γεωνόμους) are mentioned at lines 6–8.

Foundation legends' unwavering attention to the founder's quest offered colonies a precise sense of their origins and identity. The significance is clear in the history of interpolitical relations: the city in which the founder began his quest was typically recognized as the colony's mother-city. Mother-cities and colonies were bound by a less formal but also more enduring bond than those created by simple treaties (συμμαχίαι), which were notoriously subject to interpretation. Unlike allies of convenience, a colony and its mother-city were tied by religious and military obligations that were conceived, as the maternal metaphor suggests, to be permanent and irrevocable. The link is visible in the late archaic and classical periods. In 492, when Syracuse was threatened by Hippocrates, tyrant of Gela, Corinth hurried, with Corcyraean help, to save it (Hdt. 7.154.3). Corinth's remoteness did not make it indifferent to Syracuse's fate; Corinthian troops soon went to Syracuse, bringing with them a contingent from Corcyra, which overlooked its own longstanding hostility to its mother-city, to help. Corinth certainly did not act entirely from altruistic motives. Had Hippocrates taken Syracuse, he would probably have destroyed it (at least in some formal sense) and refounded it with himself as the new oecist—as he did at nearby Camarina (Thuc. 6.5.3). In that case, Corinth would have lost any future benefit it might have hoped to derive from Syracuse.

The founder's home was honored as his new city's mother-city even when a number of cities participated in the foundation.[14] The most striking example of the founder's role as a virtual symbol of the nascent city involves Epidamnus, a colony founded on the coast of Illyria in the late seventh century. According to Thucydides (1.24–25), the great majority of Epidamnus's original settlers came from Corcyra and far fewer from Corinth, but the Corcyraeans invited Corinth, Corcyra's own mother-city, to send an oecist for the expedition. Thucydides asserted that the Corcyraeans did so in deference to an "ancient law" (παλαιὸς νόμος), although there is no

---

14. The Sicilian Naxos is an apparent exception. It was founded by Chalcis and Naxos, but its founder, Theocles, was sometimes said to be Athenian (Strab. 6.2.2; ps.-Scymn. 270–76). It is very possible, however, that Theocles' Athenian origin was an invention intended to support fifth-century Athens's interest in extending its hegemony westward. On this, see Leschhorn 1984, 9.

other mention of such a requirement, and mother-cities were not always involved in their colonies' new foundations.[15] Whether or not we follow Thucydides, the Corinthian oecist certainly figured largely in the later dispute between Corinth and Corcyra over Epidamnus, the prelude to the outbreak of open hostilities between Athens and Sparta. Epidamnus illustrates the rule: conflicting attributions of colonies and founders usually derived from local political groups that supported conflicting interpolitical allegiances.[16]

The memories that colonies maintained of their founders were so closely linked to their international position that if a colony wished to change allegiances, it might be compelled to reenact its foundation. The Amphipolitans did precisely that in 422 when they tore down all civic monuments honoring Hagnon, the Athenian founder, and installed the Spartan Brasidas in his place (Thuc. 5.11.1). By enacting a symbolic destruction of their city—much as Hippocrates (Thuc. 6.5.3) or perhaps Nero (Tac. *Ann.* 15.40) did quite literally—they were able to exert political control over their own refoundation. If, at the other extreme, a colony forgot the name and origins of its founder, it took the risk that a stronger city would remember him for it or that the matter would be decided by civil conflict. Thurii, according to Diodorus (12.35.1–3), did not have an officially sanctioned oecist, which fed the rivalries of political factions. However real the danger, the inherent flexibility of foundation narrative made a solution relatively easy: Thurii sent a delegation to Delphi to ask Apollo to name the founder and the city from which the colony had originated. Apollo finessed the question by electing himself as Thurii's founder.

The memory of the founder certainly also influenced the internal political fabric of colonies, alongside their better-known international personas. Political and social unity must have been a concern in new cities. It was not uncommon for inhabitants of a new city to

---

15. Megara was involved in the foundation of Selinus by its Sicilian colony Megara Hyblaea, but the Euboeans apparently played no role in the foundation of Leontinoi by the Euboean colony of Naxos in Sicily, and Sparta was not involved at Cyrene, which was established by Thera, a Spartan colony.

16. Camarina, whose two oecists were from Syracuse (Thuc. 6.5.3), seems to be an exception to the rule of one colony—one founder, although Dunbabin (1957, 105) has proposed that one was Syracusan, the other Corinthian.

derive from all corners of the Greek world. Archilochus remarked that "the misery of all Greece ran to Thasos" (102 W), searching, in his view, for the better life that would elude them. The obvious attractions were political and economic: a fresh start as an equal in a less oppressive social system, and a workable and unencumbered plot of land (κλῆρος). It was not always possible or desirable for the founding city to restrict participation to its own citizens. Policies of exclusion seem to come late in the history of colonization and were meant to keep out undesirables, not to limit participation to a select few: Sparta, for example, excluded "Ionians, Achaeans, and a few other peoples" from Heracleia in Trachis (Thuc. 3.92.5) but did not invite only its own citizens and close allies. Simple safety in numbers was perhaps the most common reason that mother-cities invited settlers from other cities. Even when colonization became a tool of imperialistic policies, the mother-city had to maintain a balance between its colony's loyalty and efficient use of its own human resources: too few of its own people and the colony would be difficult to control, too many and the enterprise became prohibitively expensive. It is most likely that the founder and his quest for a new position of social legitimacy offered a point of identification for the heterogeneous collection of colonists that streamed to new cities.[17]

This defines the relationship between the founder's legend and his burial, whose importance for the city's sense of political identity is clearly implied in the *Tyrannus fulminatus*.[18] Burial in the agora marked the founder as a civic hero, a status that was sanctioned by his place in cult. In fact, the founder was typically considered among the most important of civic heroes; he was summoned along with the patron deities to the city's annual festivals, and his aid was sought if the city were in some way threatened. In this sense, the founder's legend, which was likely told and retold in a social and cultural context defined by cult, complemented his religious status: the city honored its founder by remembering his story—the discursive equivalent of burying him in the center of the city.

The memory of the founder seems then to have explained and

17. On the founder's quest, see also chap. 5 passim.
18. For a review of the evidence and secondary literature on cults for oecists, see the recent study by Malkin (1987, 189–260).

23

justified the institutional character of the city and its international allegiances, as though a colony's political history were a mere elaboration of its earliest moments.[19] When the Greeks remembered their early histories by analogy with their founder and crafted that analogy into narrative, they recovered and unified histories otherwise lost to them; the founder's life and quest became a moving symbol of the city itself. But if the city's history followed from the founder's own personal story, the recounting of that story was very much the city's possession. No one can write the ending to his own story, because, as Herodotus's Solon tried to explain to Croesus (1.30–32), the happiness of every mortal can be determined only after his death. So, from the city's perspective, the meaning of the founder's story—the decision about his happiness—comes, like any narrative, only with its conclusion.[20] When the city's history was narrated, the activity of remembering the past invariably underwent a split between matter and form; the founder's story became recognizably dependent on its retelling, and the city and its citizens asserted their rights to judge their history. Foundation legend thus implicitly established the city as the master of its own story at the same time that it defined the founder as that story's hero. This mastery defines the enduring political force of foundation legend. To tell the founder's story was both to invoke and to overcome the dangerous model of the individual possessing tyrantlike powers. So the city was able to remember a period of autocratic power without affirming that power as a viable political option. In short, the city sanctioned its past by narrating a happy ending to its founder's story and in so doing defined itself by implication as the heir and beneficiary of his power and achievements.

Tyrannical Memories

Rewarded for his deeds with burial in the civic center, a civic cult, and eternal fame as a symbol of the nascent city, the founder seems

---

19. On the highly compressed image of political history in Greek foundation myths, see Veyne 1988, 77.

20. So Brooks 1977, 283: "The very possibility of meaning plotted through time depends on the anticipated structuring force of the ending: the indeterminable would be the meaningless."

an obvious antithesis to the tyrant. This contrast between Greek images of the founder and tyrant is particularly clear in the paradigmatic narrative that accompanied the image of the tyrant: as the Quintilian declamation suggests, the tyrant's story ends with his expulsion *extra fines*. And the contrast gives force to the political nightmare that the *Tyrannus fulminatus* elaborates: that the city should be compelled to honor its dead tyrant—that, in other words, the tyrant should end his life happy. Happiness, in the eyes of the Greeks, was a gift of the gods. The city did not *make* the founder sacred by burying him in the agora or by recounting his achievements. Rather it *recognized* his happiness (i.e., his sacredness), of which the city itself—the founder's great personal achievement— was lasting proof. From this perspective, the figure of the *tyrannus fulminatus* utterly perverts the city's narrative self-representation. When Zeus strikes the tyrant with lightning in the agora, he preempts the city's final decision about him—whom that city tolerates during his lifetime on the condition that it may condemn him when he is dead. The city, whose tyrant is marked for honor by the gods, finds its most elementary assumption contradicted by its most important allies: the once quiescent gods reject its conviction that the tyrant is ultimately unhappy.

Thus the rhetorical exercise points to a question that lies at the very heart of the city's political integrity. If, as the declamation imagines, a tyrant were struck by lightning and buried in the agora, his city would be unable to judge him unhappy by concluding his story with the ultimate and extreme form of ignominy. Not only would the sacred areas of the city be defiled and positive values of citizens negated; in such a case, the city would yield control over the history of autocratic power and over its own sovereignty. This is clear enough from the *prior declamatio* included to elucidate the *Tyrannus fulminatus*, which announces that if the tyrant were buried in the forum, "it would be better to abandon the whole place to the tyrant's tomb and change the place of our legal business." The *pars altera*'s argument that placing the tyrant's tomb in the forum might serve, like the crucifixes of condemned criminals that lined Roman roads, as a deterrent to tyranny strains credibility in an obvious effort to circumvent this very problem: the tomb is transformed into a mark of dishonor to permit the city to exist alongside a permanently installed tyrant.

Most Greeks would clearly have found the idea of honoring tyrants equally repellent, and a threat, as the Roman exercise suggests, to the essentially narrative structure of the city's sovereignty. For Greeks from Archilochus to Aristotle, the tyrant was a politically liminal and dangerous creature, over whose story the city maintained a difficult but vital control. And both the liminality and the danger of tyranny sprang from the extraordinary personal benefits that tyrants derived from their power. First among these in the popular imagination was wealth. Gyges, the regicide and usurper of the Lydian throne and a paradigmatic tyrant, was envied from Archilochus's day for his fabulous wealth.[21] Other tyrants, such as Croesus and Polycrates, whom the Greeks also treated as paradigms of this form of rule, likewise stood conspicuously above their fellows in their remarkable accumulation of wealth.[22] The tyrant's wealth was not his only benefit. The Greeks thought that tyrants were able to reward their friends and punish their enemies in any way they wished, and that they possessed nearly unlimited sexual freedom. Herodotus's accounts of Periander's relations with his deceased wife (5.92.η3) and Cambyses' incest with his sister (3.31) perhaps represent the extension of this freedom to the grotesque. Plato captures the full range of this freedom in his story of the magical ring that allows Gyges "to take without fear whatever he desires from the agora, go into any house and sleep with whomever he wishes, kill or release from bonds whomever he wants, and do other things that the gods do to men."[23]

21. See 19.17–21 W. Herodotus's account of Gyges' rich gifts to Delphi (1.14) recalls this association. On the connection between freedom and tyranny, see Connor (1977, 102), who notes that "to the tyrant his rule is a blessing; to the city it is a curse. And in each case the reason is the same: the tyrant can do what he pleases." Also see Farenga (1981), who relates the image of the tyrant and concepts of personal identity and the proper in the ages of Archilochus and Plato.

22. On the treasures of Croesus, see Hdt. 1.30; for Polycrates' wealth, Pl. *Meno* 90a. Solon did not become a tyrant, for he refused to be swayed by the prospect of *ploutos aphthonos* (wealth free of envy and therefore unlimited: Plut. *Sol.* 14.6 = 29a GP); the stress is on *aphthonos*: the tyrant's wealth is not limited by the threat of envy. Sophocles (*OT* 380–81, 873–74; *Ant.* 1056) elaborates the connection between wealth and hubris in tyranny. The connection between power and wealth reemerges in modern clothing in Ure's (1922) image of tyrants as entrepreneurs.

23. *Rep.* 360b–c: ἐξὸν αὐτῷ καὶ ἐκ τῆς ἀγορᾶς ἀδεῶς ὅτι βούλοιτο λανβάνειν, καὶ εἰσιόντι εἰς τὰς οἰκίας συγγίνεσθαι ὅτῳ βούλοιτο, καὶ ἀποκτεινύναι καὶ ἐκ δεσμῶν οὕστινας βούλοιτο, καὶ τἆλλα πράττειν ἐν τοῖς ἀνθρώποις ἰσόθεον

Tyranny's detractors particularly chided the tyrant for the immoderate behavior that his freedom made possible. For Herodotus, tyrants are enemies both of the gods and of the city and become the common objects of divine punishment. If Herodotus appreciated the achievements of some tyrants, such as Polycrates (3.39) and Peisistratus (1.64), he nonetheless made good use of the image of the hubristic ruler, the tyrant of Greece or the Eastern monarch, whose immoderate appetites led him to violate divine law and made him subject to an implacable divine punishment.[24] This idea is elaborated in Plato's *Republic*; it is for his unrestrained ability to realize his desires that the tyrant must expect to face the greatest horrors in the remotest depths of Plato's hell (616d).

Even more self-consciously historical images of the tyrant—Aristotle offers the best examples—do not differ in essential respects.[25] In the *Politics*, Aristotle represents tyranny as a "perversion" ($\pi\alpha\rho\acute{\epsilon}\kappa\beta\alpha\sigma\iota\varsigma$) that serves the personal advantages of the ruler alone, a "despotic monarchy of the political community" (1279b5–8, 16–18), or a "despotic rule conducted according to the ruler's personal judgment" (1295a16–18). "Despotic" ($\delta\epsilon\sigma\pi\sigma\tau\iota\kappa\acute{\eta}$) is the crucial word here. For Aristotle, the tyrant establishes himself as a master of the city and inevitably treats his fellow citizens as slaves. This makes tyranny illegal, for, by the distinction that underlies Aristotle's political theory, master and slave belong to the household, not to the polis (*Pol.* 1252b16–17). Tyranny is therefore a kind

---

$\check{o}\nu\tau\alpha$. In Plato, the ring itself functions as a metaphor for tyrannical power: it comes from the gods, and it makes everything possible for Gyges. See also Plato's treatment of the tyrannical state and individual in book 9 (562a–576b). In Herodotus's story of Cambyses' relations with his sister (3.31.2–5), it is law rather than magic that underlies the monarch's extraordinary freedom: in response to Cambyses' question whether the Persians had a *nomos* (law) that permitted the king to marry his sister, the royal judges said that there was a *nomos* permitting "the king of Persia to do whatever he wanted."

24. It is not surprising that Cleisthenes of Sicyon earns the gods' anger when he threatens to displace Sicyon's legendary founder: "Adrastus is the true king of Sicyon, while you are a stone thrower," so Apollo of Delphi tells Cleisthenes (Hdt. 5.67), who has asked permission to expel Adrastus's bones.

25. Like Herodotus, Aristotle does not feel altogether constrained by his general view of the tyrant; he finds much to admire in Cypselus, Orthagoras, Cleisthenes of Sicyon (*Pol.* 1315b12–21), and Peisistratus (*Pol.* 1315b2–23; see also *Ath. pol.* 16.1–5). Like his teacher, Plato, he believed that the tyrant could be educated and reformed (*Pol.* 1313a34–1315b11).

of category mistake: the misapplication of a principle of domestic domination to the city.[26]

That the great majority of classical sources rejected the tyrant as a political anathema should not obscure the sophisticated position of his few supporters. The hatred of tyranny did not prevent sophists such as Thrasymachus and Callicles (at least as they appear in book I of Plato's *Republic*) from embracing tyranny as the model and implicit goal of all political activity. Yet the tyrant's enemies and friends agreed that tyranny was unlimited rule exercised by a single individual for his own personal benefit. As the Athenian Euphemus says in Thucydides, "For the tyrannical man or city, nothing is unreasonable that is profitable."[27]

In the popular imagination, the great freedom that the tyrant took from his power gave him a great potential for virtue. He could be benevolent and generous. (Peisistratus, for example, forgave a struggling farmer's tax burden: *Ath. pol.* 16.6.) The tyrant might even obey laws that apparently conflicted with his immediate interests. (Peisistratus came before an Athenian court on a charge of murder.)[28] But it was the tyrant's ruthlessness that most characteristically articulated his distinctive freedom. Herodotus tells that Thrasybulus, when asked by Periander's messenger how a tyrant best rules, walked into a nearby wheat field and, without speaking a single word, cut down the highest stalks. The messenger was baffled, but Periander understood the pantomime to mean that the tyrant destroys the most excellent individuals in his city as a preemptive strike against potential tyrannicides (5.92ζ).[29] Tyrants were the masters both of their virtues and of their vices. And although their

26. For Aristotle, the distinction between household and city is a characteristic of the Greek world. For the Greeks, "tyranny does not exist naturally, nor do any of the constitutions that are perversions (παρεκβάσεις), for these run counter to nature" (*Pol.* 1287b40–42). Where the distinction between the city (πόλις) and the home (οἶκος) does not exist, there can be a "despotic rule according to law" (1285b24–25). For a similar notion, see Pl. *Leg.* 832c.

27. Thuc. 6.85.1. See also Xen. *Mem.* 4.6.12 and Carlier 1984, 234.

28. *Ath. pol.* 16.8. The prosecution was too shocked by Peisistratus's appearance to proceed, and the case was dismissed. Herodotus also occasionally attributes extraordinary benevolence to Eastern monarchs, to whom the Greeks often likened their tyrants.

29. Aristotle (*Pol.* 1284a26–33) tells the same story in reverse: it is Periander who teaches Thrasybulus a silent message about political rule.

actions often sprang from whim, they were seldom believed to be stupid. Some, in fact, were credited with remarkable wisdom. Periander's treatment of Arion's kidnappers and his solution of the conflict between Athens and Mytilene over Sigeum (Hdt. 1.23–24; 5.95) suggest that the tyrant's cleverness matched his brutality. Herodotus's famous story of Peisistratus's ruse to regain the Athenian tyranny argues this for the Athenian tyrant as well. Peisistratus and his friends formed a procession featuring a tall country woman dressed to look like Athena and standing in a chariot, which was led by a herald loudly proclaiming that Athena was personally welcoming Peisistratus to her dwelling on the Athenian Acropolis (1.60). Peisistratus, Herodotus comments, found it easy to fool the Athenians, although they were "the cleverest of the Greeks." The author of the *Athenaion politeia* (15.4–5) tells another story that is only slightly less spectacular. Having taken the Acropolis, Peisistratus called the Athenians to an armed assembly. The Athenians placed their weapons on the ground to listen, but Peisistratus spoke very quietly, and they needed to step closer to hear him. When they did so, his men came behind them and collected their weapons.[30] Stories of this sort clung to tyrants. The common perception of their extraordinary acuity helps explain their presence among the Seven Sages; Periander of Corinth and Cleobulus of Lindos on Rhodes were enshrined alongside Solon, Pittacus, and Chilon as models of political and practical wisdom.

The tyrant possessed *eleutheria* in the sense that Aristotle labeled vulgar: "the ability to do what one wishes" irrespective of the interests of other citizens and the constraints that were imposed on them (*Pol.* 1310a32–33).[31] From the tyrant's almost boundless freedom came the various elements of his amorphous personal character: indifferent to the human and divine rules governing the relations between women and men and fathers and sons, the tyrant is

30. On Herodotus's story, see Connor (1987, 40–50), who makes better sense of it than Herodotus. For Cypselus's tricks, see Polyaen. 5.31. Many tyrants were skilled in the use of omens and the manipulation of oracles. Herodotus reports that Periander once consulted his deceased wife by means of the oracle of the dead in Thesprotia (5.92η).

31. The tyrant is accordingly the individual who has unlimited ability to realize his desires; in this sense, *tyrannos* serves often as a byname of the gods in the classical period. On this see LSJ s.v. τύραννος I.1.

barbarous and even bestial in his appetites and almost godlike in his ability to realize them. In his enemies' view, the tyrant's pursuit of limitless pleasures leads him down a path of self-destruction as he negates his sexual identity, his family, his humanity, and, ultimately, his own existence.[32]

Tyranny derived its popular definition as a political institution from this image of the tyrant's extraordinary personal freedom. This is clear in Otanes' description of monarchy in Herodotus (3.80.3) as the government that "can do what it wishes without rendering an account"—a description that was intended to apply to tyranny no less than to the Persian monarchy. This is the definition that Thrasymachus uses in his favorable account of tyranny at *Republic* 1.344c: injustice (ἀδικία), which tyranny realizes most fully, was, he claimed, "stronger, freer, and more despotic [ἰσχυρότερον καὶ ἐλευθεριώτερον καὶ δεσποτικώτερον] than justice [δικαιοσύνη]." And it is this notion of tyranny as the rule of a single individual who accepts no constraints on his personal freedom that Plato's *Republic* was most determined to attack (cf. 572e).

For all Greeks, the tyrant's personal freedom and the political power that gave it to him had an obvious purpose: to make him happy. The tyrant did not, however, want simple human happiness in greater quantity than his fellows. While intensely personal, the happiness of the tyrant was also completely public. Tyrants did not hoard their wealth or invest it only in private pleasure; they spent it conspicuously.[33] And they also made public the liberty they en-

32. On Plato's treatment in *Republic* 8 of the perversity and self-destructiveness of tyranny, see Farenga 1981, 5–10. Herodotus's portrait of Cambyses offers a perfect complement to Plato's theoretical account of tyranny. The reversal of gender roles in Aeschylus's presentation of Clytemnestra, the wife who becomes a tyrant and usurps the throne, and of Aegisthus, who for his support of Clytemnestra is labeled "woman" (*Ag.* 1625: see Zeitlin 1984), and in the appropriation of Clytemnestra to represent tyrannical abuse of power in Pindar's *Pythian* 11 suggests that the association of tyranny and sexual amorphousness is still earlier. Bushnell (1990, 20–25) sees this feature revived in the Renaissance image of the tyrant.

33. Their conspicuous spending has left monumental traces. That tyrants built sanctuaries, altars, temples, civic buildings, and the like as public demonstrations of their wealth does not mean that these buildings did not express some programmatic purposes; they certainly did so. On the Peisistratid building program, perhaps the most extensive undertaken by a tyrannical regime in archaic Greece, see Boersma 1970, Kolb 1977, and Shapiro 1989.

joyed from the constraints that were imposed on the domestic behavior of their subjects. The conspicuous use of consorts and illegitimate offspring was a feature common to the Cypselids, tyrants of Corinth, and the Peisistratids of Athens. The elder Dionysius, tyrant of Syracuse, in what was perhaps intended as an ultimate expression of his freedom from social conventions, celebrated weddings with his two legitimate wives on the very same day—only leaving to the speculation of his subjects which of the two marriages was first consummated.[34] The happiness of the tyrant is, therefore, the happiness that looks for, and is compounded by, a large number of admirers—who are, for the tyrant, "looking-glasses," as Virginia Woolf wrote of women, that have the "delicious power of reflecting the figure of man at twice its natural size."[35] In a passage including one of the earliest known occurrences of the word *tyrannia*, Archilochus compared himself to a city "never before conquered," which you, he says to his lover,

νῦν εἶλες αἰχμῇ καὶ μέγ᾽ ἐξήρω κλέος.
κείνης ἄνασσε καὶ τυραννίην ἔχε.
πολλοῖσί θην ζηλωτὸς ἀνθρώπων ἔσεαι.
(23.19–21 W)[36]

have now taken at spear point and made off with great fame.
Rule it and hold a tyranny.
Many will envy you.

As early as the Greeks knew tyranny, a predominant form of resistance to it was a steadfast refusal to acknowledge its attractions and to envy the tyrant for his happiness. So Archilochus in another passage:

οὔ μοι τὰ Γύγεω τοῦ πολυχρύσου μέλει,
οὐδ᾽ εἶλέ πώ με ζῆλος, οὐδ᾽ ἀγαίομαι

34. On the Cypselid and Peisistratid bastards, see chap. 5. On the marital practices and politics of tyrants, see Gernet 1968. Gernet suggests that Peisistratus was also bigamous, but this seems unlikely; on this, see also the discussion in chap. 5.

35. Woolf 1929, 35. Completing her pun, Woolf adds that "mirrors are essential to all violent and heroic action" (36).

36. On the poem, see West 1974, 118–20.

θεῶν ἔργα, μεγάλης δ' οὐκ ἐρέω τυραννίδος·
ἀπόπροθεν γάρ ἐστιν ὀφθαλμῶν ἐμῶν.

(19.1–4 W)[37]

The possessions of golden Gyges are nothing to me,
and envy has not yet caught me, nor do I wonder
at the deeds of gods; and I do not long for a great
tyranny, for that is far from my eyes.

This refusal to envy the tyrant would later gain a firmer basis. Not satisfied merely to avert their eyes, the lawgiver Solon and the political theorist Plato undertook to disprove the common opinion that the tyrant was genuinely happy.[38]

Yet this is clearly the minority position. "Everyone envies tyrants," Xenophon has Simonides say in the *Hieron* (1.9). Xenophon's Hieron protests that the popular conception is false, but his argument—that great burdens rest on the shoulders of the individual ruler—would have persuaded few in archaic or even classical Greece. And to those few who denied the value of envy, Epicharmus gives the most effective response: "Who would wish not to be envied, friends? It is clear that the man who is not envied is nothing. When you see a blind man you pity him, but not a single person envies him."[39] The enviable nature of tyranny appears prominently in the attempt Periander makes in Herodotus (3.52.4–5) to persuade his son Lycophron, who is disgruntled by reports that his father murdered his mother, to give up "the life of a vagabond" and take

37. Similar lines were at some point attributed to Anacreon, who (their author perhaps thought) was too well rewarded by tyrants to envy them:

οὔ μοι μέλει τὰ Γύγεω
τοῦ Σάρδεων ἄνακτος·
οὔθ' αἱρέει με χρυσός
οὔτε φθονῶ τυράννοις.
(8.1–4 Pr)

I do not care about the wealth of Gyges,
king of Sardis,
nor does gold attract me,
nor do I envy tyrants.

38. On Solon's reaction to tyranny, see chap. 3 passim.
39. *CGF* 285.

over the tyranny and the "goods that I now have." Lycophron, Periander hopes, will relent when he learns "how much better it is to be envied than pitied."

With the tyrant's great need to arouse the envy (ζῆλος) of his political audience came a weakness to fall prey to resentment (φθό-νος), that is, to begrudge others the public display of their happiness. Tyrants did not tolerate superiors or equals. Rival aristocrats were common victims of a tyrant's envy. And tyrants might even murder or exile members of their own family rather than tolerate them as partners.[40] Herodotus saw resentment (φθόνος) as a characteristic affliction of absolute monarchy. In the Persian constitutional debate (3.80), Otanes, who encourages the conspirators to adopt political equality (ἰσονομία), identifies two vices in the single ruler who cannot be held accountable for his power, hubris and resentment. Hubris comes from the extraordinary status that belongs to the absolute monarch alone; resentment, on the other hand, "is natural to man." The two vices make odd partners: Otanes remarks that "having every good thing"—which makes him hubristic— "the tyrant should be free from resentment." But Otanes explains that "the exact opposite characterizes his behavior toward citizens: the tyrant envies the best men their very life and presence, and he delights in the worst of the city and is the first to listen to their slanders." This makes the tyrant a hard man to please. "If you admire him moderately, he is angered that he is not courted even more," though if someone courts him as he wishes, "he would be angry at the man as a flatterer."[41] Otanes' monarch is uninterested in his subjects' wealth, for he has every material benefit that he could want. What he does not have is the good opinion of his subjects. And for this, Herodotus's Otanes—anticipating Plato[42]—insists,

40. So Polycrates (Hdt. 3.39) and Cleisthenes of Sicyon (Nic. Dam. *FGH* 90 F 61) and, among barbarian monarchs, Croesus (Hdt. 1.92) and Cambyses (Hdt. 3.30). On the other hand, Xenophon makes his Cyrus into a model ruler by characterizing him as willing to share praise (*Cyr.* 1.4.15).

41. How and Wells (1912, 1:278) compare Otanes' image of a tyrant with Tacitus's treatment of Tiberius and his subjects (*Ann.* 1.12.2), who reach the height of self-debasement in competing to flatter the princeps sincerely.

42. In the *Republic* Plato focuses on the interchangeability of freedom and slavery in formulating his own new definition of justice. It is the *eleutheria* of democracy, its greatest good, that determines its downfall, its enslavement to the rule of a single

the tyrant becomes a virtual slave. Demanding that his subjects court him abjectly, and, moreover, that they do so with sincerity, the monarch falls victim to the oxymoron of sincere flattery.

Herodotus's constitutional debate presents Greek political conceptions in Persian dress.[43] Oligarchy and democracy are political forms that belonged to the Greeks rather than to the Persians; so too Herodotus's image of the ruler trapped by an insatiable and contradictory desire for sincere praise elaborates (if also exaggerates) common Greek conceptions of autocratic rule. For Herodotus's contemporaries, the tyrant's immense resources for human happiness came at the price of considerable dangers. And if the attractions of tyranny were obvious to anyone, no one was unaware that the tyrant's happiness was provisional and threatened. The dangers of tyranny represent an answer to those, like Plato's Thrasymachus, who bluntly advocated it. But the realization of the dangers inherent in tyranny was not first made in Herodotus's time, and it was not the exclusive discovery of tyranny's enemies. The image of the tyrant as a man whose extraordinary happiness was destined to destroy itself stands in odd agreement with the self-representation of archaic tyrants themselves, who portrayed the happiness that their power gave them as conditional and fragile for the very reason that it surpassed that of other men.

A first suggestion of the complexity inherent in self-representation of tyrants, which forms a major theme of this book, can be found in the tyrannical odes of Pindar and Bacchylides, poetry commissioned by the early fifth-century tyrants of Sicily that in celebrating their athletic victories also articulated and supported the political relations that underlay their power. The epinician, or vic-

---

individual (*Rep.* 562b–c). Democracy, it follows, fashions voluntary slaves (ἐθε-λοδούλοι: *Rep.* 562d), out of free citizens. Nor does the tyrant escape the slavery of tyranny himself, for he is eventually enslaved by his own intemperate passions (*Rep.* 577e).

43. On the historicity of the debate, see the discussion in Ostwald 1969, 178–79. Ostwald is reluctant to dismiss the debate as a simple fabrication of Herodotus or his sources but does not give convincing reasons that the ideas Otanes expresses are genuinely Persian. For attempts to explain the function of the debate as a literary construct, see Evans 1981 and Lateiner 1984. Connor (1971, 199–206) suggests that the debate reflects Athenian political beliefs in the late 430s and the following decade.

tory, odes of Pindar and Bacchylides addressed the problem that Otanes noted in absolute monarchy; but they did so to profit from it, not to solve it—that is, epinician pretended to offer an answer to the problems arising from the tyrant's extraordinary power, wealth, and honor in order to characterize him as threatened by hubris and resentment and, therefore, as essentially distinct from other men. So while epinician anticipated the developed classical image of the extraordinary happiness of the tyrant, it also located within tyranny itself the tyrant's flaws and weaknesses, his dependence on language and imagery that limited and rendered temporary his political power and personal happiness. For this reason, the interaction between the epinician poetry commissioned by tyrants and an audience deeply concerned with tyrannical power merits close inspection.

The Poetics of Power: Pindar and Bacchylides

The short compositions that were danced and sung in honor of their victories at Panhellenic athletic competitions were obviously valued by Sicilian tyrants. Bacchylides' odes 3, 4, and 5 and Pindar's *Olympian* 1 and *Pythian* 1, 2, and 3 honor Hieron. Pindar also wrote *Olympian* 2 and 3 for Theron, who ruled Acragas from 489 to 473. Odes composed for other Sicilians with connections to tyrants include *Olympian* 6, which was written in honor of Hagesias, a close supporter of Hieron; *Pythian* 6, for Xenocrates, Theron's younger brother; and *Nemean* 1 and 9 for Chromius, an in-law of the Deinomenids. Both Pindar and Bacchylides also wrote other forms of occasional poetry in honor of Sicilian tyrants.[44]

The epinician poem was a species of praise poetry, and, like all praise poetry, it undertook to position its patron at the center of an admiring audience; this the epinician poet did by remembering and reenacting his patron's moment of athletic victory. But in contrast to the encomiastic compositions that were typically sung at drink-

---

44. Fragments survive from an encomion in the form of a dance in honor of Hieron (105 SM), and another (118–19 SM) for Theron of Acragas; Bacchylides wrote at least one encomion for Hieron (20C). On Pindar's Sicilian connection, see Stauffenberg 1963.

ing parties, victory odes were presented to audiences that were often public and diverse. The epinician poet could not assume that he was speaking to people who were in complete sympathy with the victor; it was incumbent on him to persuade others to share his enthusiasm for the victor. To do this, victory odes characteristically assert that the victories they celebrate were not the simple consequences of careful preparation or good fortune, but rewards that were given to victors by the gods for their good deeds, piety, or illustrious birth.[45] This predominant interest in human excellence (*aretē*) explains epinician's generic inattention to athletic skill or the vicissitudes of athletic contests—even when its patrons owed their successes to extraordinary personal efforts.[46] It also helps explain the victory poet's ability to praise victors who were only marginally responsible for their victories. Among such victors were tyrants who competed in the chariot races of Olympia and Delphi and collected prizes without driving their own teams, and even in some cases without leaving home to witness their victories.

To persuade an audience to find genuine virtue in athletic victory was the epinician poet's great challenge. How challenging it was is proved by the characteristic indirection of his argument. Epinician poetry typically expresses only passing interest in the thoughts and feelings of the immediate audience, which it clearly intends to

45. See for example Pind. *Isthm.* 2.12–19; Bacchyl. 3.5–8 and 4.14–20. The gods were in fact responsible for all human success: Pind. *Pyth.* 1.41.

46. Pindar compliments Herodotus of Thebes for driving his own team (*Isthm.* 1.15), but he does not make this the reason that Herodotus wins, nor is it for this primarily that Herodotus deserves praise. See also *Pyth.* 5.34–39, where Pindar praises Carrhotas, Arcesilas's charioteer, not for skillful driving but for remembering to entrust his chariot to the gods. Bacchylides 9 is also an apparent exception: Bacchylides honors Automedon for his extraordinary strength, but that strength is represented not as Automedon's personal achievement or private possession but as a concrete link to the mythical world with which the poet intends to connect him.

It fits Pindar's metaphor of the poet as athlete to reject the role of skill in poetry. For the metaphor, see *Pyth.* 1.41–45: "All manner of mortal virtues comes from the gods, so men are wise, mighty in body, and eloquent; I desire eagerly to praise this man, but I hope that I do not throw my bronze-edged spear that I brandish in my hand outside of the field, but far outstrip my competitors with my throws." For his rejection of the role of skill in poetry, see *Ol.* 2.86–88 and 9.100–104. And for Pindar's presentation of the poet as inspired, see 52f.1–6 SM, where Pindar calls himself the "singing prophet of the Muses," and 150 SM: "Speak your oracle, Muse, and I shall interpret."

persuade. Indeed, it directs itself in great part to an imaginary audience, which it constructs of immortal gods, heroes, and personified cities.[47] Epinician poets constantly invoke and beseech this second, imagined audience; the poems themselves are sometimes represented as gifts to it. This constant reference to an imaginary audience most clearly distinguishes epinician from epic and most of lyric. Although the epinician poet was typical in representing himself as the spokesman of the gods, he had a special need to remind his audience that he derived his inspiration from a divine source; for while the epic poet's success did not depend entirely on the veracity of his story, the epinician poet clearly needed to convince his listeners that his assertions were true to have any hope of persuading them to praise the victor.

There is another reason that the victory ode constructed a divine audience. Epinician subscribed to the view, conservative already in Pindar's day, that *aretē* derived exclusively from the gods. This view is basic to the victory ode's mission: to discover and illuminate a connection between the victor's achievement and the world of the gods and heroes. Steeped in genealogy and mythical history and skilled in manipulating poetic images—epinician's version of the Heracleian stone of Plato's *Ion*—the poet linked the quotidian reality to which his patron's victory belonged to the gods and the mythical past; at the end of a successful poem, the patron's victory emerged adorned with divine causes and mythic antecedents.

Epinician, in the words of Leslie Kurke, was a "tool finely calibrated for registering and accommodating the particular status of the victor within his civic community."[48] Within the chain that

47. On the distinction of epinician's real and ideal audiences, see Nagy 1990, 249.

48. Kurke 1991, 224. Kurke is sensitive to Pindar's interest in accommodating the political and social aspirations of his patrons: she reads Pindar's aristocratic odes as aiming to reintegrate the victor into his community by incorporating the community into the poem. But she does not, I think, pay enough attention to epinician's ability to justify and affirm those aspirations; little is made of epinician's power to reshape the relationship between the victor and his community to effect a real political difference: that, at the end of the successful ode, the victor and his victory are situated at the community's center. It is this restructuring of the relation between patron and his city that is crucial for epinician (just as the tyrannical odes aim to reorder the patron's relation to the world of gods and heroes). Epinician is less concerned to assure the community that "athletic victory is not a stepping stone to political domination" (224). On the relation between Pindar's tyrannical odes and

epinician constructed linking the gods and the victory, the victor, if a boy, could be employed as proof of the divinely bestowed *aretē* of his family; or if an aristocrat, his success might figure primarily to suggest or represent his city. In such poems—Pindar's Aeginetan odes are obvious examples[49]—the patron's family line or city stands between his victory and the gods and figures as the whole of which the patron is a part, his link to the gods, and the immediate audience of his achievements. Or, as in the odes honoring the Sicilian tyrants, the epinician poet might attempt to devise a more direct link between the *aretē* of the victor and the gods.[50] Odes honoring aristocrats typically represent the city as the final link in the chain connecting victory to the gods. But in odes honoring tyrants, the patron himself often assumes this role. So the good ruler and the good city both appear as the immediate objects of the gods' attention and both demonstrate the distinctive *aretē* that comes from the gods. Thus an important political anaalogy is made in epinician. The similar place given to the ruler and to the aristocratic patron's city allows the poet to describe them in like terms. At *Nemean* 5.47, Pindar delights that "the entire city [of Aegina] is eager for good deeds" as if Aegina were a single individual determined to prove its *aretē*. And at *Pythian* 1.75–79, Pindar includes Hieron's victory over the Etruscans in a single set with the Athenians' defeat of the Persians at Salamis and Sparta's victory at Plataea.

The significance of this chain is especially immediate when a

---

those composed for aristocrats, see Nagy (1990, 175), who challenges the conventional view that Pindar and Bacchylides wrote odes primarily for aristocratic patrons and that the odes written for tyrants are a mere variation of the aristocratic ode. Epinician, for Nagy, is a genre that is essentially related to the position and aims of tyrants and "quasityrants" (i.e., aristocrats who aspire to the political status and reception of tyrants). Nagy's view of the "quasityrant" is attacked by Stoneman (1991, 351–54), who insists (to my mind rightly) on the difference between Pindar's tyrannical and aristocratic odes. But Stoneman himself (1984, 43–49) seems to locate that difference in terms of poetic attitudes and diction, leaving aside entirely the question of epinician's complex reception and political situation. This may help us appreciate Kurke's achievement.

49. See also *Ol.* 13.1–5, composed in honor of Xenophon of Corinth, and Kurke (1991, 205–7), who constructs the relationship of the victor and his city on analogy with the Homeric relationship of the warrior and sovereign: as the warrior's success brings glory (κῦδος) to his sovereign, the victor's achievement confers a particular power and charm on the city to which he returns.

50. As Race (1986, 101) notes, "Pindar portrayed Hieron, Theron, and Arkesilas as model rulers; Aigina was his ideal *polis*."

human ruler serves as the link between the aristocratic patron and the divine source of his victory. This clearly happens in Pindar's *Olympian* 6. At the conclusion of the ode, Pindar turns from Hagesias, whose victory the ode celebrates, to speak of Hieron:

> εἶπον δὲ μεμνᾶσθαι Συρακοσσᾶν τε καὶ ᾽Ορτυγίας,
> τὰν ῾Ιέρων καθαρῷ σκάπτῳ διέπων,
> ἄρτια μηδόμενος, φοινικόπεζαν
> ἀμφέπει Δάματρα, λευκίππου τε θυγατρὸς ἑορτάν,
> καὶ Ζηνὸς Αἰτναίου κράτος. ἁδύλογοι δέ νιν
> λύραι μολπαί τε γινώσκοντι. μὴ θράσσοι χρόνος ὄλβον
> ἐφέρπων.
> σὺν δὲ φιλοφροσύναις εὐηράτοις ῾Αγησία δέξαιτο κώμων.
>
> (*Ol.* 6.92–98)

> I said to remember Syracuse and Ortygia,
> over which Hieron holds sway with an unsullied scepter,
> taking counsel for right things,
> and attending to purple-slippered Demeter
> and to the festival of Persephone with her
> white horses and to the power of Aetnean Zeus.
> Sweet-speaking lyres and dances know him.
> May time, sneaking up, not trouble him, now
> happy, and may he receive the victory celebration
> of Hagesias with well-loved acts of friendliness.

Only gods, heroes, and divine places and things could be invoked as present when they are absent. Pindar is careful to avoid addressing the absent Hieron directly; he uses the third person optative ("may he receive") instead of the vocative. Yet he comes very close to putting Hieron on a level with the gods. Hieron holds sway over Syracuse; it is he who will welcome the victory celebration in Syracuse, and it is he, therefore, who will determine the success of the ode. Hence the ode to Hagesias ends with an appeal to Hieron, who is characterized as a godlike force, whose potential anger and envy the poem acknowledges as its final task.[51]

51. The analogy that epinician constructs between the city and the tyrant supports Burnett's (1985, 42–43) suggestion that epinician praised victors in much the same way that the paean praised gods. Since the Greeks personified their cities as

In all epinician, the poet undertakes to render to god what is god's: ultimate credit for victory. In this sense, the patron reaps the victory as a return on a religious investment he has made in the past.[52] But epinician does not intend to represent the victory as a settlement of religious accounts, for even if the gods give him victory as a reward for his past loyalty, the victory puts him deeper in their debt. Epinician poetry renders this complicated relationship between the gods and the victor (or the entity whom the victor represents) in its concern with divine envy. Divine envy and resentment were, of course, important elements of the Greeks' religious vocabulary; in fact, they are among the chief qualities the gods share. "Envious more than others," Calypso calls the Olympian gods who deprive her of Odysseus's company (*Od.* 5.118). Yet, in their envy of the happiness of others, the gods were perhaps most human. Like certain men, most especially kings and tyrants, the gods put great value on the exclusive character of their happiness. Disastrous consequences met those who directly challenged the status of the gods, the Giants, or creatures such as the unfortunate Marsyas. The same fate fell upon paradigmatic tyrants, such as Croesus and Polycrates, whose wealth and power allowed them to escape the common toils of mankind.[53]

Epinician poets fully subscribed to the popular views of divine envy. To praise victors the poet needed to recognize and avert its danger. So at *Pythian* 8.71–72 Pindar prays:

> θεῶν δ' ὄπιν
> ἄφθονον αἰτέω, Ξέναρκες, ὑμετέραις τύχαις.

> I ask that the sight of the gods be unenvious
> of your fortune, Xenarkes.

But these things are not really within the poet's control; unalloyed happiness is the exclusive possession of the gods. So while attempt-

---

divine entities, the tyrant, who occupies the place assigned to the aristocratic patron's city, is implicitly separated from the rest of mankind.

52. Epinician, in this respect, follows epic. See *Il.* 23.859–83, where Teucer's loss in the archery contest is tacitly attributed to his failure to pray to Apollo before shooting. The rewards of piety are most fully elaborated in Bacchylides' version of Croesus's story.

53. See Walcot (1978, 25–26), who traces the idea to Homer. On envy in Pindar, see Bulman 1992.

ing to appease the gods, Pindar must also warn his mortal patrons that they cannot hope to escape a measure of unhappiness. "No one is or will be without a share of toil," Pindar insists at *Pythian* 5.54 and also at *Pythian* 12.28–30:

εἰ δέ τις ὄλβος ἐν ἀνθρώποισιν, ἄνευ καμάτου
οὐ φαίνεται· ἐκ δὲ τελευτάσει νιν ἤτοι σάμερον
δαίμων· τὸ δὲ μόρσιμον οὐ παρφυκτόν.

If there is some happiness in men, it does not
appear without toil; a god might bring happiness
to an end today, for it is not possible to flee what is fated.

This same reflection prompts Bacchylides to tell the story of Heracles' encounter with Meleager in Hades, which underscores the tragic dimensions of Heracles' undoing: Heracles returns from the meeting with an overwhelming pity for Meleager, which evolves into a passion for Meleager's sister, Deianira, the agent of Heracles' death. Thus the hero meets a tragic end, which Bacchylides uses to support by synecdoche his judgment on the universal condition of mankind: "No one who dwells on earth is happy in all respects" (5.54–55). Even Hieron, the poet implies, cannot expect that his favored status will always bring him an extraordinary measure of happiness.

The epinician poet's insistence on the subjects of divine envy and the inescapable suffering of man may seem to cast a shadow on the victor's otherwise bright achievements and his god-given happiness. Yet the poet clearly intends to build on the relation between the patron's achievement and the gods, not to question the value of that achievement. In fact, the anxiety about divine envy that demands the transference of praise from the victor to the gods is best equipped to do just that; for, just as the poet augments his praise for the victor when he credits the gods for the victory, so too he places his patron in a special class of men when he makes him liable to the gods' resentment. The threat of the gods is a form of attention, which confirms the victor's uniqueness. Epinician poetry thus constructs a close relationship between *aretē* and *phthonos*. The patron's great virtue—most especially, the tyrant's—invites both the gods' attention and their envy. The epinician poet lives on this problem;

41

he certainly does not intend to reject or obliterate it. In fact, he will
go to great lengths to make it seem real.

This may make us wonder about the political ethics of epinician
poetry: the poet, despite his great religious and poetic claims, was
apparently willing to praise any victor, even a tyrant, who could
pay his fee. Certainly any discrimination of the worthiness of his
patron was unrelated to his role as a praise merchant. This is most
obvious at the very places where the poet appears to instruct, and
not just to praise, his patron. So Pindar's address to Hieron at
Pythian 1.81–86:

καιρὸν εἰ φθέγξαιο, πολλῶν πείρατα συντανύσαις
ἐν βραχεῖ, μείων ἔπεται μῶμος ἀνθρώπων. ἀπὸ γὰρ κόρος
ἀμβλύνει
αἰανὴς ταχείας ἐλπίδας·
ἀστῶν δ' ἀκοὰ κρύφιον θυμὸν βαρύνει μάλιστ' ἐσλοῖσι ἐπ'
ἀλλοτρίοις.
ἀλλ' ὅμως, κρέσσον γὰρ οἰκτιρμοῦ φθόνος,
μὴ παρίει καλά. νώμα δικαίῳ πηδαλίῳ στρατόν· ἀψευδεῖ
δὲ πρὸς ἄκμονι χάλκευε γλῶσσαν.

If you speak in season, tightly weaving together many lines,
less reproach of men will follow. For persistent satiety blunts
quick expectations.
And stories especially of others' achievements weigh heavily
upon the heart secretly.
Nonetheless, envy is better than pity.
Do not give up good deeds; guide the people with a straight
rudder,
and forge your tongue with an unlying anvil.

Pindar's readers will look in vain for any specific political or ethical
message or any real program for reform in this passage. With poetic
images bordering on the trite, Pindar's moral advice can do little
to moderate or direct Hieron's political behavior. Like the semi-
fictional Timotheus in Dryden's "Alexander's Feast," the epinician
poet "cou'd swell the soul to rage, or kindle soft desire," making his
patron smile or assuaging his pain. But he did not have the power to

alter the nature of his master's power, and it certainly was not in the nature of tyranny to change by degrees. From this perspective, the poet's advice that the tyrant should behave well, and the tyrant's conspicuous reception of such advice—whether he merely pretended to listen or did so sincerely—did most to highlight the tyrant's freedom to behave just as he wished. In fact, the mixture of praise and advice that is characteristic of epinician itself serves to neutralize the claim, embraced by Herodotus's Otanes and by Plato, that the tyrant is enslaved by his huge appetite for praise.[54]

Epinician poets were likely aware that they could not really instruct their patrons; and it was not for this that they most extolled their art. What they do well, they insist, is reward virtue, and virtue that is well rewarded, they claim, is the greatest happiness available to men. In fact, as Bacchylides insists at 3.89–92, the honor that poets bestow on virtue may serve as an antidote for the inescapable march of time:

> ἀρετᾶς γε μὲν οὐ μινύνθη
> βροτῶν ἅμα σώματι φέγγος, ἀλλὰ
> Μοῦσά νιν τρέφει.[55]

> The light of virtue does not wither
> together with the body of mortals
> but is nourished by the Muse.

The power that poetry possesses to combat forgetfulness complements the inherent value of virtue ("Cheer your heart by doing things that are holy, for this is the greatest of profits": Bacchyl. 3.83–84) in rewarding victors for their glorious achievements. We may complain that epinician here praises itself in the same isolated

---

54. In this sense, the appeals in Pindar to the tyrannical patron's moral virtues function much like the image of Clementia in the principate (*Res gestae* 34; see Adam 1970 and the succinct remark in Ferguson 1970, 73: "Clementia is a reminder of the emperor's absolute power and his kindness in not using it") or like the entreaties for the ruler's forbearance that were commonplace in the court literature of monarchical Europe. On the connection between autocratic power and clemency in Greek political language, see the various remarks on the virtues of forgiveness attributed to Pittacus: Diod. 9.12.3; D.L. 1.76.

55. Cf. Pind. *Isthm.* 7.16–19; 11.13–17.

and unpolitical terms it uses to praise its patrons. But victory poets were not oblivious to the political realities of praise poetry, as a passage in Pindar that explicitly mentions tyranny argues:

τῶν γὰρ ἀνὰ πόλιν εὑρίσκων τὰ μέσα μακροτέρῳ
ὄλβῳ τεθαλότα, μέμφομ᾽ αἶσαν τυραννίδων·
ξυναῖσι δ᾽ ἀμφ᾽ ἀρεταῖς τέταμαι. φθονεροὶ δ᾽ ἀμύνονται.
ἀλλ᾽ εἴ τις ἄκρον ἑλὼν ἡσυχᾷ τε νεμόμενος αἰνὰν ὕβριν
ἀπέφυγεν, μέλανος ἂν ἐσχατιὰν
καλλίονα θανάτου στείχοι γλυκυτάτᾳ γενεᾷ
εὐώνυμον κτεάνων κρατίσταν χάριν πορών.

(Pyth. 11.52–58)[56]

Believing that those citizens in the middle flourish
with the longest happiness, I find fault with tyrannies.
I reach for common virtues. For the envious are warded off,
but if someone who has reached the heights dwells there in
     peace and avoids dread hubris,
he would come to a better end in black death, leaving for
     his sweet offspring
the grace of a good name, strongest of resources.

Tyranny receives a striking interpretation in this aristocratic victory ode. Pindar's "common virtues" are not common to all men; instead, they are virtues that deserve the community's collective honor. Conversely, behavior labeled as "hubris" is unwelcomed and isolated and, for that reason, entices no poet to celebrate it. From this perspective, it makes sense that Pindar elsewhere chooses Phalaris of Acragas as his paradigmatic political villain. Phalaris, in his hubris, roasted his enemies inside a bronze bull, and he suffers eternal damnation as a result ("Hateful infamy holds [him] down in every way") and is deprived of all the benefits of song (Pyth. 1.96–98).

It is likely that Pindar's mythological presentation of athletic victory kept tyranny in the minds of his audience. If so, Pindar's interest in addressing tyranny explicitly is perhaps a preemptive

56. On the passage, see Young 1968, 12–22, and Kurke 1991, 215–18.

move. Pindar, in other words, incorporates tyranny within the distinct conceptual framework of epinician in order to insist on a strictly moralistic interpretation of it. Tyranny, for Pindar, is hubris deserving the silence that the poet bestows just as he bestows praise. The poet's threat of "hateful infamy" may not seem impressive. Like the *condemnatio memoriae* of the enervated Roman Senate, his refusal to praise evil deeds seems to articulate his powerlessness; Pindar does not speak against, but can only refuse to support, actions that he deems tyrannical. Pindar's powerlessness becomes all the more obvious in his example of actions that deserve silence: his Phalaris is a fiction with little resemblance to real tyrants. But although—or, indeed, because—his claim to power is imaginary, Pindar's interpretation of tyranny offers real power to his patron. When he asserts for himself and incorporates in his poem the final judgment over tyranny, Pindar in fact appropriates the power of praise from the community, his audience, and gives it to his patron. In the hands of the praise poet, the final decision over the patron and his victory becomes poetic. The beginning, middle, and end of his story, which epinician narrates and sanctifies with myth, is told by the patron's own agent, who supports his account of his patron with poetic proof of his credibility. The epinician poet allows the tyrant to replace his audience, preempt its decision over him, and exercise sovereignty over his story. The tyrant becomes a virtual narrator of his own story, the form, as Walter Benjamin has said, in which "the just man encounters himself"[57]—or, in which any man is able to invent his own justice.

Of course, the epinician poet did not serve his patron just by composing prayers, and divine jealousy did not itself diminish the power of tyrants or the reputation of aristocrats. Danger to tyrants and aristocrats came from their fellow citizens, the real audience of epinician poetry.[58] Although the poet's talk about divine envy is

57. Benjamin 1977, 410: "Der Erzähler ist die Gestalt, in welcher der Gerechter sich selbst begegnet."

58. Kurke (1991, 220) observes that Pindar's tyrannical odes treat the problem of envy far more cavalierly than his aristocratic odes: "The enviers are mocked rather than mollified." Pindar's disdain is, I think, strategic: he means to suggest that the audience's envy of his tyrant-patron is proved to be foolish by the considerable divine support the patron enjoys.

indirect, it is neither incidental nor insignificant. The acknowledgment and appeasement of the envy of the gods provided in fact the uniquely satisfactory solution to the very real problem of human envy. This is at times explicit: in one place, the envy of mortals is taken as proof of the victor's *aretē* (*Ol.* 6.72–76); in another, praise, which links mortal achievements with the gods, overcomes human envy:

μή νυν, ὅτι φθονεραὶ θνατῶν φρένας ἀμφικρέμανται ἐλπίδες,
μήτ᾽ ἀρετάν ποτε σιγάτω πατρῴαν,
μηδὲ τούσδ᾽ ὕμνους.

(Isthm. 2.43–45)

Not now, that envious hopes cling about the hearts of men,
must he ever let his ancestral virtue be silenced,
nor these songs.

Thus epinician links the victor and his divine patrons by means of mythical narrative and the invention of a divine audience. This link is intended as an appeal to the poem's human audience to honor the victor. And the appeal is powerful for the very reason that it is indirect. The audience that follows the music and dance of epinician watches and participates in a spectacle that anticipates and answers all doubts about the victor's *aretē*. Bacchylides makes it clear that this aim is traditional:

χρὴ δ᾽ ἀλαθείας χάριν
αἰνεῖν, φθόνον ἀμφοτέραισιν
χερσὶν ἀπωσάμενον,
εἴ τις εὖ πράσσοι βροτῶν.
Βοιωτὸς ἀνὴρ τᾷδε φώνησεν, γλυκειᾶν Ἡσίοδος πρόπολος
Μουσᾶν, ὃν ἂν ἀθάνατοι τιμῶσι, τούτῳ
καὶ βροτῶν φήμαν ἕπεσθαι.

(5.187–94)

It is necessary for the sake of truth to give praise,
shunning envy with both hands,

when someone of mortals fares well.
That Boeotian man, Hesiod, servant
of the sweet Muses, said these things:
whomever the immortals honor
should be followed with the good fame of mortals.

Thus epinician poets attempt to win honor for their patrons by asserting that they already possess the special honor that gods give men; some patrons, particularly rulers, possess so much honor that they risk the gods' envy. Because the gods have recognized the victor, the poet's real audience should find it easy and even necessary to honor him as well. This is the sophisticated aim of the victory poet. If he is successful, the patron emerges outfitted like Aeacus, whom, according to Pindar at *Nemean* 8.8–10,

πολλοὶ λιτάνευον ἰδεῖν.
ἀβοατὶ γὰρ ἡρώων ἄωτοι περιναιεταόντων
ἤθελον κείνου γε πείθεσθ᾽ ἀναξίαις ἑκόντες.

many pray to see.
And unsummoned the flower of the heroes living nearby
wish, though not forced, to obey his commands.

Victory, the poet asserts, is the source of praise, and praise is the source of honor, the public acknowledgment that victory comes from the gods. With this claim, epinician seems to complete its refutation of Herodotus's Otanes. While in the Persian debate the ruler's desire for the regard of his subjects is a logical contradiction that renders his power irrational, in epinician that regard is a necessary and inevitable consequence of the divine origin of his special *aretē*.

The victory poet obviously needs to present the relationship between the victor and the gods as real. Like the student arguing the Quintilian declamation, his theology is axiomatic; the victorious patron, like the *tyrannus fulminatus*, must be honored because the gods have marked him for honor. The poet is not guilty of insincerity. From his perspective, *alētheia* (truth), the opposite of con-

47

cealment,[59] insists on the celebration of *aretē*. The obligations of his politics and poetics dovetail perfectly: the poet serves truth when his song echoes in his audience's praise for the victor. But the victor also has his obligation. He must avoid the supreme impiety of failing to acknowledge in song that the gods are responsible for the victory. So Pindar at *Pythian* 5.23–25:

τῶ σε μὴ λαθέτω
Κυράνᾳ γλυκὺν ἀμφὶ κᾶπον Ἀφροδίτας ἀειδόμενον,
παντὶ μὲν θεὸν αἴτιον ὑπερτιθέμεν.

Therefore do not let it escape you, when you are
honored in song in the sweet garden of Aphrodite in Cyrene,
for each to hand over credit to the god.

The victor, in other words, must not forget poetry. And if the victor is pious and the poet is successful, the result is a poem of great power. As Pindar insists, "The song of good deeds makes a man fortunate like kings."[60]

It is not difficult to see why Sicilian tyrants were attracted to victory odes as a poetic supplement for the glory they won in their wars against the Carthaginians, the Etruscans, and rival cities and tyrants in Sicily.[61] The epinician poet undertook to reorder poetically the relationship between his audience and his patron. Tending

59. In Pindar, see *Nem.* 8.24–26 (Homer on Odysseus). In general, see Detienne 1967 and Cole 1983. Pindar's aesthetics are hardly naive; they concur with Hesiod and Solon ("Poets tell many lies": Sol. 25 GP), not with Homer ("Poets are not to blame" for the stories they tell: *Od.* 1.347–48). For Pindar, the poets may lie by revealing what did not happen, as Homer does in telling the tale of Odysseus (cf. Pind. *Nem.* 7.20–21).

60. *Nem.* 4.83–85:

ὕμνος δὲ τῶν ἀγαθῶν
ἐργμάτων βασιλεῦσιν ἰσοδαίμονα τεύχει
φῶτα.

61. Athletic victory and martial victory are occasionally linked in epinician. In *Pyth.* 1, Pindar extends his praise for Hieron's chariot victory in 470 to celebrate his defeat of the Etruscans at Cumae several years earlier. For the link between victory in war and victory in games, see also *Pyth.* 8.25–27, where the subject, however, is not a Sicilian tyrant but the city of Aegina.

by nature to collusion rather than confrontation, epinician used meter, music, and myths to draw the audience into a celebration of the *aretē* of the victor. For all its patrons, the celebration aimed to translate athletic victory into civic stature. For aristocratic patrons, it was enough that the celebration offered an image of the community—brief but repeatable—in which the patron and his family appeared as first citizens. But the tyrant clearly wanted more from victory odes. Epinician attempted to bring the tyrannical patron's fellow citizens, like Aeacus's, to "obey his commands willingly" (Pind. *Nem.* 8.10), or, if we may gloss Pindar with Machiavelli (*Discourses* 1.8), "to yield him the first place without deeming themselves degraded thereby."

But was epinician successful? Performances of victory odes were intense but also fleeting; the poet tried to convince the audience of the gods' immediate interest in his patron's victory, but he could not hope to make that conviction outlast the performance by very long. It is not only the remoteness of modern sensibilities that makes the victory ode now seem rather pompous and hollow. Pindar and Bacchylides might temporarily elevate their patrons in the eyes of their audience, but they did so by pretending to offer eternal proof that the patron's victory stemmed from divine *aretē*. As masters of mythical narrative and interpreters of the divine, epinician poets asserted complete control over their audiences' judgment of their patrons. Yet temporary success seems to have come at the price of ultimate failure. To make the patron seem honorable, the poet also made him seem threatened. The gods are powerful, but also fickle; they want the victor to be honored now, but they may feel very differently later. Every argument that epinician gives for its patron's distinctiveness is also an argument for his fragility. In its own terms, then, epinician seems to question, even as it proclaims, the happiness of the poet's tyrant-patron; and its listeners, even if they are brought to praise him, are left with the impression that the victor's fate is still very much in doubt.

If this is correct, epinician's very effort to control the tyrant's reception unwittingly invokes the rule implied by the Quintilian *Tyrannus fulminatus*: the tyrant, despite all his efforts, could not exert final control over his own reception. In turn, the declamation implies the city's obvious response to the representation that poets invented for tyrants: holding the power to expel the body of the tyrant *extra fines*, the city was able to replace with lasting infamy the temporary honor that rulers created by their own self-representation or purchased from praise merchants.

So read, the Quintilian exercise suggests that stories about the tyrants and founders offered Greek cities a kind of narrative power over their past. The lives of tyrants and founders functioned as fables to which cities could append their own morals: burial in the civic center made the founder's story a happy one, while expulsion *extra fines* redefined the tyrant's entire life as miserable. By adding its own conclusion, the polis embedded a narrative reversal in both stories. The founder's quest, which usually began and often progressed ignominiously,[62] ended in complete success, while the tyrant lived for a short time as the happiest of men to end life perfectly unhappy. And the narrative reversal served a political reversal. In honoring its founder, the city, which remembered him as its maker, honored him as its own possession; likewise, in oppressing its tyrant with dishonor, the polis was able to spurn its onetime master as if he were chattel that it might keep or discard at its discretion. The honor and dishonor detailed in the declamation thus celebrate the maturity and mastery of the city in the form of a story that retains the founder and tyrant as both decidedly significant and utterly finished. So Greek city-states did not need to conceal their early histories: when they wrote conclusions to the stories of their autocratic masters, they rendered innocuous their debt to founders and marked their subjugation to tyrants as forever past.

In Quintilian's day, the *Tyrannus fulminatus* could only have been appreciated for the quandary that it offered schoolboys. I have argued that the quandary (should the tyrant be buried in the civic center because he died as a result of Zeus's special attentions, or should he be cast from the city because he lived as a tyrant?) reflects the opposition between the tyrant and the founder and the city's mastery over their stories, both of which are basic to the polis's political identity and to its conception of sovereignty. But in reflecting the political language of the polis, the rhetorical exercise also

---

62. On this, see chap. 5 passim.

captures its distinctive political achievement: the Greek city-state solved the very quandary at the heart of the Quintilian exercise. Unfettered by the conventional logic that made the *Tyrannus fulminatus* a puzzle for the Roman schoolboy, poleis found ways to honor the tyrant as *fulminatus*—that is, as marked by the gods—at the same time that they utterly devalued his memory and negated his claims, as *tyrannus*, to happiness.

CHAPTER TWO

Justice and Power: The Language
of Early Greek Tyranny

ἐνίοις δηγμοῦ δεομένοις καὶ κολάσεως ἐμβαλὼν ὁ θεὸς πικρίαν
τινὰ τυράννου δυσμείλικτον καὶ τραχύτητα χαλεπὴν ἄρχοντος, οὐ
πρότερον ἐξεῖλε τὸ λυποῦν καὶ ταράττον ἢ τὸ νοσοῦν ἀπαλλάξαι
καὶ καθῆραι.

Sometimes the god applies the implacably bitter and harsh rule of a
tyrant to peoples needing a caustic and correction, and does not
remove the pain and annoyance until he has expelled and purged the
disease.

Plutarch, De sera numinis vindicta 553a

The sophist Hippias reports that *tyrannos*, the Greek word for
autocratic ruler (the individual who dominates a state through his
own strength and abilities rather than by perceived conceptions of
right), was first used in Archilochus's time, the seventh century
B.C.[1] In his extant poetry, Archilochus labels only one ruler a *tyrannos*, Gyges, the fabulously fortunate king of Lydia. But Archilochus clearly did not see tyranny as something entirely foreign
or strange. When he drew on it to construct metaphors for love
(23.18–21 W) and greed (19 W), he was exploiting a political situation that his Greek audience must have known, although perhaps
not yet from personal experience.[2] If Archilochus and his genera-

1. Cf. *FGH* 6 F 6. On the origin and original meaning of *tyrannos*, see Labarbe
1971.
2. For Archilochus on tyranny, see also chap. 1.

tion were the first Greeks to label individual rule as *tyrannia*, they were certainly not the first to form ideas about the political domination of single individuals and small groups. Homeric epic incorporates complex models of kingship that much predate tyranny. But the political institution that Archilochus and his contemporaries marked with a new word, was a new and very different form of political power. To frame the political innovation that this new word reflects and, most important, to understand its close relationship with the concept of justice (δίκη), I begin with a discussion of kingship in Homer and Hesiod, who record the ideas and images of political domination in the generations that saw tyranny come to exist.

Kings in Homer and Hesiod

When Louis Gernet made his provocative suggestion that archaic tyrants deliberately revived images of Homer's kings in order also to recapture their privileges and power,[3] he was ignoring much that Homer's narratives offered their early archaic audiences on the subject of kings and kingship. Tyrants could not help being intrigued by the godlike status of Homeric kingship, but they would hardly have wished to resurrect its tenuous and fragile social and political basis. The kings of the *Iliad* and *Odyssey* are, as a rule, preeminent warriors who enjoy power and privileges in proportion to their martial achievements.[4] The Lycian king Sarpedon suggests this relation in *Iliad* 12 (310–14) when, on the verge of battle, he asks Glaucus why their people honor them like gods, and immediately defines his question as rhetorical by answering it himself with an exhortation to Glaucus to join him at the head of the army.[5]

---

3. Gernet 1968.
4. On Homeric kingship in general, see Carlier 1984, 165–68, Drews 1983, Andreev 1979, Descat 1979, and Deger 1970. On the fragile nature of Agamemnon's power as king of men (ἄναξ ἀνδρῶν), see McGlew 1989; and on the ideology of Homeric power see also Rose 1975 and Thalmann 1988.
5. To the question,

> Γλαῦκε, τίη δὴ νῶϊ τετιμήμεσθα μάλιστα
> ἕδρῃ τε κρέασίν τε ἰδὲ πλείοις δεπάεσσιν

And what Sarpedon stresses by leaving unsaid—that kings live well because they fight well—explains the peril as well as the power of Homeric kingship. The prerogatives of kingship obligate Homer's warrior-kings to face repeatedly the possibility of death in the heroic duels that kings characteristically fight. In this fundamental sense, victory is the first condition of the Homeric king's royal status.

Yet, despite the conditional nature of their power, Homer, like Thomas More, saw kings as "the springs both of good and evil."[6] A good king ensures social harmony, while a bad or weak king threatens it. And for Homer the king is necessary even if his power is insecure and his devotion to his community wavers. The absence of a king is an important feature of the perfectly uncivilized society of the Cyclopes; and, although Homeric kings never rule entirely alone, a community with too many kings, as Odysseus suggests at *Iliad* 2.204, courts political disaster. This ambiguous image of kingship as necessary but fragile fits the narrative demands of the *Iliad* and *Odyssey*, which plot the fates of communities through the personal trials of their kings, but it does not exhaust Homer's thoughts on the subject of royal power. Interspersed within his stories of the struggles of Agamemnon and Odysseus, Homer offers occasional glimpses of a less heroic world and less heroic forms of power, which have been thought "ordinary" from the

---

> ἐν Λυκίῃ, πάντες δὲ θεοὺς ὣς εἰσορόωσι,
> καὶ τέμενος νεμόμεσθα μέγα Ξάνθοιο παρ' ὄχθας,
> καλὸν φυταλιῆς καὶ ἀρούρης πυροφόροιο;

Sarpedon answers:

> τῷ νῦν χρὴ Λυκίοισι μέτα πρώτοισιν ἐόντας
> ἑστάμεν ἠδὲ μάχης καυστείρης ἀντιβολῆσαι.
> (*Il.* 12.310–16)

Why have we been rewarded most of all
with a seat of honor and meat and many goblets
in Lycia, and everyone regards us as gods,
and we dwell on a great estate by the banks of the Xanthus,
lovely in its vineyards and grain-bearing fields?

So now we must go forward and stand among the first
of the Lycians and meet the raging battle.

6. More 1964, 5.

perspective of the poet's own world.[7] These glimpses, much like Homer's similes, were intended to frame the distinction between the world of his heroes and that occupied by himself and his audience, men who, in the language of the similes, could not lift stones even half as large as those heaved about by his heroes. But even if Homer turns to his contemporary world only to highlight the stature of his heroes and their struggles, his images of his own world offer much of value on the character of political power in the generations before tyranny.

This is particularly true of the shield scene in *Iliad* 18, Homer's description of the images Hephaestus etches into the new shield he makes for Achilles. The shield scene is an elaborate microcosm that provides dynamic and static images of the heavens, Ocean, the worlds of agriculture and urban life, and the points of intersection between civilized life and nature. In this world within a world, Hephaestus places two cities, one of which is at war, the other at peace. The former is simultaneously beset by two hostile armies, while the latter enjoys weddings and feasts and witnesses the peaceful arbitration of a blood dispute between two citizens. The poet's account of the two cities is particularly terse, and details of the cities' social, political, and economic institutions are sparse. Yet is clear and important that Homer accords no place in the two cities to the sort of royal power that elsewhere dominates the political, social, and economic center of heroic society. No king is involved in the activities of either city, while the one anonymous king of the shield is busy tending his kingly estate at the periphery of the shield,[8] as if to suggest that his remoteness from the shield's social activities reflects the unimportance of kingship in the world that the shield depicts. The absence of kings certainly does not hamper the two cities. In the battle surrounding the less fortunate of Hephaestus's two cities (the sort of activity that Homer's kings would not usually miss), the shield men are obviously able to fight to protect their city or to destroy someone else's without the leadership of Homeric kings and without the heroic duels that they fought.

---

7. So Edwards (1988, 279–86) refers to the Iliadic shield scene.

8. *Il.* 18.550–57. On the function of the Homeric royal estate (τέμενος βασιλήϊον), see Carlier 1984, 158–60.

The people of Achilles' shield are also able to solve their legal problems without the help of kings.[9] In his account of the legal dispute in the more fortunate of the two cities, Homer relates that a man offers a certain sum as restitution for killing a fellow citizen, while a relative of the victim rejects the offer. The community's elders listen to the arguments of the two litigants and then take turns offering solutions, each announcing his opinion with a scepter in hand. Although the scepter is elsewhere in Homer a symbol of exclusive god-given power in legal matters (θέμιστες: *Il.* 2.206; 9.99), the elders do not themselves determine or enforce the final judgment in this case. For "two talents of gold lay in the middle" (18.506), which the litigants,[10] or, more probably, the assembled people who also hear the litigants (18.500), award to the elder whose "judgment is most straightforward" (18.508). Established legal procedures now perform the function performed elsewhere in Homer by kings. The change is apparently for the better. The orderly assembly bears little resemblance to those that Homer positions in the crucial second books of the *Iliad* and the *Odyssey*, which prove disastrous because of the weakness or absence of the ruling king.

Throughout the *Iliad* and *Odyssey*, Homer constructs and exploits an elaborate analogy between the worlds of gods and kings. In the shield scene, too, theology is closely related to politics. The role of the Olympian gods, who are otherwise prominent in Homer as the patrons of kings, is much curtailed in this world lacking royal power. Zeus himself does not appear, and no Olympians are pictured among the immortal bodies with which Homer encircles his two cities. Instead we are offered brief glimpses of Athena and Ares in the thick of battle around the city at war (18.516), fighting apparently as patron gods of warring groups and as divine soldiers of fortune, but not, as far as we are told, in the service of a supreme god or as patrons of individual warriors.

Epic, which was both product and ingredient of early archaic Greece, frames its own relation to its world as antithetical rather than mimetic. The shield scene is obviously included in the *Iliad* for

9. On the legal scene and controversies, see Gagarin 1986, 26–33.
10. So Gagarin 1986, 31.

literary, not historical, purposes: it is an antiheroic image created by the artist-god Hephaestus and exhibited (paradoxically) by the incomparably heroic Achilles. But that it also reflected the social concerns of Homer's own world is argued by the marked similarity of the shield scene to the world described by Hesiod's more didactically oriented *Works and Days*. Like the shield scene, Hesiod's *Works and Days* shows little interest in the claim that kings owe their position to their divine ancestors.[11] Hesiod's kings ($\beta\alpha\sigma\iota\lambda\hat{\eta}s$), again more like the elders of the shield scene than the kings who dot Homer's battlefields, function as arbiters rather than warriors. And the parallel extends to the gods: the Olympian gods who appear in the *Works and Days* have entirely shed their roles as the personal patrons of powerful kings.

In fact, the most important god in the lives and social dealings of men in the *Works and Days* is not an Olympian at all, but Dike, a thin personification of the principle of political order and responsibility. Her mythological shallowness perhaps explains Dike as a relatively new invention, but it also articulates her essence and function. Unmotivated by anthropomorphic passions, without mortal children, and unwilling to play favorites among men and women, Dike is defined by a single concern: to punish the devotees of Injustice (= Adikia or Hybris), her antithesis and eternal enemy. Though clearly one-dimensional, Dike is hardly peripheral: Hesiod makes it clear that "the gift-devouring kings ($\beta\alpha\sigma\iota\lambda\hat{\eta}s$) who sell themselves to the largest bidder" (*Op.* 36–39) keep her very busy.

Hesiod's kings resemble Homer's in one important respect: they are responsible for the goodwill of the gods and the prosperity of the city. This is apparent in Hesiod's image of the fates of the good and bad cities. The good city, where "kings give straight judgments and do not transgress the just, fares well and the people flourish" (*Op.* 225–27).[12] But the evil city, in which kings give crooked judgments, suffers all sorts of torments. Dike watches over men

11. See, however, *Th.* 96, where Hesiod, in discussing kings who listen to the voices of the Muses, concedes vaguely that "kings are from Zeus."

12. On Hesiod's notion of justice, see Vernant 1978, 42–79. The forswearing of oaths and taking of bribes are characteristic of injustice for Hesiod; so also in Heraclitus (B28 DK) and Alcaeus (see below, n. 31). Few would have argued with the Orphic saying, "The oath is justice" (D.L. 8.33).

and records their transgressions, comes to the city in a mist, "bringing evil to the men who drove her out" (*Op.* 223–24), while Zeus, her partner in punishment, exacts vengeance on a broader scale: "The son of Cronus puts great trouble upon the people, famine and plague at the same time; the people wither away; the women do not give birth; households are diminished" (*Op.* 242–44). Hesiod's ideas of *dikē* and *adikia* extend into the political sphere the religious notions of pollution and purification.[13] Injustice, like pollution, troubles the entire community, not kings alone, although kings most often commit the offending acts. Yet there is one clear difference between religious purification and the Hesiodic notion of punishment; Hesiod never speaks of restoring *dikē* by expelling or killing an unjust individual or by designating and eliminating a scapegoat. Only the suffering of the entire community will appease the divine Dike: "It often happens that a whole city is punished on account of a single bad man," Hesiod writes (*Op.* 240). In this notion of justice there lies perhaps the first trace of an acknowledgment of the demos's (people's) political rights.

Hesiod's kings are no less vital for the welfare of their communities than are Homer's. But while Homer's kings, with the exception of Alcinous, seem oblivious to social and political responsibilities off the battlefield, Hesiod's are never permitted to forget that they must maintain justice in their cities; in fact, Hesiod sees it as his duty to remind them. The poet does not always find this easy; Hesiod at one point compares himself to a nightingale who pleads for mercy from a hawk who has captured her, but the hawk says, "One far stronger than you holds you tight, and you, though a songstress, must go where I take you" (*Op.* 207–8). Hesiod's point is perhaps less the poet's weakness than the implacable rule that strong dominates weak: "He is a fool," the hawk tells the nightingale, "who wishes to fight against his superiors" (*Op.* 210). It is a rule that Hesiod probably thought applied to kings as well, for Zeus, who supports the cause of justice, is much stronger than kings.[14] The poet thus performs a moral duty that exceeds his social position, and "kings who understand," Hesiod adds (*Op.* 202), will

13. See Parker 1983, 257–80. For the significance of purification in the legends of founders, see chap. 5.
14. See Lamberton 1988, 121–22.

avoid committing acts of injustice against him. As Hesiod insists in the *Theogony* (81–93), the good king and the poet share the Muses' attentions: the king owes his ability to make straight judgments to the Muses (93), whom the poet also claims to serve (100).[15]

Epic's idealized view of the heroic past and Hesiod's severe view of his contemporary society offer very different pictures of kingship. In Homer, cities and nations are each dominated by a single king. Homer's heroes (and his gods) are driven by a desire for honor and vengeance, but not for *dikē*. In Hesiod (and in the Homeric shield scene), on the other hand, there is no one single king, no master of the city, whose political actions articulate his personal desires. Instead the many leaders of each community are responsible for the preservation of justice. The character of the relation between the gods and kings changes along with the definition of kingship. Hesiod's gods define the responsibility and irresponsibility of kings and scrutinize their behavior with great care; Hesiod seems convinced that without divine supervision kings would gladly ruin their communities to indulge their personal interests. This transformation of the nature of the gods, and of Zeus especially, is no less dramatic than the change in the conception of royal power. In Hesiod, Zeus and Dike, goddess of justice, become father and daughter (*Th.* 902); and in the moralistic spirit of Hesiod's reflections on power, Zeus will soon trade in the scales with which he measures the fates of heroes for a set that weighs the crimes and punishments of all men.[16]

As the struggle between justice and hubris dominates Hesiod's political conceptions, so it also pervades his view of the history of mankind. In his tale of the history of mankind (*Op.* 109–201), hubris plagues the ages of man that perish at the hands of Zeus, but is clearly absent from the Golden Age and the Age of Heroes, which Zeus honors with a measure of immortality. The notion that injustice cannot escape divine punishment enjoyed a long life in the

---

15. The Muses have a dual role: they teach the poet to "sing of the glories of earlier men and of the blessed gods" (*Th.* 100–101) to charm away his audience's sorrows, and they lend him authority to advise kings and the demos.

16. Scales of Justice (τάλαντα Δίκης) appear first in *Hymn. Hom. Merc.* 324 and *Bacchyl.* 4.11–12 and 17.24–26. For the idea, see also Aesch. *Ag.* 250–51 and *Cho.* 61.

poets and philosophers in the centuries after Hesiod. Archilochus insists that no injustice, no matter how petty, escapes the gods: "The hubris and justice of the wild beasts interest Zeus" (177 W). And, as always, fictions of divine or natural necessity serve moral ends. In his own unique way, Archilochus transforms Hesiod's *dikē* into a personal code of honor: "There is one great thing that I know: to respond with terrible wrongs to him who wrongs me" (126 W). Sappho adopts a similar idea of the inevitability of punishment when she proclaims unrequited love to be a wrong for which Aphrodite will force her reluctant lover to make amends (1.20–24 LP; 37 LP). Eventually the notion of *dikē* would surface as a law of nature in the Ionian cosmologies from Anaximander through Heraclitus and, somewhat later, in the medical writers, who viewed health as a kind of political balance (ἰσονομία) of the body's powers and disease as the disturbance of such a balance (Hippoc. *Arch. iatr.* 14).[17]

Amidst the personal and cosmological extensions of *dikē* after Hesiod, there was also a deepening sense of the relation between *dikē* and political leadership and unity. The connection is particularly striking in the common metaphorical representations of the city as a ship that sails on a sea of political turmoil and is doomed to destruction if it is without the "just rudder" of good leaders. It lurks also in the less common representations of the city as a human body whose parts are symbiotically linked with one another and with their common environment.[18]

But it is perhaps in the new form of political power that the Greeks after Archilochus labeled *tyrannia* that Hesiod's intensely moral conception of politics is most completely preserved. Although the causes and events that led to the establishment of tyranny on the Greek mainland are difficult to know (not because they have been silenced by time, but because later Greeks remembered them as events of legendary significance in the early history of their

17. See Gentili 1972. On Sappho, see Bonanno 1973. On Ionian cosmologists and the medical writers, see Vlastos 1970 and Kahn 1979, 272–75.

18. For ship metaphors, see Archil. 105 W; Alc. 6, 208, 249 LP (cf. Heraclit. *All.* 5); Pind. *Pyth.* 1.86 ("guiding the people with a just rudder": δίκαιον πηδάλιον) and 10.72 ("steering of cities": πόλιων κυβερνάσιες); or. ap. Plut. *Sol.* 14.4 (= 15 PW); Soph. *Ant.* 163; and for body metaphors, Alcmaeon B4 DK.

cities), a few traces of the political language and reception of early Greek tyranny survive to allow us to reconstruct tyranny's relationship with the predominant concern for justice that characterizes archaic Greece.

Justice and the Cypselids

Both the historical value and limitations of the Greeks' memories of their earliest tyrants are evident at Corinth, where Cypselus established tyranny in the middle of the 650s.[19] The popular story of the Cypselids' rise was reported in somewhat different versions by Herodotus and Nicolaus of Damascus, who borrowed from the fourth-century world history of Ephorus.[20] In Herodotus, the story is told by Sosicles, Corinth's delegate at an assembly of Peloponnesian states that met in the last decade of the sixth century to discuss recent events at Athens. The Spartans intended to establish a tyranny at Athens, and the Corinthian delegate sought to dissuade them by recounting Corinth's own experiences with tyranny. In his account, Cypselus's mother, Labda, belonged to the ruling Bacchiad clan, while Aetion, his father, did not. The Bacchiads did not generally allow marriages outside their clan; they permitted this one because Labda's lameness left her without a Bacchiad husband. But oracles made the Bacchiads fear the offspring of this union. When the news of a son's birth came to them, they went to kill the child. But the infant's sudden smile stunned them, and before they could steel their nerves, Labda concealed Cypselus in a chest (which became his namesake). When he grew to a man, Cypselus heard another oracle that encouraged him to make himself "king" of Corinth, and, as Corinth's tyrant, he executed or exiled many of the Bacchiads and stole their property.

Nicolaus's version also mentions Cypselus's great fortune as a child in avoiding the Bacchiads and the oracles that encouraged Cypselus's ambitions, but it is less interested in miracles than in

19. For the chronology of the Cypselids, see Mosshammer 1979, 234–45, and Servais 1969. Among recent studies of the Cypselid tyranny, see Bockisch 1982 and Salmon 1984, 186–95.

20. Toher (1989) shows, however, that Nicolaus was more than a mere compiler.

Cypselus's qualifications for the position of tyrant. In this account, Cypselus begins his public career as the polemarch in the Bacchiad administration, where he becomes famous for his justice and integrity. At an opportune moment, Cypselus consolidates his support among the Corinthians, kills the reigning Bacchiad king, and exiles and expropriates the land of many of the Bacchiads. Although his actions against the ruling elite were harsh, Cypselus did not apparently damage his general popularity. According to Nicolaus, Cypselus "ruled in a kindly manner without a bodyguard and was not hateful to the Corinthians" (*FGH* 90 F 57.8).

With its extended report of Cypselus's clouded social origins and the miraculous smile that saves him from the Bacchiads, Herodotus's account offers a fairy tale of the tyrant's rise to power that implicitly classes Cypselus with the likes of mythical kings and city founders. Like Oedipus (cf. Soph. *OT* 1178–81), Cypselus survives because the ironic and irrational pity of his future victims overcomes their own best interests.[21] Here Nicolaus parts ways with Herodotus. His Cypselus is a competent and sensitive leader whose political opportunism cannot obscure his justice and mildness. It is difficult to know which version the Corinthians preferred: Herodotus's, which mythologizes Cypselus's rise, or Nicolaus's, which prefers to stress his abilities and virtues. There is even less hope of knowing what actually happened. This has been effectively— albeit unintentionally—demonstrated by Stewart Oost and Robert Drews, who have carefully combed the two accounts to arrive at opposite conclusions about who Cypselus was and what he did to make himself tyrant.[22] Yet there is a crucial point of agreement in Delphi's involvement in Cypselus's rise, which, though probably a historical fiction, was likely invented in the time of the Cypselids' rule and its immediate aftermath, when the Cypselids were still very much on the Corinthians' minds. On this we will focus our attention.

21. See Vernant 1982 and Jameson 1986. For parallels of miraculous beginnings in Greek foundation legends, see chap. 5 passim. A story featuring a miraculous survival was also told about the Sicilian tyrant Gelon (Diod. 10.29.1). Pity also saves Cyrus (Hdt. 1.112).

22. Oost (1972) uses the reports of Herodotus and Nicolaus to show that Cypselus was in reality a Bacchiad who consolidated and preserved Bacchiad rule, while Drews (1972) uses the same material to show that Cypselus was not a Bacchiad or even Corinthian.

The Language of Early Greek Tyranny

Delphi figures most prominently in Herodotus's story. When Cypselus's father, Aetion, came on a pilgrimage to Delphi, he was told about the son his wife was soon to bear:

> Ἠετίων, οὔτις σε τίει πολύτιτον ἐόντα.
> Λάβδα κύει, τέξει δ᾽ ὀλοοίτροχον· ἐν δὲ πεσεῖται
> ἀνδράσι μουνάρχοισι, δικαιώσει δὲ Κόρινθον.
>
> (5.92β.2)

Aetion, though you deserve honor, you are dishonored.
Labda carries a child and will bring forth a great rock
that will fall on the exclusive rulers and set Corinth right.

The Corinthians heard much the same thing when they visited Delphi to ask about another matter:

> αἰετὸς ἐν πέτρῃσι κύει, τέξει δὲ λέοντα
> καρτερὸν ὠμηστήν· πολλῶν δ᾽ ὑπὸ γούνατα λύσει.
> ταῦτά νυν εὖ φράζεσθε, Κορίνθιοι, οἳ περὶ καλὴν
> Πειρήνην οἰκεῖτε καὶ ὀφρυόεντα Κόρινθον.
>
> (5.92β.3)

An eagle conceives in the rocks and will
bring forth a lion, a mighty hunter of flesh,
who will weaken the knees of many.
Be warned of this, you Corinthians who live
around the fair Pirene and the heights of Acrocorinth.

Cypselus was given a third oracle when he visited Delphi:

> ὄλβιος οὗτος ἀνὴρ ὃς ἐμὸν δόμον ἐσκαταβαίνει,
> Κύψελος Ἠετίδης, βασιλεὺς κλειτοῖο Κορίνθου,
> αὐτὸς καὶ παῖδες, παίδων γε μὲν οὐκέτι παῖδες.
>
> (5.92ε.2)

Happy is this man who enters my house,
Cypselus, son of Aetion, king of renowned Corinth,
himself and his children, but the children of his children
no more.

These oracles are the focus of most efforts to reconstruct the ideological aura that came to surround the Cypselids' rise. It is certain that the oracles are not the genuine *ante eventum* products of Delphi that Herodotus and Nicolaus took them to be, but it is widely believed that they predate the version of Cypselus's rise that Sosicles used to dissuade the Spartans from establishing a tyranny in Athens.[23] There is also considerable agreement about their purpose before they were interwoven as narrative elements in Sosicles' tale. Commentators take the oracles as fabrications originally intended to create the impression that the tyranny was favored or hated by the gods. This view pervades the attempt to assign authors for the three fabrications: most see the first as favorable to the tyranny and attribute it to a camp of Cypselid supporters and interpret the second as hostile and credit it to the Cypselids' enemies.[24] The third, which shifts in midstream from language apparently favorable to Cypselus to terms that seem hostile, has complicated this method of attribution, and most scholars believe that it underwent revision.[25]

Yet the various disagreements about the date and authorship of the Cypselid oracles are ultimately less troubling than the agreement about their function and significance: that the oracles were the ideological products of a regime determined to disguise its power or the inventions of its enemies, who were equally determined to represent that regime in the worst possible light. Are the oracles well understood as either "favorable" or "hostile" to the Cypselids? Are they likely either to have helped consolidate support for Corinth's tyrants or to have justified opposition to them?

The first oracle, which is usually regarded as pro-Cypselid, seems most obviously to resist these assumptions. It announces Cypselus's rise as a restoration of the honor of his father, Aetion, who, the oracle implies, was dishonored by the ruling Bacchiads. According to the accompanying story, Aetion went to Delphi distressed by his

23. PW 1:116–17 makes the point explicitly.
24. So Salmon 1984, 186–87, and Drews 1972, 132 n. 11. Drews takes the first oracle as contemporary or nearly contemporary with Cypselus's coup d'état; Salmon agrees only to place it before the tyranny's fall. Oost (1972, 18) and PW 1:116–17 interpret the tone of both the first and the second oracle as pro-Cypselid.
25. See the discussion below.

wife's failure to bear a child. The oracle told him that "Labda will bear a rolling stone that will fall upon the exclusive rulers." The image of the rolling stone (*olooitrochos*) deserves close scrutiny. Elsewhere in Herodotus (8.52), rolling stones (*oloitrochoi*) are used as weapons that are let loose from an acropolis upon a siege force; and in a simile at *Iliad* 13.137, Hector is compared to an *olooitrochos* when he rushes in the madness of battle at the Achaeans. The *olooitrochos* is an object of fear as well as a tool of destruction; it can be aimed, but once set in motion, it is impossible to stop or control. In that sense, the *olooitrochos* very much resembles the natural disasters that follow injustice in Hesiod: famine, plague, the withering away of the people, and barrenness (*Op.* 242–44). An undiscriminating, arbitrary, and apparently senseless force, the *olooitrochos* seems a perfect archaic punishment for a breach of justice. As Solon wrote, the injustice of even a single individual in the city brings forth a "common evil" that "comes into the house of every man"—whether innocent or guilty—passing through closed gates and jumping hedges, seeking out even the man "who hides in his own room" (3.26–29 GP).[26] The Corinthians may well have despised their *monarchoi* (single rulers), as the oracle labels the Bacchiads, and believed that they deserved all they got, but they would have been very careful to stay out of Cypselus's way.

It does not seem that the first of the three oracles was designed to win Cypselus conventional political support. Like the elder Cato's remarkable rhetoric in his campaign for censorship (Plut. *Cat. Mai.* 16.6–7; Livy 39.41.1–3), the oracles perversely argue for Cypselus by promising that his rise to power will be extraordinarily harsh. In fact, the oracles do not suggest that the Corinthians will benefit from Cypselus's rule, and make it very clear that Cypselus's own motives are entirely personal; he falls on the Bacchiads in order to avenge his father. But this does not mean that the Bacchiads were guilty only of a single personal insult. They are explicitly labeled *andres monarchoi* (men ruling alone). In the political language of archaic Greece, *monarchoi* are rulers who arrogate powers and privileges that belong to all *aristoi* (the nobility) or possibly to the entire

---

26. See also *Theog.* 39–52; for Solon's view of justice, see Vlastos 1946, 69; and chap. 3 passim.

city. In Solon (12.3–4 GP), "the demos falls to the slavery of the monarch" through its ignorance and the injustice of its leaders, and in Theognis (39–52), *monarchia* emerges from the wrongs of the unjust. *Monarchia* was likewise construed as an evil in the Hippocratic tradition and in the Ionian school of natural philosophy,[27] which the Corinthian who narrates Cypselus's story in Herodotus reflects when he characterizes the Spartan proposal to establish a single ruler in Athens as a perversion of the cosmic order.[28]

That oracles announcing a tyranny should label the preceding regime a monarchy seems incongruous; in fact, this incongruity has fueled the suggestion that the Cypselid oracles were invented at an early point in Cypselus's rule, before he determined to become, and before he was perceived as, a tyrant.[29] But this suggestion is not necessary. The notion of justice that the Cypselid oracles invoke and that Solon and Theognis echo implies a reciprocity between crime and punishment that makes them at times seem identical. "The city is pregnant," Theognis feared at 39–40, "and will give birth to an *anēr euthuntēr* (reformer) of our hubris." This man, who must be one of the *monarchoi* Theognis mentions at 52, is both an evil and a good: he makes the city suffer for the wrongs of its leaders, but he also restores justice.[30] Conversely, good order (εὐνομία) in Solon performs many of the deeds of Theognis's *monarchos*, if in a far gentler manner: good order "often chains the feet of the unjust, smooths over the rough, brings an end to satiety, obscures hubris, withers the waxing buds of ruin, straightens crooked judgments," and the like (3.32–36 GP).[31] Both Theognis and Solon would have

27. For passages and a general discussion, see Vlastos 1970, 57–60.

28. Hdt. 5.92α.1: "The heavens will be beneath the sea, and the earth will be elevated above the heavens, and men will live in the sea, and the fish will take the dwellings of men, now that you, Lacedaimonians, prepare to dissolve freedom (ἰσοκρατία) and introduce tyrannies into cities. For nothing is more unjust (ἀδικότερον) or murderous (μιαφονώτερον) among men than tyranny."

29. So Forrest 1966, 111.

30. The related *euthunos* (corrector) similarly appears in Aeschylus as an executor of divine justice, once in connection with Zeus (*Per.* 828) and once with Hades (*Eum.* 273). For its relation to the project of Solon, the Athenian lawgiver, see the next chapter. On *dikē* in Theognis, see also Nagy 1985, 22–81.

31. The antityrannical poetry of Alcaeus is different, for he tailors his notions of *monarchia* and *dikē* to suit "the great contest" that is now "visible" (6.10 LP): the tyranny of Pittacus. For the conservative Alcaeus, the monarch (Pittacus) alone is

wished "that Dike had had a share in these matters from the first," as Pelasgus cries in Aeschylus's *Suppliants* (344), for Dike is more fearful by far when she arrives late.

This may explain the significance of *dikaiōsei Korinthon* in the first oracle, a phrase that has been variously understood to mean "set Corinth right" or "punish Corinth," but perhaps means both: Cypselus will set Corinth right by punishing it. This interpretation in turn suggests that the second of the Cypselid oracles ("An eagle conceives in the rocks and will bring forth a lion, a mighty hunter of flesh, who will weaken the knees of many") confirms the first. Even as it focuses on the less pleasant side of the emergence of an agent of *dikē*, it defines, rather than rejects, his rule. In fact, the second oracle makes good rhetorical sense in pretending to remind the Corinthians that they were once warned of Cypselus's coming but chose to ignore the warning. Cypselus's rule is made to look inevitable and is neatly described: he is the lion who will exact punishment by eating Corinth's evil leaders alive.[32]

It seems then that the first two oracles, as religious arguments for political power sometimes do, justify the Cypselids' power by its very harshness. The Cypselid oracles might in this respect be compared with the oracle that was included in the story of the rise of the Orthagorids, the contemporaries of the Cypselids who ruled the neighboring city of Sicyon. The Orthagorid oracle, which survives in a prose version,[33] bluntly informs the Sicyonians that they will be "ruled by scourge" for one hundred years. The accuracy of the prediction dates the oracle to the post-tyrannical period. But although the oracle was certainly produced after the Orthagorids'

---

the evil that is sinking the scales of the city (141 LP), for he himself has broken oaths and devours the city (129.23–24 LP; cf. 167, 200, 306g.10–11). The city is chastised for tolerating Pittacus (348 LP), but punishment must be directed primarily against him, and it is the task of the exiled aristocrats to exact it (cf. 6, 70, 298 LP).

32. On the lion's significance as a political symbol, see the account of Hipparchus's dream at Hdt. 5.56 and Arist. *Pol.* 1284a15–17. At 7.131.5, Herodotus mentions the lion that Agariste dreams she will bear, when she is pregnant with Pericles; the lion characterizes the remarkable power that the Alcmaeonids wielded in fifth-century Athens. For the lion as an image of divinely willed destruction see also Aesch. *Ag.* 717–36. For late fifth-century appropriation of that imagery, see Ar. *Ran.* 1431. Elsewhere (Alc. 129 LP) *ōmēstas* (eater of raw flesh) is an epithet of Dionysus, who, like early tyrants, was viewed both as fearful and as irresistible.

33. Diod. 8.24 = 23 PW; cf. *POxy.* 1365 = *FGH* 105.2; Plut. *Mor.* 553a.

fall, it does not represent the punishment of tyranny as unwarranted or illegal. Plutarch (*Mor.* 553a) thought the Orthagorid tyranny was sent by the gods to punish the Sicyonians for their crimes. In all probability, the Sicyonians believed this as well.

The second of the Cypselid oracles purports to be a response to an inquiry from the Corinthians. In this it differs from the first, which Sosicles reports to have been delivered spontaneously to Aetion as he entered Apollo's temple. This is made obvious in the third oracle ("Happy is this man who enters my house"); a dramatic sense of the spontaneity of the priestess's response is written into the text itself. Among legendary and literary oracles, spontaneous responses are awarded to many of Delphi's most prestigious visitors: Lycurgus (29, 216 PW), Hesiod (206 PW), Battus (39 PW), and Ancaeus, founder and ruler of Samos (233 PW).[34] Like these, Cypselus is already known to Apollo as a man marked for exceptional deeds, and Aetion, Cypselus's father, for bearing such an illustrious son. The spontaneity of the second and third oracles also underscores the significance of their messages.[35] As in fictional oracles in which the response is unrelated to the inquiry,[36] Delphi's voice rings more genuine and divine as it appears less influenced by the inquirer's question.[37]

In the third oracle Delphi confirms its support for Cypselus by addressing him as "king of famous Corinth."[38] But the tone of this oracle changes in the third line ("himself and his children, but his children's children no more"), which predicts an abrupt end to the Cypselids' good fortune after only two generations. The shift from a greeting supportive of the Cypselids to a prediction of their

34. The prestige attached to such oracles continued beyond the classical period. Alexander the Great (270 PW) and Attalus I of Pergamum (431 PW) were also awarded spontaneous oracles.

35. An obvious example is the gloomy prediction of defeat that the Athenian delegation is given when it comes to Delphi in search of a plan against the Persians (Hdt. 7.140.1 = 94 PW).

36. See, for example, 37, 39, 79, 114, 160, 410 PW. In a related type (e.g., Myscellus's question about his childlessness: 43 PW), the god solves the private concern of the consultant by engaging his support for a much larger project. See also chap. 1.

37. This was to become a literary topos (321, 514, 516 PW); see Parke 1962.

38. Oost (1972, 19) took this as a sign that Cypselus was regarded as a king in Corinth, but see Oliva (1982, 368).

demise complicates attempts to attribute this oracle according to its tone; some scholars have proposed that the first two lines were written during the family's reign, while the final line was appended by its enemies, at Delphi or Corinth, after the Cypselids' fall.[39]

Yet this solution does not take into account other political and legendary oracles that show similarly mercurial shifts in tone. The oracle that welcomes Gyges' rule but quickly announces the limit of its duration is an obvious example (Hdt. 1.13 = 51 PW).[40] What underlies this similarity is not Delphi's indecision but a certain ambivalence toward autocratic rule. It must have seemed to the authors of both genuine and spurious oracles to fit Apollo's duties as the manager of the great gulf separating men and gods to maintain a precise balance between human happiness and misery. It follows that oracles celebrating mortals and their achievements without qualification are rare exceptions. The point of the exceptions is to suggest that those so honored are not quite mortal—for example, Lycurgus, whom Delphi decides is probably a god (29, 216 PW); and Archilochus (321 PW), whom the oracle specifically labels immortal (ἀθάνατος).[41] In this sense, shifts from good fortune to ruin may be seen to translate into oracular form the familiar commonplaces of archaic and classical thought that too much happiness will inevitably lead to misfortune (cf. Hdt. 3.40) and that it is impossible to know whether or not a life is truly happy before it is over (cf. Hdt. 1.29–32).

This is not to attribute the entire oracle to the Cypselid era, which is clearly inconceivable. But it is to argue against the conclusion that the oracle must have been written in two distinct stages. The oracle's concluding line does more than just negate the message of the

39. So PW 1:116–17, which is followed by Oost (1972, 18) and Salmon (1984, 187). Crahay (1956, 240–41) and Berve (1956, 2:522–23) treat the entire oracle as post-Cypselid.

40. Another, addressed to Attalus I of Pergamum (431 PW), begins optimistically ("Take courage, bull-horned, you will have the office of king") and concludes very much like the last line of the third Cypselid oracle ("and the children of your children, but the children of these no longer"). PW (cf. 431) explains the great similarity between Attalus's oracle and the third Cypselid oracle as direct imitation.

41. Delphi did not apparently think quite so highly of Hesiod: a spontaneous oracle (206 PW) addressed to him closes, like the third Cypselid oracle, with a prediction of his death. On the similarity, see Fontenrose 1978, 117.

first two lines. Rather than reject the impression of Cypselus's happiness, it constructs a close relationship between the success of the Cypselid tyranny and its demise. Much like a French leftist daily's succinct announcement, in an obituary for John Paul I, that His Holiness's death offered further proof that all men are mortal, the oracle closes in an obvious spirit of schadenfreude. As Apollo bestows his blessing on the tyranny in his salutation, he marks the limit of their good fortune by predicting their fall. So the third oracle closes the Cypselids' story, just as it begins it, by invoking divine agency. From this perspective, the third oracle functions much like the fairy tale in which all three Cypselid oracles were embedded and preserved; it is pervaded by the same irony as the Bacchiads' pity for the child who will destroy them, and it appeals to the same cosmological proposition that the gods direct human affairs, including the rise and fall of tyrannies.[42]

The question of the third oracle's date and authorship frames a larger and more important point. Whether the oracles' authors at Delphi or Corinth appended new lines to old oracles or devised their own from scratch, they were continuing and elaborating a genre and a method of representation whose origin was closely related to tyrants. And even when they meant to subvert the message of the Cypselid oracles, the Corinthians, who preserved and apparently believed the stories preserved by Herodotus and Ephorus, appropriated and implicitly accepted the political language and conceptions of political authority that the tyrannical oracles invoke. From this perspective, the consistent presentation of tyranny in all three oracles is more important than their date and attribution, more important even than their value as propaganda. For the oracles, tyranny rises from injustice, and the ultimate responsibility for the establishment of a tyranny lies with the city's leaders, not with the tyrant's personal ambitions and motives. The greatest enemies of tyranny, Solon and Theognis, agree; the social ruin that results in tyranny comes from the city's leaders, who, in Solon's words, "do not watch for the holy roots of Justice, who silently knows what is

42. Herodotus's account of the Peisistratids (1.59–64; 5.55–65) seems also largely drawn from local stories that attribute divine necessity to both the rise and the fall of the tyrannical dynasty (cf. 1.62; 5.56). On this, see Lavelle 1991, 317–24.

and what was" (3.14–15 GP). It is true that Solon and Theognis warn their cities in the hope of preventing the social chaos that leads to tyranny, while the first two Cypselid oracles pretend to be *pro eventu* warnings that the Corinthians have heard and ignored. But this difference in rhetorical function builds upon a basic agreement: tyranny, for its friends and enemies, comes to exist as a consequence of injustice.

The first two oracles, though they may have been written when the Cypselids were in power and enjoyed Delphi's support, nonetheless stress the fearfulness, rather than the advantages, of tyranny. If they were hardly calculated to win Cypselus the regard a popular ruler wanted and needed, they would encourage the Corinthians to appreciate the formidable quality of a tyrant's rule; and fear possessed a distinct value for tyrants. A story attributed by Diodorus (9.30) to Phalaris, the philosopher-tyrant of Acragas, tells of a flock of doves that flees from a hawk not because the hawk is invincible, for they could defeat it if they dared, but because of fear: no dove could count on the support of its fellows. The Cypselid oracles inspired a second fear that was less blatant but equally effective: that the tyrant was not a mere man but a divine agent whom the Corinthians could not, and should not, resist. For this reason, the oracles are not well understood as an ideological veil that obscured the Cypselids' power. Even if the Cypselids manufactured the oracles as part of a complex ideological program (which is unsure), they would not entirely deserve the charges of insincerity or impiety that such a program might seem to invite. The Cypselids did not need to doubt what they wanted others to believe: that injustice was rampant in Corinth, that Apollo was personally interested in the restoration of justice, and that it was their job to see it through.[43]

This suggestion is supported by Nicolaus's presentation of Cypselus as a just man who begins his public career as Corinth's pole-

43. So the Cypselids' conviction reflects the complex relationship of myth and ideology characteristic of Greek belief systems. As Veyne (1988, 84) notes: "Like the Dorzé, who imagine both that the leopard fasts and that one must be on guard against him every day, the Greeks believe and do not believe their myths. They believe in them, but they use them and cease believing at the point where their interest in believing ends."

march (*FGH* 90 F 57.5). In Nicolaus, this position, despite the military tone of the name, is a civil magistracy with judicial and police functions.[44] The polemarch judges criminal cases and ensures that the Corinthians pay public fines. He can imprison delinquents and is entitled to keep a portion of the fines for himself. The job, like a tax collector's, must have been highly prized: the honest polemarch could not help but make money, and the corrupt polemarch might become very rich. The Bacchiad polemarchs, according to Nicolaus, pursued their personal interests exclusively; they were "hubristic and violent" (ὑβρισταὶ καὶ βίαιοι). But Cypselus exercised his powers as polemarch in a "manly, prudent, and public-minded [δημωφελής]" manner. "He did not imprison or enchain anyone, instead he accepted surety, or offered it himself," and in every case he gave up the percentage of the public fine that he was entitled to keep by Corinthian law (*FGH* 90 F 57.4–5).

Herodotus, though finding miraculous events in their rise, clearly thought the Cypselids were anything but just. But even Herodotus's account offers hints of the Cypselid representation and reception as agents of justice when he casts Cypselus's son and successor, Periander, as a perspicacious judge in the tale of Arion's miraculous rescue (1.23–24) and as a mediator between Athens and Mytilene in the dispute over Sigeum (5.95).[45] Periander's judgment in this second, more credible case must have involved a complex demarcation of the spheres of interest of two rival cities and probably gave new significance to Corinth's role in the northeastern Aegean—as the roughly contemporaneous foundation of Potidaea suggests.[46] Yet Herodotus's brief account was more concerned to capture the terms in which the agreement was presented: according to him, "Each of the two states kept what it originally possessed." Periander's judgment restored an original balance, in keeping with the role of Theognis's *anēr euthuntēr*, the monarch who ensures justice.

The oracles and stories of the Corinthian tyrants, although among the most important sources for early Greek tyranny, offer

44. For the question of Nicolaus's reliability with regard to the polemarchy and to the Cypselids in general, see the discussion in Salmon 1984, 188–92.

45. On the latter, see Piccirilli 1973, 28–35. Alcaeus seems to mention Periander's role as mediator (μεσίτης) in 306f.19 LP, which is probably from a poem Alcaeus wrote to Melanippus describing the event (Hdt. 5.95).

46. On this foundation, see Salmon 1984, 211–17, and Graham 1983, 30; on the Cypselid colonies, see also chap. 5.

evidence that is old, indirect, and partial. We do not escape the problems of historical reconstruction when we look at the Cypselid stories for the language and reception of early Greek tyranny, rather than for chronologies or formulas of social and political patronage. But in defense of this reconstruction, we should note that the tyrant's persona as an agent of justice is not unique to the stories of Cypselus's rise. Other stories suggest that other tyrants courted similar receptions. In a fragment of the Aristotelian *Constitution of Naxos* (fr. 558 = Ath. 8.348B–C), Lygdamis starts his reign as Naxos's tyrant by leading a group of fellow citizens against some aristocratic youths who had unjustly attacked a widely admired man named Telestagoras. The theme of punishment also looms large in at least one version of the rise of the Orthagorids at Sicyon. In Plutarch's account, Delphi announces that tyranny will come to Sicyon as punishment for the accidental killing of Teletias, a victor in the boys' race at Delphi, whom the Sicyons tore to pieces while attempting to take him away from the Cleonaeans, who also claimed him. For this, Plutarch says, the god told the Sicyonians that "their city needs the whip," which materialized in the form of the Orthagorid tyranny. The punishment, Plutarch believed, did the Sicyonians good; the Cleonaeans did not receive the benefit of such treatment (*ἰατρεία*), and, as a result "they never amounted to anything."[47] "Sometimes," Plutarch noted, "the god applies the implacably bitter and harsh rule of a tyrant to peoples needing a caustic and correction, and does not remove the pain and annoyance until he has expelled and purged the disease" (*Mor.* 553a). Plutarch's medical analogy implies a belief in three conditions of the body politic: disease, treatment, and health. Health is a balance of all powers (*κράτη*) that act upon or reside in the body.[48] A condition of disease exists when a single power becomes dominant to the detri-

---

47. *Mor.* 553a–b. The story is not found in the fragmentary accounts of Diodorus (8.24) or the Oxyrhynchus papyrus (11.1365 = *FGH* 105.2), but it is consistent with them.

48. Cf. Alcmaeon of Croton (B4 DK); Hippoc. *Arch. iatr.* 14, 19.53–57. It is this perhaps that Heraclitus meant when he defined strife as justice (B80 DK; cf. B60, A22). Another passage (B58 DK) suggests that Heraclitus himself made use of medical conceptions of disease and treatment to explain the working of *dikē* in nature. The same thought finds expression in Aristotle's discussion of constitutional change (*Pol.* 1307b28): "Opposites give rise to opposites, and ruin is the opposite of safety."

ment of the whole. Treatment consists of isolating and removing the source of disease. The cure is not at all pleasant, but a return to health demands it.

As a rule in such stories, a tyranny begins its correction of injustice with an act of violence against the former leaders of the city—the *monarchoi* in the language of the Cypselid oracles. Nicolaus reports in his account of the Corinthian tyranny that Cypselus killed the last Bacchiad king, Patroclides, and gives his reason: Patroclides was "lawless and burdensome" (παράνομος καὶ ἐπαχθής: *FGH* 90 F 57.6). Theagenes, Megara's late seventh-century tyrant, was said to have slaughtered a herd of cattle belonging to Megara's aristocrats.[49] Theagenes' precise motive has been lost, but it seems most likely that he understood and represented his action as retribution, a correcting of past injustices committed by the nobility against himself and Megara. Aristotle seems to think Theagenes' act marked the beginning of his reign; if so, it must have been intended to define the spirit as well as the fact of Theagenes' tyranny.

Punishment and Power in Athens and Mytilene

Retribution may also have played a role in the rise of the Peisistratids at Athens. According to Herodotus (1.59),[50] Peisistratus began his first tyranny by inflicting wounds on himself and his mules, and then riding into the agora claiming that he had been wounded by his enemies. Fooled by his ruse, the demos granted Peisistratus a contingent of *korunēphoroi* (club-bearers), which he employed to make himself tyrant of Athens for the first time.

We might find Peisistratus's *korunēphoroi* puzzling. As Plato makes clear in the *Republic* (566b), bodyguards of spear-bearers were a common instrument for the establishment of tyrannies. But club-bearers would obviously stand little chance against the entire citizen body or even a relatively few hoplites. In a celebrated study,[51] John

49. Arist. *Pol.* 1305a25–26. Theagenes probably used the bodyguard that Aristotle (*Rhet.* 1357b) says the demos of Megara granted him. For a different interpretation, see Legon 1981, 95–96.

50. See also Plut. *Sol.* 30 and *Ath. pol.* 14, who repeat the story with variations.

51. "Herakles, Peisistratos, and Sons" (1972); see also Boardman 1975. Boardman (1978) also argues that Cleisthenes of Sicyon had a similar interest in Heracles.

Boardman proposes to solve the problem by rendering the guard as a symbolic tool rather than a military force. Associating the guard and its distinctive weaponry of clubs with the Heraclean symbolism that he takes to be fundamental in Peisistratid Athens, Boardman argues that a bodyguard armed with clubs supported Peisistratus in his effort to identify himself with the greatest of Greek heroes and the darling of Athena. The bodyguard of Peisistratus's first attempt to make himself tyrant thus anticipates his second effort several years later, when he was conducted by an Athena look-alike to the Athenian Acropolis (Hdt. 1.60), like (Boardman suggests) Heracles, who was introduced to the home of the gods by the real Athena.[52]

Boardman's solution is ingenious. But it is worth questioning whether it makes good sense of the historical function that Herodotus attributed to the *korunēphoroi*. Herodotus does not present the club-bearers as an ideological support for Peisistratus's reign. Instead, the acquisition of the guard marks the inception of his tyranny. Peisistratus's bodyguards seem for that reason incompletely understood as mere symbols of Heracles. I will suggest, to paraphrase Freud freely, that sometimes a club is a club, or rather, that the club has its own distinctive symbolic content that makes better sense of the bodyguard's place in Herodotus. In a simile in Homer (*Il.* 11.558–62), boys take a club (ῥόπαλον) to beat an ass that does not behave as it should. Odysseus uses the royal scepter as a club against Thersites, who behaves like an ass in *Iliad* 2. Thersites suffers no great physical damage, but the welts that the royal scepter leaves on his back will remind him of the greater punishment that continued defiance of royal authority will bring. As a weapon, the club is neither efficient nor elegant; the soul escapes more neatly through the hole made by a spear or a dart. The club for that reason

---

52. Boardman's important suggestion that Peisistratus exploited a propagandistic value in religious and mythological imagery is alternately criticized (see most recently Cook 1987, 167–69, and Connor 1987) and placed on the pedestal of orthodoxy (so Hurwit 1985, 235). Boardman answers his critics; see Boardman 1984 and 1989. But he passes over the problem addressed here: how Peisistratus's use of religious imagery (his club-bearers, the disguised Phye) actually helped him establish his tyranny. Shapiro (1989, 15–16) supports Boardman's interest in deciphering Athenian political imagery but is more cautious about the link between Peisistratus and Heracles. On Peisistratus's march into Athens with the remarkable Phye, see Connor (1987), who explains the episode in conjunction with the highly ceremonial religion of archaic Athens.

is less fitting for warfare. It has its place rather in situations where the intention is to correct and reform, to hurt without necessarily inflicting permanent harm. It is true that Heracles and Theseus sometimes club their enemies to death, but the choice of weapon in such cases defines and justifies the violence as punishment—as the severity of the punishment meted out to their victims defines them as beyond reform.[53]

These hints about the sense and function of clubs may help clarify Peisistratus's *korunēphoroi*. Herodotus says that Peisistratus asked the demos for some protection ($\varphi\upsilon\lambda\alpha\kappa\acute{\eta}$ $\tau\iota\varsigma$), but Peisistratus certainly did not intend to use the bodyguard (nor, perhaps, did the demos expect it to be used) for defensive purposes alone, for which club-bearers were not necessarily better suited than for open warfare. It is most likely that Peisistratus took advantage of his *korunēphoroi* as a tool of revenge against rival aristocrats, who, he claimed, had wounded him. The Athenian aristocracy seems therefore to play the same role that the Cypselid oracles assign to the Bacchiads, who, by dishonoring Cypselus's father, invited the punishment of Cypselus's tyranny. Herodotus adds briefly to his account of the ruse that Peisistratus used the club-bearers to take the Acropolis (1.59.5), as if this were no more than a natural result of the acquisition of a personal bodyguard. In one sense, this may be true. The demos's grant of a guard of club-bearers is what most clearly separated Peisistratus from the failed tyrant Cylon, who could afford to equip his supporters with more serious weapons than clubs but was easily defeated when he attempted to use them to take the Acropolis.[54] Peisistratus, on the other hand, seems to have encountered no

53. Pindar notes at *Ol.* 9.30 that Heracles used his club against Poseidon's trident at Pylos, but he quickly drops the tale, fearing the charge of impiety (*Ol.* 9.35–38). Other Greeks were probably not so squeamish about the story; Poseidon's reputation for brutish behavior made the club an appropriate weapon to use against him. Like Heracles and Theseus, Oedipus in the *OT* (811) beats his father to death with a club ($\sigma\kappa\tilde{\eta}\pi\tau\rho o\nu$); the tool suggests a rationale for the action, which Oedipus represents as retribution (see below in chap. 6). Finally, Plutarch notes that the enemies of Tiberius Gracchus attacked him with clubs and cudgels ($\dot{\rho}\acute{o}\pi\alpha\lambda\alpha$ $\kappa\alpha\grave{\iota}$ $\sigma\kappa\upsilon\tau\acute{\alpha}\lambda\alpha\varsigma$: *Ti. Gracch.* 19.8.1). Their intention, of course, was to kill Tiberius and his followers, not to reform them; but it is probable that they also wanted to represent their action as civic punishment rather than civil war—hence the significance of the clubs and cudgels.

54. On Cylon, see Thucydides' account at 1.126. Aristotle notes at *Rhet.* 1357b that Theagenes and Dionysius the Elder had guards given them by the demos.

serious resistance. Taking the demos's grant of a band of club-bearers as a license to exact vengeance, he established a reign of justice—justice as Auden describes it in his "Marginalia": "permission to peck a wee bit harder than we have been pecked."[55] In the club-bearers there lies, therefore, a conspicuous claim to an exclusive right to retribution. Thus Peisistratus seems, like Cypselus, Orthagoras, Theagenes, and Lygdamis, to have begun his tyranny with conspicuous acts of retribution.

The Peisistratid club-bearers give up much of their force when viewed exclusively as symbols. Yet Boardman is right that they possess important symbolic associations. Clubs and justice are linked on the famous Chest of Cypselus at Olympia, described by Pausanias, where on one panel Dike was pictured clubbing Adikia (Paus. 5.18.2). The same image appears again on an Athenian red-figure neck amphora that has been dated to 520, when Peisistratus's sons were in power in Athens.[56] By necessity, the struggle between Dike and Adikia continues forever, for Dike can chastise but not destroy her rival: the existences of Dike and Adikia are ultimately inseparable. The club is for that reason a perfect weapon for Dike. It is of course true that the club is also linked very closely with Heracles. And it is not improbable, as Boardman suggests, that the distinctive weapons of Peisistratus's bodyguard encouraged the Athenians to think of Heracles when they saw Peisistratus. But Heracles' persona as a civilizing hero probably held greater significance for Peisistratus than his link to Athena. Pindar found it natural to use the verb *damazein* (tame) of Heracles (*Ol.* 10.30; *Nem.* 3.23, 7.90), a verb he also used to describe a tyrant's victory over a barbarian army (*Pyth.* 1.73). Elsewhere Pindar recounts that Teiresias, upon hearing that the infant Heracles had killed Hera's serpents, predicted "how many Heracles would kill on land and how many ignorant of justice [ἀϊδροδίκας] at sea" (*Nem.* 1.63). And in a famous fragment quoted by Plato (*Grg.* 484b = 169 SM), Pindar remarks that the deeds of Heracles demonstrate how *nomos* (law) makes violence just.[57] Al-

55. Auden (1976, 591).
56. On the personification, see Shapiro 1976, 42–48. On the vase, see Frel 1963. Frel believes the vase registers Athenian dissatisfaction with the Peisistratids, without considering the more likely possibility that the image reflects Peisistratid self-representation.
57. Theseus is sometimes praised in the same way; cf. Bacchyl. 18.38–44, where he is urged on by a god to bring justice against unjust acts.

ways packing a club for his trips, if (perhaps like Peisistratus's bodyguard) using other weapons as the occasion warranted, Heracles civilized nature by punishing its injustice and lawlessness; as Bacchylides wrote, Heracles "put an end to arrogant hubris by ordaining judgments [δίκας] among mortals" (13.44–45). In this sense, the image of Heracles certainly might help define the persona of Peisistratid power.

Peisistratus was perhaps not the only Greek tyrant to have a bodyguard armed with clubs. According to later sources (Poll. 3.83, 7.68; Steph. Byz. s.v. Xíos), Cleisthenes, the most important of the Orthagorids of Sicyon, also had club-bearers. Clubs and sticks pop up in other contexts featuring tyrants. The Spartan Cleomenes is said in Herodotus (6.75.1) to have beaten fellow citizens with a scepter, an abuse of royal power that Herodotus takes as evidence of Cleomenes' insanity.[58] And when they were not busy beating their rivals with clubs, autocratic leaders sometimes resisted the appropriation of the imagery of justice by others. According to Aristotle (*Pol.* 1311b26–28), Megacles, Mytilene's first tyrant, began his reign by gathering followers to overcome the Penthilids, who were unjustly beating the Mytileneans with clubs. There is a striking modern parallel to the ancient political imagery of the club: the colossal bronze statue of Mussolini planned (but never erected) for the Foro Mussolini in Rome was to bear in its left hand a club to symbolize the Fascist victory over the Italian left.[59]

Retribution thus appears as a dominant element of early archaic tyrants' political posture, so much so that Xenophon (*Lac.* 8.4) grouped tyrants with officials of games and the Spartan ephors for their determination to punish wrongdoing the moment they recognized it. But tyrants also found other ways to articulate their interest in *dikē*. According to Nicolaus of Damascus, Cypselus made a serious effort to correct the injustices committed by the Bacchiads by recalling their exiles and restoring citizenship to them (*FGH* 90 F 57.7). Likewise Aristotle praised the Orthagorids of Sicyon for obeying the law and Cleisthenes in particular for his treatment of a

---

58. It is unclear whether Cleomenes' *skēptron* is a mere walking stick or a symbol of Spartan royal power—and therefore unclear whether Cleomenes' behavior perverts only his royal power or also the very image of Spartan royal power.

59. On the statue and its significance, see Bondenella 1987, 199.

judge who had denied him a victory (*Pol.* 1315b15–22), while Peisistratus was commended for answering a summons to appear before the Areopagus (*Pol.* 1315b23–24; cf. *Ath. pol.* 16.8). There is some evidence that tyrants were responsible for substantive political and social reforms. Peisistratus was credited with establishing traveling judges to increase access to Athenian legal procedures (*Ath. pol.* 16.5); other tyrants, Cleisthenes of Sicyon and perhaps the Corinthian Cypselids, instituted major changes of their cities' tribes.[60] Ancient authors represent these innovations as the simple consequences of tyrants' interests in consolidating power. In particular, Herodotus (5.67–68) reported that the Cleisthenic redivision was intended to favor his own tribe at the expense of Sicyon's Dorian population,[61] while the author of the *Athenaion politeia* (16.5) read Peisistratus's judicial reform in connection with his new taxes and his determination to keep the Attic peasantry busy and away from Athens. But Herodotus and the *Athenaion politeia* probably confuse motive and result; centralization and consolidation do not belong to the political language of archaic Greece. It is far more likely that the authors of these changes drew their inspiration from their contemporary concepts of justice and represented them as corrections of past evils.

Justice played a particularly dramatic role in the regime of Pittacus, sole ruler of Mytilene in the 580s. Pittacus was called *tyrannos* by his contemporaries, but Aristotle (*Pol.* 1285a35–37), noting uncharacteristic features in his reign, chose to classify him not as a tyrant but as an *aisymnētēs* (the word Dionysius of Halicarnassus later used to translate the Latin *dictator*). In classifying Pittacus as *aisymnētēs* rather than tyrant, Aristotle gave greater weight to Pittacus's method of acquiring power than to his way of exercising it.[62] Pittacus, Aristotle believed, was set up in a position of autocratic

---

60. On Cleisthenes, see Hdt. 5.67–68. On the reorganization of Corinth's tribes that may have taken place under the Cypselids, see Jones 1980 and Salmon 1984, 207–9, 413–19.

61. Cogent doubts are expressed by Bicknell (1982).

62. Berve (1967, 1:94) is wrong to say that Pittacus "stellt keinen eigenständigen politischen Faktor neben dem Gemeinwesen dar, er ist vielmehr dessen Beauftragter, dessen Organ, und seine Machtfülle" ("represents no independent political presence alongside the community, he is rather its delegate, its instrument and the realization of its power").

power by the people of Mytilene, who were harassed by the recent political exiles under the leadership of Alcaeus and Antimenides. Aristotle, for this reason, called Pittacus "an elected tyrant" and gave the *aisymnēteia* a special position between tyranny and hereditary monarchy. For evidence, Aristotle offers a fragment of Alcaeus noting that the Mytileneans "established as tyrant [ἐστάσοντο τύραννον] of the cowardly and ill-starred city the lowborn Pittacus, praising him greatly in a single voice." It is far from certain that a definite political procedure is implied by Alcaeus's remark that Pittacus was "established as tyrant"; the poem is obviously intended as an attack on the Mytileneans, not as a simple description of an event.[63] Later sources (Strab. 13.2.3; D. L. 1.75) that report that Pittacus resigned his position after ten years may indicate that Pittacus was a benevolent ruler, but not that his position was regular, for he seems to have resigned at his own discretion.

We cannot be sure that Pittacus actually employed the title *aisymnētēs*, though it is more likely that Aristotle borrowed Pittacus's title to designate his new political category than that he used a term unrelated to Pittacus, since Pittacus is his only example of an *aisymnētēs*.[64] If Pittacus was called an *aisymnētēs* (and this not because he was tyrant by election), it is not entirely clear what the term meant before Aristotle. *Aisymnētēs* probably derives from *aisa* (rightful dispensation) and *mnaomai* (recall, keep in mind); the *aisymnētēs* therefore "holds in mind what is due."[65] This derivation is supported by the fact that *aisymnētai* outside Aristotle are typically engaged in activities appropriate for judges: for example, the nine *aisymnētai* who are appointed to supervise athletic contests in the *Odyssey* (8.258). The *aisymnētēs* is not a regular political official.[66] So in the *Iliad* (24.347), when Homer likens a young herald (Hermes in disguise) to a *kouros aisymnētēr* (youthful judge), he seems to imply that the herald carries himself like a noble youth who is the measure

63. See Romer 1982.
64. See Andrewes 1956, 95–97.
65. So Frisk 1960–72; Chantraine (1968) notes that even if the word is foreign, the Greek popular imagination probably associated it closely with *aisa*.
66. Admittedly, Medea's nurse in Euripides (*Med.* 19) says Creon, the hereditary king of Corinth, "judges the land" (αἰσυμνᾷ χθονός), but the phrase describes his rule; it does not suggest a title.

of his fellows. Whether or not Pittacus's contemporaries called him *aisymnētēs*, the title, with its subtle flavor of archaic justic, is well suited to his activities as the sole ruler of Mytilene. Aristotle says (*Pol.* 1285a35–37) that the Mytileneans appointed Pittacus as *aisymnētēs* "to counter the exiles, whom Antimenides and Alcaeus the poet led." Alcaeaus's antagonism toward Pittacus and his supporters at Mytilene argues that Aristotle is right.[67]

Dikē provides the point of intersection between the personal ambition of the aspiring tyrant and the political expectations of his fellow citizens. Aristotle was speaking more of the archaic period than of his own when he noted that "constitutions and aristocracies are dissolved for the most part because of a departure from justice in the constitution itself."[68] And it seems likely that archaic tyrants used justice not only as an argument for establishing their power but also as a program for exercising it.

In this sense, *dikē*'s significance for Greek tyranny is perhaps made most clear by the account that Herodotus gives (1.96–101) of the rise of Deioces as king of the Medes. In the story, which is a political essay on the nature of government rather than a historical account (for Herodotus knew little about the Medes),[69] Deioces appears as a near-perfect tyrant. Like the Spartan Lycurgus (1.65.1–2), Deioces is a man of unique insight and integrity in a context of nearly complete social and political chaos. But unlike Lycurgus, Deioces is not willing to forgo all personal ambition in the establishment of a perfect state; Deioces, Herodotus says, is "a lover of tyranny" (ἐρασθεὶς τυραννίδος). Desiring to make himself sole ruler of the Medes, he realizes his ambition by exploiting his reputa-

---

67. Berve (1967, 1:94) excuses Pittacus's possession of a bodyguard on the grounds that the demos granted it to him. But if my treatment of Peisistratus's bodyguard is correct, the demos's grant of a bodyguard made its tyrant. Pittacus's title of *aisymnētēs* is aptly compared to Solon's designation as *diallaktēs* (arbiter) in the *Constitution of Athens* (5.2) and Plutarch (*Sol.* 14.2) by Romer (1982, 37). On the relation between the mediation that Solon performed in Athens and Pittacus's in Mytilene, see the next chapter.

68. *Pol.* 1307a6–7: λύονται δὲ μάλιστα αἵ τε πολιτεῖαι καὶ αἱ ἀριστοκρατίαι διὰ τὴν ἐν αὐτῇ τῇ πολιτείᾳ τοῦ δικαίου παρέκβασιν.

69. So How and Wells 1912, 1:380–84, and, more recently, Helm 1981. On the story, see also Flory (1987, 122–28), who reads it against Herodotus's presentation of Athenian tyranny.

tion for justice. Offering himself as an impartial judge in his neighbors' disputes, he builds his reputation for justice to an extent that the Medes come from all over to have him arbitrate their conflicts. But once he had made himself indispensable, Deioces suddenly resigns; to those who continue to seek his judgments, he replies that "it brings him nothing to ignore his own affairs." Deioces is sorely missed. The Medes fall once more into a state of "pillage and lawlessness" (ἁρπαγὴ καὶ ἀνομία), which their recent experience of justice perhaps makes all the more intolerable. Faced with the choice between anarchy and monarchy,[70] they elect to establish a monarchy and to install Deioces in that position. Deioces makes it immediately clear what sort of king he intends to become. He insists that the Medes give him a personal bodyguard and a palace surrounded by a magnificently fortified city. When he has these things, he suddenly ends all personal interaction with his fellow Medes, instituting the practice of Eastern monarchs that encourages their subjects to view them as beings of a different nature.

Although Deioces is for Herodotus a paradigm of barbarian monarchy (rather than of political virtue), the historian does not doubt the value of Deioces' justice. Before he becomes king, Deioces "alone renders straight judgments" (μοῦνος κατὰ τὸ ὀρθὸν δικάζων: 1.96.3), and after he is established, he remains "strict in the observance of justice" (τὸ δίκαιον φυλάσσων χαλεπός: 1.100.1). Herodotus sees no contradiction between Deioces' drive for power and his determination to render justice: his form of justice is not simply a tool of power, nor does his tyranny serve exclusively private interests. As Herodotus observes, "Deioces did all these things when there was much lawlessness throughout Media, for he understood that injustice is inimical to justice" (καὶ ταῦτα μέντοι ἐούσης ἀνομίης πολλῆς ἀνὰ πᾶσαν τὴν Μηδικὴν ἐποίεε, ἐπιστάμενος ὅτι τῷ δικαίῳ τὸ ἄδικον πολέμιόν ἐστι: 1.96.2). But Deioces also understood something else: that justice and power

70. The choice seems rather typical of Greek conceptions of their neighbors. The Persian conspirators, at Hdt. 3.80–82, make a show of deciding among monarchy, oligarchy, and democracy for the new government of Persia. But the point of that debate is that the ancestral laws (πατρίοι νόμοι) of the Persians, not just the inherent defects of oligarchy and democracy, decide the question in favor of monarchy.

($\dot{\alpha}\rho\chi\dot{\eta}$ or $\kappa\rho\acute{\alpha}\tau os$) are essentially linked.[71] His experiment in justice
shows the Medes the difference between justice and injustice; his
sudden refusal to continue the experiment teaches them the second
lesson, that justice is impossible without government. Hearing
Deioces say that "it did not profit him to judge his neighbors'
concerns day after day" (1.97.1), the Medes decide that they have no
choice but to accept Deioces as their king—that is, as someone who
will benefit from making their concerns his own. Deioces has
cleverly finessed this result; now he can lay down his hand. When he
assumes the trappings of monarchy, he makes himself the supervisor of the Medes' interests, and he makes them over into his
political subjects.

The Punishment of Tyrants

There was, however, no such thing as a perfect tyranny—at least
not in archaic Greece. Tyrants could not wall themselves up in
palaces. Their extraordinary freedom came with a real need to use
it; tyrants could maintain their position only as long as they preserved the fiction of its necessity. Yet although tyrants had to exercise their power to justify it, nevertheless they did so at their own
expense. Tyrants found retribution a slippery political tool. This
was perhaps inevitable. When, as Aeschylus notes in the *Agamemnon* (1560–61), "rebuke follows upon rebuke, it is difficult to distinguish" justice from injustice; indeed, even the gods, as the *Eumenides* shows, found it sometimes difficult to know one from the
other. For that reason, *dike* could not provide an enduring foundation for individual power. In exact proportion to the tyrant's success
in diminishing the danger presented by his predecessors, his own
acts would eventually seem arbitrary, unjust, and in need of correction. That tyrants could not monopolize the language of justice is

71. Protagoras makes the same point in his myth of the origin of man (Pl. *Prt.*
320a–322d), but, for Protagoras, justice is Zeus's gift to all men, and hence society's
very nature is democratic. Not only tyrants parlayed a reputation for wise arbitration into real power; the same can be maintained for aristocrats such as Themistocles
(Plut. *Them.* 5.6) and Aristides (Plut. *Arist.* 4.2; 7.1).

the message of Hippias's dream, which Herodotus includes as part of the Athenians' story of the Peisistratids' fall:

τλῆθι λέων ἄτλητα παθὼν τετληότι θυμῷ.
οὐδεὶς ἀνθρώπων ἀδικῶν τίσιν οὐκ ἀποτίσει.
(Hdt. 5.56)

Endure, like a lion, the unendurable with an enduring spirit;
no man avoids paying the penalty for doing wrong.

Herodotus here employs much the same language and imagery that is marked in the Cypselid oracles, but to a different end. Once the tyrant's fury in punishing injustice was lionlike; but now his lionlike heart must prove equal to a fate that the dream's almost unendurable repetition adorns with tragic pathos: that he is no more able to escape the consequences of injustice than other men. The sparse historical record of tyrants gives occasional indications that the tyrant's rhetoric could be turned against him. Alcaeus freely appropriated the language of *dikē* in his quest to upset Pittacus. Polycrates' exiles very probably intended to dispute his claim to justice when they named their new home in Italy Dicaearchia, Just Rule (Steph. Byz. s.v. Δικαιάρχεια). That, as Aristotle observed (*Pol.* 1312b21–25), tyrants of the second generation were generally crueler than their fathers probably reflects their increasing desperation to prevent the same sort of political revolution as that which brought them to power. But, like Jack at the end of Wilde's *Importance of Being Earnest*,[72] the tyrant suffered the terrible experience to "find out suddenly that all of his life he has been speaking nothing but the truth": that the reformer's power is invincible.

An element of necessity seems, therefore, to lie in the evolution of tyranny from the rule of the *anēr euthuntēr* to the most unjust form of government.[73] "It is hard for a tyrant to act piously," Sophocles has Agamemnon admit in the *Ajax* (1350); for, as the chorus says in the *Oedipus Tyrannus* (872), it is overweening pride and selfish ambition (ὕβρις) that "gives birth to the tyrant [φυτεύει

72. Wilde 1965, 108.
73. As Sosicles says at Hdt. 5.92α.1, "Nothing is more unjust (ἀδικώτερον) than tyranny."

84

τύραννον]," not, as in the case of Herodotus's Deioces, a profound understanding of the working of justice. But the tyrant's transformation into the perfectly unjust ruler is also a part of a general change in the nature of the relation of justice and power. Where justice and rule are virtually inseparable in the archaic period, they are viewed in classical political thought as antagonistic or even mutually exclusive. The requirements of justice are then perceived as impeding the exercise of power; and the truly just man, like the man Plato believed to be most qualified to govern his utopic state, feels most comfortable living far from the city's political center and dressing in the clothing of the philosopher, not the statesman.

This new view of political and moral activity appears most clearly in late fifth-century Athens, which developed its own practical politics of injustice while playing host to the philosophical disputes engendered by the rift between justice and power. The new politics of injustice are captured particularly well in Thucydides account of the debate following Mytilene's revolt in 428/427 (3.37–49). There Cleon and Diodotus clash in all respects but one: they agree completely that self-interest is the first principle of Athenian politics. This sort of agreement also links Cleon and Pericles, whom Thucydides otherwise presents as opposites: both Cleon and Pericles assert that Athens rules a tyranny (2.63.2; 3.37.2), and insist that the Athenians must therefore act accordingly to a deliberate and concerted plan. Thucydides' later account of the Melian Dialogue (5.84–113) confirms the priority of self-interest over justice in fifth-century discussions of political power. The Athenians force the Melians to debate the Athenian and Melian interest without any reference to justice, for the Athenians announce that self-interest will alone determine their actions. When the Melians attempt to resort to arguments based on divine justice, the Athenians emphatically insist that "our actions agree with the beliefs men hold about the gods and the principles that guide their acts" (5.105)—namely, that the gods do what they believe benefits them most. The philosophical position that underlies the Athenians' argument finds its clearest expression in Thrasymachus's rejection of any other standard of justice than "the interest of the stronger" (Pl. *Rep.* 338c) and in Antiphon's *On Truth*, or in the satyr play *Sisyphus*, with its striking image of *dikē tyrannis* (B25 DK), the unnatural imposition of social convention on men.[74] From this perspective, it often lies in the ruler's interest to seem just, but it is always necessary for him to act unjustly. Thus a somewhat changed tyrant begins to haunt the discussions of political power in the late fifth century. Freed from the constraints of just action (which is a personal ethic for others but a divine or social necessity for no one), the new tyrant defines his self-interest in direct opposition to *nomos*. As Euphemus generalizes in Thucydides (6.85.1), "Nothing is unreasonable for a tyrant or a tyrant city that lies in their interest."[75]

The emergence of the amoral *tyrannis polis* and the theoretical undressing of the *anēr euthuntēr* that accompanied it are important aspects of the story of the "liberation" of power from justice. In its fullest scope this liberation involves a widening of the relatively narrow political horizons of the early archaic city: its discovery, far beyond the concern for justice, of the enormous power and dangers that exist in tyranny. We will begin to trace this story of the Greeks' struggle with the idea and reality of tyranny with a discussion of the Athenian lawgiver Solon, who was the first of the Greeks to present a genuine political understanding of tyranny and the first to attempt to harness its power without falling victim to its dangers.

74. The play is traditionally thought to be by Critias. But Dihle (1977, 28–42) and Scodel (1980, 124–26) attribute it to Euripides. The change in the perception of justice is evident in Plato: justice, he insists, is seen by the many as something "useful for the profits it brings and for one's good reputation, but which in itself is avoided as if burdensome" (*Rep.* 358a).

75. Protagoras seems in this sense an exception, for, unlike Antiphon and Critias, he makes a serious effort to reunite the social and natural orders. See the recent discussion by Farrar (1988, 117–19).

CHAPTER THREE

The Lawgiver's Struggle with Tyranny: Solon and the Excluded Middle

δελφῖνες καὶ φάλαιναι πρὸς ἀλλήλους ἐμάχοντο. ἐπὶ πολὺ δὲ τῆς διαφορᾶς σφοδρυνομένης κωβιὸς ἀνέδυ καὶ αὐτοὺς ἐπειρᾶτο δι- αλύειν. εἰς δέ τις τῶν δελφίνων ὑπολαβὼν ἔφη πρὸς αὐτόν· "ἀλλ᾽ ἡμῖν ἀνεκτότερον ἔσται μαχομένοις ὑπ᾽ ἀλλήλων διαφθαρῆναι ἢ σοῦ διαλλακτοῦ τυχεῖν."

The dolphins and whales were at war with one another. When the dispute became quite vehement the anchovy rose and tried to recon- cile them. But one of the dolphins interrupted him and said, "It would be more bearable for us to fight to the death than to accept you as a mediator."

Aesop 116 (Halm)

It is impossible to consider resistance to tyranny in archaic Greece without focusing on the political activities and poetry of Solon, whose life spanned the years between Cylon's unsuccessful attempt to make himself tyrant of Athens in the late seventh century and Peisistratus's success in the middle of the next century. Solon made it his personal mission when named archon and mediator in 594 to institute political reforms in Athens without assuming a tyranny and to prevent the establishment of tyrannies by the leaders who followed him.[1] Solon has been much celebrated for his per- sonal integrity in not becoming the tyrant of Athens, but he also has been blamed since antiquity as a political failure. As Plutarch notes

---

1. On the date, see Wallace 1983, 81–95.

(*Comp. Sol. et Publ.* 3.3), Solon looked on helplessly as Peisistratus swept away Solon's reformed *politeia* (constitution) and established himself as tyrant of Athens. Plutarch paints a picture of Solon as a tragic figure who was responsible in some crucial, if hidden, way for his own fate. By leaving Athens after enacting his reforms, Solon, in Plutarch's view, left the Athenians without a defender, and he compounded his guilt on his return by not resorting to armed resistance to protect his measures against Peisistratus (*Comp. Sol. et Publ.* 3.4). Plutarch's assessment of Solon is complex. He agrees with the *Athenaion politeia* that Solon left Athens in order to force the Athenians to entrust themselves to his laws without his interpretation (*Sol.* 25.4–5; *Ath. pol.* 11.1; cf. Hdt. 1.29), and he adds that Solon acted in conformity with his own laws when he failed to resist with violence Peisistratus's attempts to make himself tyrant (*Comp. Sol. et Publ.* 2.2). For Plutarch, then, Solon condemned his reforms to failure by his very attempts to make his new laws strong and independent. This view of Solon is paradoxical, but it can be defended. As we will see, the lawgiver's quest to prevent the rise of tyranny at Athens helped in many ways to make it more possible for an individual to establish himself there as tyrant.

Solon's Justice

Solon fought against tyranny both as a statesman and as a poet. If the combination of reformer and poet was new at least to Athens, Solon's political views were conventional in important ways. Solon's ideas about the social ills that plagued archaic cities (tyranny in particular) followed from and developed those of the poets of the early archaic period. In a passage from a poem that was famous in antiquity, he warns of the consequences of injustice with natural images that are especially reminiscent of Hesiod:[2]

ἐκ νεφέλης πέλεται χιόνος μένος ἠδὲ χαλάζης,
βροντὴ δ' ἐκ λαμπρῆς γίγνεται ἀστεροπῆς·

2. See chap. 2.

ἀνδρῶν δ' ἐκ μεγάλων πόλις ὄλλυται, ἐς δὲ μονάρχου
δῆμος ἀϊδρίῃ δουλοσύνην ἔπεσεν.

(12.1–4 GP)

Out of a cloud comes the power of snow and hail,
and thunder comes from bright lightning;
so a city comes to ruin through its great men,
and the people fall to the slavery of single rule
through their ignorance.

The domination of the city by a single individual thus emerges from
the behavior of the city's leading men. Another passage elaborates
this link between the unjust behavior of Athens's leading men and
the punishment that the city can expect to suffer as a result:

οὔθ' ἱερῶν κτεάνων οὔτε τι δημοσίων
φειδόμενοι κλέπτουσιν ἀφαρπαγῇ ἄλλοθεν ἄλλος,
οὐδὲ φυλάσσονται σεμνὰ Δίκης θέμεθλα,
ἣ σιγῶσα σύνοιδε τὰ γιγνόμενα πρό τ' ἐόντα,
τῷ δὲ χρόνῳ πάντως ἦλθε' ἀποτεισομένη.
τοῦτ' ἤδη πάσῃ πόλει ἔρχεται ἕλκος ἄφυκτον,
ἐς δὲ κακὴν ταχέως ἤλυθε δουλοσύνην,
ἣ στάσιν ἔμφυλον πόλεμόν θ' εὕδοντ' ἐπεγείρει,
ὃς πολλῶν ἐρατὴν ὤλεσεν ἡλικίην.

(3.12–20 GP)

Sparing neither the goods of temples nor of the city,
in their greed, all of them steal somewhere
and ignore the venerable foundations of Justice,
who silently knows the present and future,
and who without fail comes in time to exact punishment;
this intractable wound is upon the entire city,
and the city quickly comes to evil slavery,
which raises from sleep internecine strife (*stasis*) and war,
which destroys the lovely youth of many.

Solon paints the social evil of injustice in gloomy tones; to make
injustice appear still more fearful he adds a few lines later that not a

89

single individual will be able to flee from the *stasis* (civil strife) to which injustice leads, no matter how hard he may try.[3] Injustice brings about inevitable and unavoidable consequences for the city: the injustice of even a single member of the community threatens every other member. Nothing remains hidden; no injustice goes unpunished. This emphasis on the necessity and universality of punishment proceeds directly from Hesiod. Like Hesiod, too, Solon stresses the religious character of justice: behind *dikē* stands Zeus, who is vigilant and uncompromising. So in one elegy:

ἀλλὰ Ζεὺς πάντων ἐφορᾷ τέλος, ἐξαπίνης δὲ
ὥστ᾽ ἄνεμος νεφέλας αἶψα διεσκέδασεν
ἠρινός, ὃς πόντου πολυκύμονος ἀτρυγέτοιο
πυθμένα κινήσας, γῆν κάτα πυροφόρον
δηιώσας καλὰ ἔργα θεῶν ἕδος αἰπὺν ἱκάνει
οὐρανόν, αἰθρίην δ᾽ αὖτις ἔθηκεν ἰδεῖν,
λάμπει δ᾽ ἠελίοιο μένος κατὰ πίονα γαῖαν
καλόν, ἀτὰρ νεφέλων οὐδ᾽ ἓν ἔτ᾽ ἐστὶν ἰδεῖν.
τοιαύτη Ζηνὸς πέλεται τίσις.

(1.17–25 GP)

Zeus sees the end of all things, and suddenly
as a wind of spring scatters the clouds,
disturbing the foundation of the rough barren sea,
laying waste fine works through the grain-bearing land,
it reaches to heaven, the sheer seat of the gods;
but then once more it makes the heavens visible,
and the strength of the sun shines beautiful over the rich land;
and then it is no longer possible to see a single cloud.
Such is the retribution of Zeus.

Hence Solon agrees with Hesiod on the not entirely obvious point—to judge from Homer—that men are responsible for the

3. See 3.26–29 and 1.11–25 GP and the discussion in the preceding chapter. On Solon's terminology, see Nagy 1983, 84. Solon uses *stasis* only here; the compound *dichostasia* appears, however, at 3.36 GP, as the object upon which *eunomia* (order) works its corrective powers.

evils that beset them.[4] The gods, as Solon insists at the beginning of his *Eunomia* (3.1–5 GP), seeks to protect the city from harm; and if the city comes to harm, he warns in another poem, the Athenians should not "blame the gods for [their] own corruption" (15.1–2 GP). Yet though Solon places blame in the same place as Hesiod, his view of the character of divine punishment is less naive. The storms and intractable wounds that beset the unjust city in Solon are not meant as literal descriptions of the punishment that comes upon injustice, but as metaphors. *Dikē*, according to Solon, is fully as uncompromising as the natural disasters in which Zeus deals; however, the city would do better to look for the consequences of retribution in its social dynamics and institutional structures. The unjust city is particularly liable to suffer *stasis*, which comes from the evils that the rich unleash upon the city to make themselves its masters (cf. *Ath. pol.* 5.3), and which leads inevitably to the rule of a single individual.

Solon's Persona as Athenian Mediator

The differences that separate Solon's view of justice from the views of his predecessors derive from the crucial distinction marking Solon among archaic social commentators: he was also a reformer. Solon did not wish to persuade his audience of its helplessness against injustice; the didactic character of his elegies makes it clear that he reviews the dire consequences of injustice in order to persuade his listeners to prevent them.[5] Behind his fierce rhetoric stand specific political aims. No one, Solon insists, can remain unaffected by a breach of justice; it is therefore everyone's responsibility to deal with such infractions. In Plutarch, Solon accordingly defines the best state as "that in which those who have not been wronged denounce and punish wrongdoers no less than those who have been wronged" (ἐκείνη, ἐν ᾗ τῶν ἀδικουμένων οὐχ ἧττον οἱ μὴ ἀδικούμενοι προβάλλονται καὶ κολάζουσι τοὺς ἀδικοῦντας: *Sol.* 18.5).

4. On blame in Homer, see Adkins 1960, 10–60, and Lloyd-Jones 1983, 1–27.
5. See 3.26–29 GP and the preceding chapter.

Solon's conviction that the community possesses a fundamental interest in justice played a large role in the reforms he drafted in 594 as archon and mediator. According to the *Athenaion politeia* (9.1), Solon wrote a law that opened the Athenian legal system to anyone wishing to prosecute an injustice, even if the prosecutor was not related to the victim,[6] and he established a procedure of appeal to the popular courts against magisterial decisions that were perceived as unjust. The *Athenaion politeia*, looking forward to the extraordinary power that the Athenian popular courts held beginning in the fifth century, numbered these among Solon's most democratic reforms. But Solon did not intend to promote the domination of the courts by the demos.[7] He was also not primarily concerned to guarantee some elementary legal rights for all Athenian citizens, for which modern scholars celebrate his measures.[8] Plutarch (*Sol.* 18.5) gives a better explanation when he says that Solon opened courts to increase the Athenians' feelings of empathy for one another. More precisely, both this measure and Solon's establishment of a court of appeals seem to have been designed to promote the understanding of injustice as a collective matter and to establish the city's unique responsibility to rectify public and private acts of injustice. Solon's restrictions on legal self-help, which disallowed private justice even when the state was threatened by the machinations of an aspiring

6. Plutarch (*Sol.* 18.5) offers a paraphrase: καὶ γὰρ πληγέντος ἑτέρου καὶ βιασθέντος ἢ βλαβέντος ἐξῆν τῷ δυναμένῳ καὶ βουλομένῳ γράφεσθαι τὸν ἀδικοῦντα καὶ διώκειν ("When a man is struck or violated or harmed, anyone who is able and willing is permitted to prosecute the wrongdoer and pursue the case"). Solon is traditionally credited with the distinction between *dikai* and *graphai*, that is, private and public law (see the discussions in Harrison 1968–71, 2:74–70, and MacDowell 1978, 57. If this is correct, Solon's own conviction that every injustice threatens the entire community argues that the distinction was new and important in defining and protecting a large portion of Athenian legal activity as public.

7. This is confirmed by the use Solon made of the aristocratic Areopagus and his new Boule of 400, which Plutarch (*Sol.* 19.2) rightly explains as deterrents to potential disturbances of the polis by the demos, and by Solon's serious reservations about the political role of the demos. On the Areopagus before and after Solon, see Wallace 1985, 3–69.

8. See, for example, Rhodes (1981, 160), who, following Ruschenbusch, 1966, explains Solon's measure allowing anyone to prosecute injustice as a nascent form of legal representation (those who, perhaps as a result of the crime itself, were unable to prosecute their cases personally would therefore have some recourse to legal retribution).

tyrant, argue that a principal and abiding concern behind his legal reforms was to maintain the city's exclusive legal authority.[9]

If Solon's concern with injustice and its consequences, *stasis* and tyranny, places him securely among archaic political thinkers, the legal character of his measures clarifies his particular brand of political reform. Unlike the legendary Lycurgus at Sparta, Solon did not undertake to prevent injustice by completely overhauling the social and economic fabric of the city.[10] He was just as concerned to remedy injustice as to prevent it—or, more precisely, to give the Athenians the language and legal procedures that would allow them to remedy injustice for themselves. In this way, Solon sought with his reforms to overcome the threat of tyranny by anticipating and neutralizing the tyrant's strongest argument: that he possessed a unique responsibility to correct the injustices of the city.[11] Solon made it clear that the good city could maintain its own justice through its laws.

Solon approached the problem of reform with surgical precision. If he was greatly concerned to create a state in which injustice was a universal concern, he also wished to effect reform in as economic a fashion as possible. According to Plutarch (*Sol.* 15.2), Solon was aware that the Athenians would not allow him to impose an ideal *politeia*, and sought the best laws that they would tolerate. It was perhaps Solon's conservatism that kept him from solving Athens's greatest problem, the wide disparity in wealth and power between rich and poor. As long as the disparity remained, it might appear that Solon's laws were dependent on the goodwill of the rich and powerful Athenians. But Solon denied that this was a problem.

---

9. For Solon's restrictions on legal self-help, see Ruschenbusch 1966, 83. On Solon's law against tyranny, see below. On the importance of legal procedure for Solon, see Gagarin 1986, 73–74. There was one exception to Solon's rule that injustice was the concern of the entire state: a husband could kill an adulterer apprehended in flagrante delicto (see Plut. *Sol.* 23.1 and Hoffmann 1990, 95–98). Like later Athenians, Solon apparently did not believe that individual initiatives taken against adulterers were likely to compromise the city's legal integrity.

10. Spartan legend confirms that Lycurgus's reforms involved more radical social and economic changes by inserting elements of civic violence in Lycurgus's story (Plut. *Lyc.* 11.1; cf. *Sol.* 16.1) that are absent from Solon's. Solon enforced his laws without suffering physical injury and without imposing physical coercion.

11. On the tyrant as reformer (ἀνὴρ εὐθυντήρ), see chap. 2.

When the visiting sage Anacharsis questioned his efforts by comparing laws to a spider's web that can hold the weak but not the strong, Solon responded that "men preserve agreements that profit no one to violate," and he himself "fit [ἁρμόζεται] the laws to the citizens in such a way that they realize that just action is preferable to illegal action" (συνθήκας ἄνθρωποι φυλάττουσιν, ἃς οὐδετέρῳ λυσιτελές ἐστι παραβαίνειν τῶν θεμένων· καὶ τοὺς νόμους αὐτὸς οὕτως ἁρμόζεται τοῖς πολίταις ὥστε πᾶσι τοῦ παρανομεῖν βέλτιον ἐπιδεῖξαι τὸ δικαιοπραγεῖν: Sol. 5.2–3). The story is perhaps improvised, but Plutarch, even in improvising, is probably echoing the language of Solon's political poetry. The words "to fit" (ἁρμόζειν and συναρμόζειν) are conspicuous in Solon's poetic defense: claiming that he "fit together force and justice" (ὁμοῦ βίαν τε καὶ δίκην ξυναρμόσας: 30.16 GP), he announced that he meant his laws "alike for the good man and the bad, fitting straight justice to each" (θεσμοὺς δ᾽ ὁμοίως τῷ κακῷ τε κἀγαθῷ, εὐθεῖαν εἰς ἕκαστον ἁρμόσας δίκην: 30.18–19 GP). Hoping to draft laws that would strike the Athenians as inherently rational, Solon seems to have tailored them to fit the existing tribal order and, despite considerable economic innovation, existing disparities in individual wealth.

But the precision and rationality of Solon's laws tell only part of the story of his difficult struggle with tyranny. Solon was determined to avoid tyranny himself and render it impossible in Athens, but he could not defeat his enemy without arming himself with similar weapons. Plutarch asserts, and his own poetry seems to confirm, that Solon was not originally commissioned to revise Athenian law or to design a new political structure but to act in the capacity of a mediator—a position of considerably greater power and one that links him closely with some archaic tyrants.[12] If this is true, Solon reformed Athens the way a tyrant ruled his city: alone and in possession of extraordinary political power. If he determined not to exercise his own powers to the limit of his mandate, this decision was entirely his own.

Both the *Athenaion politeia* (5.1) and Plutarch (*Sol.* 14.2) call

12. On Periander's role as mediator, see Hdt. 5.95, where Periander acts as a mediator (μεσίτης) between Athens and Mytilene; see also the preceding chapter.

Solon a *diallaktēs* (mediator) and note that he was selected by the two dominant factions of Athens (rich and poor) as a defender of the special interests of each. While Plutarch adds that Solon was also named a lawgiver (νομοθέτης), his account of Solon's political struggles with the Athenians makes it clear that he was not originally commissioned to revise the Athenian laws and constitution.[13] Solon was certainly not the only mediator of the archaic period.[14] He was perhaps not even the first to be selected as a mediator to resolve Athens's internal political disputes; the law code of his predecessor Dracon may have come to exist as the solution of a mediator. But Solon's closest parallel, the only other known to have mediated in his own state, was not at Athens but at Mytilene, where, almost at the same time that Solon was made *diallaktēs*, Pittacus was installed with full discretionary power to resolve the political crisis that Mytilene's many political exiles were causing. Aristotle considered Pittacus to be an *aisymnētēs*.[15] We cannot know what he was called by his contemporaries (except Alcaeus, who called him a tyrant), but Pittacus's status and activities seem well described if, as seems probable, an *aisymnētēs* in Pittacus's day was in some sense a judge. Pittacus probably enjoyed the endorsement of Mytilene's contending factions. Born an aristocrat, in his youth he joined two of Alcaeus's older brothers in a conspiracy to kill Melanchrus, who was ruling Mytilene as tyrant. That Pittacus was not later exiled with other aristocrats suggests that he also enjoyed the favor of Mytilene's demos. Once made *aisymnētēs*, he reformed Mytilene through his own personal decisions and actions. According to Aristotle, he made no real changes in the constitution and drafted only a few minor laws.[16] Yet in his actions Pittacus most

13. See especially *Sol.* 16.3: "But soon, realizing the benefit of [the *seisachtheia*] and giving up their private complaints, they made a sacrifice in common, which they called the *seisachtheia*, and they appointed Solon correcter and lawgiver of the state [τῆς πολιτείας διορθωτὴν καὶ νομοθέτην], not just of some things but entrusting everything to him."

14. See Gagarin 1986, 60. Gagarin's examples include Demonax, Andromadas, and Philolaus.

15. On Pittacus, see also chap. 2.

16. *Pol.* 1274b18–23. Aristotle mentions one bestowing more serious penalties on crimes committed when drunk, which was certainly directed against the politics and social organization of the *aristoi* of Mytilene; on wine and the politics of the *aristoi*, see Burnett 1983, 155.

definitely sided with the Mytilenean demos against the other dominant faction, which was composed of Mytilene's aristocrats. Alcaeus himself gives us the best proof of this in his surviving poetry:
writing like a man who feels betrayed, he labels Pittacus an impos-
ter (κακόπατρις: 75.12, 348 LP; cf. 72) and a coward (141 LP), and
he castigates Mytilene for electing Pittacus as its tyrant (348 LP). It
is very unlikely, however, that the demos perceived Pittacus as a
tyrant or regretted having made him *aisymnētēs*, of which Pittacus's
voluntary and peaceful return to private life after ten years in power
(something that no tyrant ever managed) was the best proof.

Solon's position in Athens shares much with that of Pittacus in
Mytilene. Like Pittacus, Solon was invested with nearly absolute
power to solve a set of social problems caused by escalating feuds
between hostile factions. To be sure, for the *Athenaion politeia* and
Aristotle's *Politics*, Solon was selected in part because of his connections with the Athenian "middle" (οἱ μέσοι), a group of citizens
of common birth (κακοί) whose wealth separated them from the
poor.[17] This cannot be maintained of the aristocratic Pittacus. But
we may wonder if the Aristotelian tradition understands Solon
rightly. That Solon belonged to the "middle" sector of Athenian
society agrees with Aristotle's conviction (*Pol.* 1297a3–5) that this
group made an important political contribution by providing mediators in times of civic conflict. The *Athenaion politeia* (5.3) supports
its social identification of Solon by quoting from one of his political
poems. But it wrongly assumes that Solon wrote the poem in his
own voice, and, in fact, even if he had, the passage shows only that
Solon wished to disassociate himself from the injustices of the
rich.[18] With its description of Solon as "among the first in birth and

17. On Solon and the political "middle" see Arist. *Pol.* 1296a19–21. Cf. also
1295b34–35, where Aristotle makes his general view quite clear: δῆλον ἄρα ὅτι καὶ
ἡ κοινωνία ἡ πολιτικὴ ἀρίστη ἡ διὰ τῶν μέσων. Plutarch offers little help, noting
only (*Sol.* 14.1) that "the most sensible" (οἱ φρονιμώτατοι) of Athens looked to
Solon in the moment of civic conflict; we cannot know whether he is referring to a
separate group or to "the most sensible" within each of the two dominant factions.
On the rise of a social and economic "middle" in archaic Greece, see Starr 1977,
123–28.

18. 5 GP: "Keep your great heart quiet in your breast, you who push to the
overabundance of goods, and hold your great ambition in bounds. For neither will
we obey nor will these things behoove you" (ὑμεῖς δ' ἡσυχάσαντες ἐνὶ φρεσὶ
καρτερὸν ἦτορ, οἳ πολλῶν ἀγαθῶν ἐς κόρον ἠλάσατε, ἐν μετρίοισι τίθεσθε

reputation, but among the middle in wealth and property" (ἦν δ' ὁ Σόλων τῇ μὲν φύσει καὶ τῇ δόξῃ τῶν πρώτων, τῇ δ' οὐσίᾳ καὶ τοῖς πράγμασι τῶν μέσων: *Ath. pol.* 5.2)—that is, from a family apparently on its way to becoming impoverished gentry—the *Athenaion politeia* leaves unclear the exact nature of Solon's political link to the relatively well-off commoners who seem to have been typical of the "middle." The import of Solon's reforms seems also to have been misunderstood. The *Politics* (1296b35–36) makes the general remark that lawgivers do well to promote the political status of the "middle," and it celebrates the political balance that Solon achieved by mixing oligarchic and democratic elements (1273b35–74a5). In turn the *Athenaion politeia* (7.3–4) emphasizes those aspects of Solon's constitution, such as his redivision of the Athenians into classes according to wealth, that weakened the prerogatives of the noble in their relations with their political opponents (κακοί). For the Aristotelian tradition, therefore, Solon avoided the exclusion of any segment of the citizen body from at least some participation in political affairs. But this is something quite different from asserting that Solon designed a "constitution of the middle" (μέση πολιτεία) that would place the economic "middle" at the political center of the city.[19] Rather than clarifying Solon's position in the Athenian state and the directions of his reforms, Aristotle and the *Athenaion politeia* suggest that there was confusion about Solon's social and economic allegiances. Solon's contemporaries were perhaps also confused.

If not a compromise from the "middle," then Solon, much like Pittacus in Mytilene, was probably made a mediator because the Athenians did not know whether he would side with the rich or the poor, or, more probably still, because each of the two factions regarded him as a potential advocate. An elegy mentioned by the *Athenaion politeia* (5.2 = 4 GP) in which Solon "did battle on behalf

---

μέγαν νόον· οὔτε γὰρ ἡμεῖς πεισόμεθ', οὔθ' ὑμῖν ἄρτια ταῦτ' ἔσεται). Rhodes (1981, 124) suggests that the author of the *Athenaion politeia* abbreviated and misparaphrased his source, who included a more appropriate poetic proof that Solon belonged to the political "middle." But we do not have any such passage in what survives of Solon's poetry, and it is doubtful whether he ever wrote an unambiguously autobiographical poem.

19. The *Athenaion politeia*'s first reference to a "constitution of the middle" (μέση πολιτεία) (13.4) comes in its discussion of the followers of Megacles after it has finished with Solon's reforms.

of each of the groups against the other and then mediated" between them and "urged them to abandon their ambitions" suggests that Solon embraced each faction's complaints against the other without committing himself to either political program.[20] Plutarch (*Sol.* 14.2) notes that the Athenians were impressed by Solon's phrase "Equality does not make war" (τὸ ἴσον πόλεμον οὐ ποιεῖ) but understood it in opposite ways: the rich were thinking of equality in terms of substance and virtue (ἀξίᾳ καὶ ἀρετῇ), while the poor thought Solon was praising equality of numbers (μέτρῳ καὶ ἀριθμῷ). Solon himself claimed in a poem (29b GP) that although he did not satisfy either rich or poor, he "fulfilled with the help of the gods the things [he] promised" (ἃ μὲν γὰρ εἶπα, σὺν θεοῖσιν ἤνυσα: 29b.6 GP). But he might not have been entirely innocent of this confusion; one ancient scholar, Phanias of Lesbos, accused Solon of winning support as mediator by deceiving the Athenians.[21]

Even if the Athenians were not deceived in commissioning Solon to solve their social and political problems, they were certainly surprised at the solution he offered. The "first of his measures" (Plut. *Sol.* 15.3) and his most immediate response to the crisis that led to his selection was the *seisachtheia* (shaking off of burdens), the immediate cancellation of outstanding debts on persons. The reform attests to the remarkable power that Solon held over the public and private matters of the Athenians. But the *seisachtheia* was not a permanent solution. It eased the immediate political crisis in Athens, which was caused by a growing number of indebted poor, but did not alter the economic circumstances that caused such debt. Solon eliminated debt bondage, which protected the Athenians from slavery but not from poverty. He did not attempt to make debt an effective means to achieve social parity (for example, by imposing usury laws), nor did he mitigate the basic needs that

20. Some of the extant fragments of Solon's poetry (e.g., 5–8 GP) may belong to the same elegy. Passages 7 and 8 GP are placed in the past; if they were part of the elegy mentioned at *Ath. pol.* 5.2, it was not, as the *Athenaion politeia* treats it, a poem that anticipated political events. For Solon's remarkable manipulation of narrative voices, see the discussion below of 29a GP, and see Will 1958.

21. Cited by Plut. *Sol.* 14.1 Plutarch (14.2) answers Phanias by disputing his assumption that Solon wanted to be mediator: "Solon had at first shied from taking on the *politeia*, fearing the greed of some and the arrogance of others."

forced the poor to contract debts (by redistributing land).[22] The economic conservatism of the *seisachtheia* was certainly intended. Elements of the *politeia* that he subsequently drafted, such as his division of the Athenian citizen body into economic groups with distinct political privileges,[23] show that Solon did not believe that erasing the distinction between the poor and rich would itself solve Athens's political problems. Taking advantage of the moral terminology of archaic politics, he says in his poetry that "bad and good [i.e., poor and rich] should not have equal shares of the rich earth of the fatherland" (οὐδὲ πιείρας χθονὸς πατρίδος κακοῖσιν ἐσθλοὺς ἰσομοιρίαν ἔχειν: 29b.8–9 GP).

According to Plutarch (*Sol.* 15.3–16.3), Solon exerted himself to demonstrate the wisdom of the *seisachtheia* to the Athenians, but they were not persuaded easily and did not remain persuaded for long.[24] What did the opposed factions want? Different things, obviously. The Athenian demos seems to have been upset by the very existence of an economically and politically superior class and wanted the aristocracy rendered indistinct—most effectively by a radical redistribution of land. The aristocracy was annoyed that the demos could threaten to use political means to extricate itself from its legal debts. The aristocrats would apparently have liked a political guarantee that the poor would honor their debts; that is, they wanted the demos reduced to political impotence. Each saw the selection of Solon as mediator as a good risk. According to Plutarch, "many, not excluding those of the middle, viewed change by reason and law to be troublesome and difficult, and welcomed a single man who was most just and sensible to direct their affairs" (πολλοὶ δὲ καὶ τῶν διὰ μέσου πολιτῶν, τὴν ὑπὸ λόγου καὶ νόμου μεταβολὴν ὁρῶντες

22. Ober (1989, 62) stresses that the reform threatened to worsen the economic status of the lower classes most dependent on debt by diminishing their "capital," although it would eventually have important implications for the definition of Athenian citizenship. In Solon's defense, the elimination of the system of hectemors (the Athenian version of sharecroppers) must have involved some effort to give land to the landless, and other changes (e.g., restricting exports of foodstuffs to olive oil and limiting ownership of large estates) helped the poorer Athenians.

23. See *Ath. pol.* 7.3–4; Plut. *Sol.* 18.1–2.

24. The *Athenaion politeia* (13.3) notes that the *seisachtheia* became a fundamental issue in the resurgence of factionalism after Solon's departure from Athens.

ἐργώδη καὶ χαλεπὴν οὖσαν, οὐκ ἔφευγον ἕνα τὸν δικαιότατον καὶ φρονιμώτατον ἐπιστῆσαι τοῖς πράγμασιν: *Sol.* 14.3). Plutarch believed that they could support their political argument with religious evidence: Solon, he tells us, received an oracle from Delphi that said, "Sit in the middle of the ship, setting straight the pilot's task; many Athenians will help you" (ἧσο μέσην κατὰ νῆα κυβερνητήριον ἔργον εὐθύνων· πολλοί τοι Ἀθηναίων ἐπίκουροι: *Sol.* 14.4). The image of the "straightener" (εὐθύνων) echoes the tyrant's persona as an *anēr euthuntēr*, Theognis's fearful image of the reformer of the unjust city (39–40). It is not surprising that the Athenians in Plutarch put forth Pittacus—who was clearly a tyrant in the eyes of his enemies—as the model of the sort of mediation they expected from Solon.

Yet Solon refused to oblige the Athenians. In a fragment that may refer to this period, Solon said that the Athenians "came for plunder with hopes of wealth, and each of them expected to find much happiness" (29b.1–2 GP). And elsewhere:

εἰ γὰρ ἤθελον
ἃ τοῖς ἐναντίοισιν ἥνδανεν τότε,
αὖτις δ᾽ ἃ οὕτεροι φρασαίτο,
πολλῶν ἂν ἀνδρῶν ἥδ᾽ ἐχηρώθη πόλις.
(30.22–25 GP)

For if I wanted the things
that appealed to one group
or, again, what the others designed,
the city would have lost many men.

What the Athenians wanted from a mediator—what Pittacus had done for Mytilene—Solon himself understood as a formula for tyranny, that is, the "slavery of the monarch" to which injustice ultimately leads if uncorrected (12.3–4 GP). Solon seems to have distinguished mediation and reform: reform would remedy injustice, but the mediation demanded by the Athenians was tantamount to tyranny, which, though some would gladly be flayed alive to possess it, was a mistake even for the tyrant, for tyranny is "a nice place to be," Plutarch quotes Solon, "but a hard place to get out of" (*Sol.* 14.5).

Solon's extant poetry gives few details about his legislation, even about his redivision of the Athenian citizen body according to income. But it is full of his struggle with the Athenians over the definition of reform and the nature of his political role. In his poetry Solon often paints himself as the protector of the Athenians against themselves. He stands among them, at one moment, "like a border stone in the space between two armies";[25] at another, he bears "a strong shield to protect both, not allowing either to win unjustly."[26] He makes it clear, however, that his position is not at all an easy one. In another poem Solon says he is "making defense from every quarter, like a wolf holding a pack of hounds at bay" (30.26–27 GP). Once a predator, he now is hunted, for the Athenians, Solon implies, are very inclined to turn against him. At other moments in his political poetry, Solon seems locked in a competition with the Athenians. Having spared Athens tyranny and violence, for which his enemies think him foolish, he claims, "Rather I think that in this way I will win victory over all men."[27] He also freely expresses contempt for his competition, the Athenians who have different ideas of his political responsibility and their own:

> ὑμέων δ᾽ εἷς μὲν ἕκαστος ἀλώπεκος ἴχνεσι βαίνει,
> σύμπασιν δ᾽ ὑμῖν χαῦνος ἔνεστι νόος·
> ἐς γὰρ γλῶσσαν ὁρᾶτε καὶ εἰς ἔπη αἱμύλου ἀνδρός.
>
> (15.5–7 GP)

Each one of you walks with the footsteps of a fox,
and the thought in all of you is frivolous,
for you look to the tongue and words of a wily man.

It is with an emotion very near pride that Solon says that those "who come for plunder . . . all look to me cross-eyed as an enemy"

25. 31.8–9 GP: ἐγὼ δὲ τούτων ὥσπερ ἐν μεταιχμίῳ ὅρος κατέστην. On this fragment see the important treatment by Loraux (1984).

26. 7.5–6 GP: ἔστην δ᾽ ἀμφιβαλὼν κρατερὸν σάκος ἀμφοτέροισι, νικᾶν δ᾽ οὐκ εἴασ᾽ οὐδετέρους ἀδίκως.

27. 29.4–5 GP: πλέον γὰρ ὧδε νικήσειν δοκέω πάντας ἀνθρώπους. That the other Athenians do not win is an implication made explicit at 7.6 GP.

(οἳ δ' ἐφ' ἁρπαγαῖσιν ἦλθον . . . λοξὸν ὀφθαλμοῖσ' ὁρῶσι πάντες ὥστε δήιον: 29b.1–5 GP).

The *Athenaion politeia* and Plutarch agree that the immediate effect of Solon's efforts to reform Athens was to make him the enemy of both political factions, rich and poor.[28] This conclusion was almost certainly based on Solon's poetry and should be read as a commentary on his self-representation, not his political reception. Enough of Solon's poetry survives to suggest that he deliberately cultivated the image of himself as embattled, unpopular, and un-appreciated. This is perhaps clearest in the remarkable poem quoted at length by Plutarch (*Sol.* 14.6), in which Solon constructs a dramatic debate featuring a political opponent who blasts him for refusing to accept the Athenian tyranny:

οὐκ ἔφυ Σόλων βαθύφρων οὐδὲ βουλήεις ἀνήρ·
ἐσθλὰ γὰρ θεοῦ διδόντος αὐτὸς οὐκ ἐδέξατο.
περιβαλὼν δ' ἄγραν ἀγασθεὶς οὐκ ἐπέσπασεν μέγα
δίκτυον, θυμοῦ θ' ἁμαρτῇ καὶ φρενῶν ἀποσφαλείς·
ἤθελον γάρ κεν κρατήσας, πλοῦτον ἄφθονον λαβὼν
καὶ τυραννεύσας Ἀθηνῶν μοῦνον ἡμέραν μίαν,
ἀσκὸς ὕστερον δεδάρθαι κἀπιτετρίφθαι γένος.

(29a GP)

Solon was not a deep thinker or an intelligent man,
for he himself did not accept goods offered by the god.
Though he has cast out his great net, he is amazed
and does not pull it in, failing in strength and lacking sense.
For to rule and acquire bounteous wealth
and reign over Athens for even a single day,
I would be willing to be flayed alive and have my line exterminated.

The fragment exhibits the free manipulation of narrative voice that also characterizes Solon's remarkable poem (4 GP) that, in the *Athenaion politeia*'s account, persuaded the opposed factions of Athenians to trust their affairs to Solon.[29] In this poem, however,

---

28. Cf. *Ath. pol.* 6.3: ἀμφοτέροις ἀπεχθέσθαι; also 11.1 and Plut. *Sol.* 16.1.
29. See the discussion above.

Solon is yet more daring, giving (or pretending to give) a critical voice to a position that is opposite his own. There is considerable vigor to his imaginary opponent's charge, for though Solon implicitly belies any political justification for tyranny by stressing (and exaggerating) the pleasures that the many and wretched (οἱ πολλοὶ καὶ φαῦλοι) saw in it, his opponent is correct that Solon refused a tyranny that he might have had without losing his life and family, for (as Solon's oracle suggests) the gods had offered it to him without cost (and not only for a single day). In the poem, the indictment of Solon's critic was almost certainly followed by a response from Solon; the fragment Plutarch quotes a few lines earlier probably belonged to this rebuttal:

> εἰ δὲ γῆς ἐφεισάμην
> πατρίδος, τυραννίδος δὲ καὶ βίας ἀμειλίχου
> οὐ καθηψάμην, μιάνας καὶ καταισχύνας κλεός,
> οὐδὲν αἰδεῦμαι· πλέον γὰρ ὧδε νικήσειν δοκέω
> πάντας ἀνθρώπους.
>
> (29 GP)

> If I have spared my fatherland
> and did not take up a tyranny and violence,
> polluting and shaming my fame,
> I am not ashamed; for rather in this way shall I,
> I think, win a victory over all men.

Solon might have answered his critic with a political explanation of his refusal to accept the tyranny. Instead, he counters the critic's talk of the pleasure and wealth to be had from tyranny with ideas of personal honor and shame, implying that the best things in life come to the man who avoids tyranny. This was a cogent (and possibly true) answer, but it was deliberately confrontational; Solon rejects, without really answering, his opponent's principal assertion that tyranny is good for the tyrant. The poem shows no trace of compromise, no reconciliation, nothing but a blunt statement of opposing views. Indeed Solon's accounts of the pleasure that the average Athenian saw in tyranny and of the prizes that came to the man who avoided it seem both exaggerated and strained. The poem cannot be considered an exercise in political debate; it is less concerned to bring the dissatisfied over to Solon's side than to mark, if necessary to invent, the differences that divide him from them.

Thus Solon uses his poetry to construct for himself a solitary position in the middle of Athens surrounded by his fellow country-men, who need him but do not appreciate him. This is a highly personal characterization of Solon as a lawgiver and the Athenians as his involuntary beneficiaries, but it betrays genuine political significance. Using the language of inclusion and exclusion that he employs elsewhere to characterize the human condition vis-à-vis the gods,[30] and to describe the consequences of unjust actions and the corrective force of *eunomia* (order),[31] Solon draws an unflatter-ing picture of the political unity of the Athenians, to whom his poetry is addressed and about whom it often speaks. "*Each one of you* [ὑμέων δ' εἰς μὲν ἕκαστος]," Solon says, "walks with the steps of a fox," and "there is no sense in the *lot of you* [σύμπασιν δ' ὑμῖν]" (15.5–6 GP), but "I expect to win a victory over *all men* [πάντας ἀνθρώπους]" (29b.5 GP)—in each of these passages, the Athenians are intrinsically united only by their common inability to under-stand and act on common interests and concerns. As the existence of man is defined by his fear of injustice and his inferior status in relation to the gods, the political unity of the Athenians appears to come directly from Solon, who stands in their middle, Proteus-like in his changes in form, appearing at one moment as a common benefactor and at the next as a common enemy. That Solon allows no one (except himself) to escape inclusion in one or the other of the political factions, rich and poor, confirms his conviction that the Athenians lacked collective political insight.

Solon's poetic invention of his political persona as isolated was certainly related to his perception that Athens was deeply divided and to the aims of his reforms. Unlike a mediator of Pittacus's mold, Solon was not out to fool one of the two parties that joined to

30. "No man alive is happy, but all are wretched, whomever among mortals the sun looks down upon" (οὐδὲ μάκαρ οὐδεὶς πέλεται βροτός, ἀλλὰ πόνηροι πάν-τες, ὅσους θνητοὺς ἠέλιος καθορᾷ: 19 GP), and "Everywhere the mind of the immortals is concealed from men" (πάντη δ' ἀθανάτων ἀφανὴς νόος ἀνθρώ-ποισιν: 21 GP).

31. So in the *Eunomia* (3 GP): "The intractable wound comes upon the entire city [πάσῃ πόλει]" (17); "in every way [πάντως]" will the man be found out who seeks to hide (28). *Eunomia* makes "everything [πάντα] among men fitting and wise" (39).

support him: he apparently preferred to fool them both. He was determined not to act as a catalyst, resolving the growing problem of the increasing gap between rich and poor by guiding and hastening the end to which it naturally aimed, the domination of the city by a single faction. This is what others would have done who had possession of the goad that the Athenians had entrusted to him (30.20 GP), and this is what the Athenians expected "who hoped to find much happiness" and foolishly imagined Solon "would show himself to have a jagged mind that prattled glibly" (29b.2–3 GP). But Solon felt compelled to disappoint them. Intent on keeping from tyranny by restraining the demos (30.21–22 GP), he imposed a *seisachtheia* and disallowed debt bondage, which prevented the abuse of wealth not in order to erase the division between rich and poor but to preserve it.[32] Reform for Solon clearly lay less in economic solutions than in legal reform: invalidating the laws of Dracon "because they were too harsh and burdensome in their penalties" (Plut. *Sol.* 17.1)—because, in other words, they exacerbated the consequences of injustice rather than mitigating them—and writing new ones, "for good and bad, fitting straight justice to each" (θεσ-μοὺς δ' ὁμοίως τῷ κακῷ τε κἀγαθῷ, εὐθεῖαν εἰς ἕκαστον ἁρμόσας δίκην, ἔγραψα: 30.18–19 GP).[33]

Solon therefore construed reform as a matter of imposing laws on all, which he contrasted with pressing the will of one faction on another. Solon's was a solution that balanced restraint and retribution, solving the problem caused by the injustices of the rich without inviting their vengeance. It realized politically the *eunomia* that Solon captured metaphorically when he described it as "often chaining the feet of the unjust, smoothing over the rough, bringing an end to satiety, obscuring hubris, withering the waxing buds of ruin, straightening crooked judgments," and the like.[34] As an imper-

32. See the remarks above.
33. Cf. 29.3–5 and 29a.5–7 GP.
34. 3.32–36 GP:

> καὶ θαμὰ τοῖς ἀδίκοις ἀμφιτίθησι πέδας·
> τραχέα λειναίνει, παύει κόρον, ὕβριν ἀμαυροῖ,
> αὐαίνει δ' ἄτης ἄνθεα φυόμενα,
> εὐθύνει δὲ δίκας σκολιὰς ὑπερήφανά τ' ἔργα
> πραΰνει, παύει δ' ἔργα διχοστασίης.

sonal and enduring replacement for the mediator's brief and self-interested expression of his will,[35] Solon's laws were not *nomoi* (a word that Solon does not use) but *thesmoi*, which Martin Ostwald has defined correctly as things "imposed by a higher power upon those for whom the authority of the imposing agency makes the θεσμός an obligation."[36] His laws, as Solon implies in his assertive "I wrote laws for good and bad alike" (30.18–19 GP), were born from the power that the Athenians had invested in him, owed their validity to his authorship, and were beyond the Athenians' power to revoke.[37]

Nevertheless Solon could change his own laws. According to Plutarch (*Sol.* 25.4–5) and the *Athenaion politeia* (11.1), when the Athenians were confused by the new laws or annoyed with them, they pestered Solon to interpret them or tried to convince him to make improvements. Solon found the role the Athenians were forcing on him as the supervisor and interpreter of his laws to be intolerable (ἄτοπος: Plut. *Sol.* 24.5); both Plutarch and the *Athenaion politeia* say that he wanted neither to change his laws nor to incur the enmity of the Athenians for refusing. More cogently, Solon wanted, as lawgiver rather than tyrant, to place his laws beyond change—that is, to endow them with a power of their own, so that they would provide straight justice and a political center for Athens. It was not enough for him to refuse to explain his laws; he needed also to vitiate his own power over them. To do this he removed himself from Athens; on the pretext of conducting trade abroad, he embarked on his long and famous voyage through the lands of the eastern Mediterranean (*Ath. pol.* 13.1; Plut. *Sol.* 25.5).

Solon's achievement, then, was essentially dramatic: he acted out in his own person a solution to the political dilemmas he saw in Athens. The history of his reform of Athens was therefore in-

35. The *Athenaion politeia* (7.2) and Plutarch (*Sol.* 25.1) say the laws were to be valid for a century, which is also the period for which the Orthagorid oracle (Diod. 8.24 = 23 PW) predicts that the Sicyonians will be "ruled by the scourge" of tyranny. But Herodotus (1.29) limits the authority of Solon's laws to a period of ten years.

36. Ostwald 1969, 19; cf. 1–8.

37. See Hdt. 1.29: "The Athenians themselves were not able to do this [i.e., change or annul the laws], for they were bound by great oaths to use Solon's laws for ten years."

herently biographical (as also inherently poetic); Plutarch shaped, touched up, and added his own distinctively moral flavor to Solon's story, as the *Athenaion politeia* abbreviated it—but neither missed the principal lines of its plot: Solon's attempt to prevent tyranny by establishing law (θεσμός) in the place he himself had held as the mediator/lawgiver of Athens. Solon's achievement required him to gain possession of the same sort of discretionary power that tyrants and mediators wielded, but also to alienate that power from himself. Thus Solon offers and dramatizes a solution to the problem that underlies his efforts to combat tyranny: how to win without becoming a tyrant. The remarkable insight in Solon's political solution is apparent in his poetic self-representation and his biographer's commentary on the major chapters of his story, his selection as *diallaktēs* of Athens, the ambivalence of his relationship with the Athenians, and his renunciation of autocratic power. It serves as a sort of confirmation of the reality of the problem and significance of Solon's solution that his political maneuvers reverberate elsewhere.

The conspicuous act of self-removal that concluded Solon's tenure as lawgiver was a prominent feature of the stories of archaic lawgivers.[38] Admittedly, many of these stories differ from Solon's in that they spring from the collective imagination of their cities. If there was a core to which legends have adhered, it cannot be known. But this amounts to a difference in authorship, not in political significance: Solon molded his own political persona, as those of lawgivers were molded by the generations of citizens who celebrated and followed their laws, in response to the same need to establish and maintain the integrity of their *thesmoi*.

The theme of the lawgiver's self-removal dramatizes the autonomy of the laws, which comes to exist only when they assume the political authority of the individual who has drafted them.[39] It provides narrative support for the Greeks' conceptions of the au-

38. For the patterns and significance of lawgiver legends, see Szegedy-Maszak 1978. Szegedy-Maszak views the patterns, which he ingeniously discovers, as fictions that are valuable "because they illustrate so clearly the transformation by and into myth" (200). Perhaps because he views the lawgivers' stories purely as myth, Szegedy-Maszak does not recognize their relationship with Solon's poetic self-representation.

39. So Szegedy-Maszak (1978) notes.

thority of law. As a rule, the Greeks customarily claimed they were adhering to their legal tradition, even when they were not. The Athenians continued to believe that they were operating on the foundation of Solon's laws. The Locrians prided themselves on having left Zaleucus's laws virtually unchanged for 200 yars. The Spartans apparently viewed their laws, their *rhētra* (verbal contract) with Lycurgus, rather than their assembly, kings, ephors, or their land, as the principal object of their loyalties. The immutability of laws appears as a first criterion of the stability of the state in both of Plato's literary visions of the state, the *Republic* and the *Laws*. Law possesses compulsive power and for that reason could represent an alternative to individual rule. Comparing laws and rulers, Aristotle maintained that laws were free of the personal element ($\tau\grave{o}\ \pi\alpha\theta\eta\tau\iota$-$\kappa\acute{o}\nu$) that marks the commands of the king, who in restraining the natural desires of men was likely to earn their hate (*Pol.* 1286a18). Plato's representation of the laws in the *Crito* as living, speaking, and reasoning beings takes this conception of law to its natural limit.

The lawgiver himself represents an implicit danger to the autonomy of the laws he has created.[40] He may yield to political pressure to change them; or if he disregards them himself, he effectively vitiates their force. As long as the lawgiver is alive, his laws are regarded as his creation, and he (rather than the laws themselves) is sovereign. Plato stresses in his *Seventh Letter* (337a) that the success of laws depends on the willingness of the laws' makers to exercise personal self-control. The legendary lawgiver brutally solves the problem by obliterating the threat at its source. Lycurgus, lawgiver of Sparta, for example, forced his countrymen to swear obedience to his laws until he returned; he then left Sparta permanently, and in some versions committed suicide. The story of Charondas, lawgiver of the Chalcidian cities of Sicily, is still more graphic. When he was accused of violating his own rule that forbade bearing weapons within the city, Charondas plunged the knife that he forgot to leave at home into his own heart. The accuser's point was presumably that the law should not be applied without regard for circumstances. But Charondas was determined to prove his laws to be

40. See Szegedy-Maszak 1978, 207.

inviolable and absolute.[41] The Romans had the comparable story of Brutus's execution of his sons, who had conspired to return the Etruscans to power in Rome: in Livy's highly dramatic version of the story (2.5.5–10), Brutus himself supervises the execution of his sons, thus acting as the responsible agent of his own family's demise as he is responsible for the birth of the new Republic.

Like the founder and tyrant, the legendary lawgiver does not render account to the city. His greatest personal achievement, his self-destruction, is a purely voluntary action. In this sense, the lawgiver holds an intermediate place between founders and tyrants. Unlike the founder, the lawgiver is seldom buried within his city; unlike the tyrant, his removal is itself a mark of honor rather than dishonor. The Greeks recovered the remains of a number of legendary founders but were less interested in lawgivers, as if, while importing Theseus gave new strength to Athens, returning a Lycurgus would weaken the autonomy of Sparta's laws. So the lawgiver's (and tyrant's) death seems crafted by legend very differently than the founder's. While the founder, as a hero, in some way survives his death as a personal force that is acknowledged and invoked by his city, the lawgiver lives on only in his impersonal laws.

The self-restraint that looms large in Solon's self-characterization was echoed in the stories of a second semilegendary group that counted Solon as a member: the Seven Sages. Consider once more the passage quoted above (29 GP) in which he celebrates his moderation. By reversing the popular view of the desirability of tyranny (which he seems deliberately to exaggerate),[42] Solon made himself an example of his new ideas of civic virtue. This becomes the theme of the popular, albeit chronologically impossible, story of Solon's encounter with the Lydian king Croesus. Yet its thematic origin is in Solon's own poetry:

$$\pi o\lambda\lambda o\grave{\iota} \ \gamma\grave{\alpha}\rho \ \pi\lambda o\upsilon\tau\epsilon\hat{\upsilon}\sigma\iota \ \kappa\alpha\kappa o\acute{\iota}, \ \grave{\alpha}\gamma\alpha\theta o\grave{\iota} \ \delta\grave{\epsilon} \ \pi\acute{\epsilon}\nu o\nu\tau\alpha\iota\cdot$$
$$\grave{\alpha}\lambda\lambda' \ \dot{\eta}\mu\epsilon\hat{\iota}\varsigma \ \alpha\grave{\upsilon}\tau o\hat{\iota}\varsigma \ o\grave{\upsilon} \ \delta\iota\alpha\mu\epsilon\iota\psi\acute{o}\mu\epsilon\theta\alpha$$

41. See Szegedy-Maszak 1978, 206. Philolaus (Arist. *Pol.* 1274a42–43) seems to be an exception to the rule.

42. Solon was certainly not the first to hate tyranny. For Archilochus on tyranny, when tyranny was new to the Greeks, see chap. 1.

$$τῆς ἀρετῆς τὸν πλοῦτον· ἐπεὶ τὸ μὲν ἔμπεδον αἰεί,$$
$$χρήματα δ' ἀνθρώπων ἄλλοτε ἄλλος ἔχει.$$

(6 GP)[43]

Many bad men are rich, many good men are poor,
but we would not exchange with them
virtue for weath. For virtue stands fast,
while money changes hands frequently.

A similar motif dominates the charter legend of the Seven Sages, which is preserved in Plutarch (*Sol.* 4.13) and Diogenes Laertius (1.27–33). A golden ornament (or a tripod, bowl, or cup in the versions Diogenes presents) was designated for the wisest of the Greeks. It was first presented to Thales, who accepted the prize but passed it on to another whom he decided was wiser yet than himself. This second sage likewise found a more worthy recipient, and onward the prize traveled until it reached Thales a second time (or, in some versions, Solon), who dedicated it to Apollo. Those who had received and passed on the prize became members of the group, which was constituted by its members' rejection of self-delusory claims of wisdom and the transitory honor of material gain as a condition of permanent fame. The sages do not reject honor; like Solon, the mediator who made himself a lawgiver, they redefine it.[44]

Understanding tyranny as the result of injustice, Solon undertook to render injustice a matter of procedure and thereby to demystify it—to make sure that its punishment remained a political rather than an extrapolitical matter. But Solon knew that tyranny involved a displacement of political power from the hands of the socioeconomic elite to the demos,[45] and, moreover, that when tyranny

43. Cf. also 29b.1–2 and 29a GP.

44. The theme intrudes into Plutarch's *Life of Solon* at other points. Plutarch (12.4–6) reports that Epimenides, who is sometimes included among the Seven Sages (D.L. 1.42–43), was invited by the Athenians to solve their political problems. The Athenians were impressed with his reforms (which anticipated Solon's) and offered him much money and many honors, but Epimenides asked for "nothing more than" a branch of the sacred olive tree of Athens, rejecting the expedient honor for the eternal.

45. Solon suggests a link between tyrants and the demos at 30.21–25 and 31.6–10 GP.

displaced political power it also consolidated it, personalized it, gave it a location, and made it something that belonged to someone. Although Solon was hostile both to the tyrant's *monarchia* over the city and to the typical byproduct of that *monarchia*, the unleashing of the demos's power, his response to the displacement of power inherent in tyranny was more complex. As much as he wanted to avoid the dangers of tyranny, he also wanted to exploit its political strength. To neutralize the tyrant's persona as a mediator and a corrector of injustice, Solon took on this very persona, canceling old laws and imposing new ones no less autocratically than Pittacus or any tyrant. As Nietzsche succinctly remarked about Solon in *Menschliches, Allzumenschliches* (1886), "to be a lawgiver is a sublimated form of tyranny."[46] More important still, when Solon's laws and *politeia* were no longer dependent on him, they retained some of the more important aspects of the tyrant's power: his demand for unquestioned obedience, his authority, and his exclusive hold on political matters. In Solon's laws, the Athenians found a master who, though impersonal and not self-interested, demanded fully as much as any tyrant. According to Herodotus (1.29), Athens was bound to Solon's laws by "great oaths," which, according to Plutarch (*Sol.* 25.2), were sworn by the Council and the incoming guardians of the laws (θεσμοθέται).

Solon as Political Failure

In exact proportion to the credit we give Solon for his insight into tyranny, we must also seek to understand why his conceptions of law and government proved failures—why, in other words, his departure from Athens was followed within a decade by further outbreaks of *stasis* and anarchy, and why Peisistratus, while Solon still lived, found it relatively easy to establish himself as tyrant (*Ath. pol.* 13–14). The answer offered here will absolve Solon of some blame but will also in part implicate him. On one hand, Solon wanted an enduring sovereignty of law, which was impossible for one man to achieve—unless he were godlike Lycurgus. Yet Solon must also share some blame, if not that tyranny came to Athens, nonetheless

---

46. Nietzsche 1969, 1:606: "Gesetzgeber sein ist eine sublimierte Form des Tyrannentums."

that it came so soon. What Solon did to accelerate tyranny's arrival should become clear when we consider how Solon actually thought tyranny might be prevented—when, in other words, we examine the specific laws Solon designed to protect his constitution from the fate to which it quickly fell. We know of two: one outlawed the establishment of tyranny itself, and a second forbade neutrality in periods of *stasis*.

The *Athenaion politeia* refers to the first law briefly and somewhat imprecisely when noting that the Areopagus, along with its other duties, "tried those conspiring to put down the democracy, for Solon had established a law of impeachment concerning these things" (τοὺς ἐπὶ καταλύσει τοῦ δήμου συνισταμένους ἔκρινεν, Σόλωνος θέντος νόμον εἰσαγγελίας περὶ αὐτῶν: *Ath. pol.* 8.4). Solon did not share the concern of later Athenians for the political status of the demos, which did not in Solon's day exercise an active control over the state, and which he clearly did not wish to make sovereign. Here the *Athenaion politeia* is using an abbreviation based on later laws against tyranny, which equated the dissolution of the demos with the establishment of tyranny. It is very nearly certain, however, that the *Athenaion politeia* here refers to a Solonian law against tyranny, and that that law established a procedure for impeaching tyranny. It was not the first law against tyranny; that there was an earlier one is implied by a passage in Plutarch (*Sol.* 19.3) in which Solon is said to have amnestied all Athenians convicted of crimes before his time except those whom the Areopagus, the *ephetai*, or the prytaneum had convicted for homicide or tyranny. On the basis of historical probability, this earlier law has been attributed to Solon's predecessor, Dracon.[47]

The exact provisions of neither law are known. The *Athenaion politeia* explains the rise of Peisistratus with the suggestive note that "all the laws concerning tyrants were mild at this time and especially that referring to the establishment of a tyranny; for there was this law: 'these are the laws [θέσμια] and customs [πάτρια] of the Athenians, if some rise to rule as tyrant or if anyone joins in setting up a tyranny, he and his family are outlawed.'"[48] Although the

47. See Ostwald 1955, 105–9.

48. *Ath. pol.* 16.10: ἦσαν δὲ καὶ τοῖς Ἀθηναίοις οἱ περὶ τῶν τυράννων νόμοι πρᾶοι κατ' ἐκείνους τοὺς καιροὺς οἵ τ' ἄλλοι καὶ δὴ καὶ ὁ μάλιστα καθήκων πρὸς

Athenaion politeia seems to present the quotation as the text of an archaic law, the reference to "laws [θέσμια] and customs [πάτρια]" suggests that the passage was taken from a later inscription of an archaic law.[49] Scholars,[50] assuming that the *Athenaion politeia* has incorporated a single archaic law in its entirety—"If some rise to rule as tyrant or if anyone joins in setting up a tyranny, he and his family are outlawed"—have argued that the passage could not refer to Solon's law against tyranny, for it notes a precise punishment for tyranny but says nothing about the impeachment procedure (εἰσαγγελία) that the *Athenaion politeia* (8.4) attributes to Solon. But the inscription may not have rendered its archaic precedent either literally or completely: if the procedures for prosecuting tyranny were no longer used, they would hardly be included. In any case, taking *Athenaion politeia* 16.10 as an exclusive reference to the pre-Solonian, and presumably Draconian, law against tyranny seems to require rejecting Plutarch's notice (*Sol.* 27.1) that Solon repealed all of Dracon's laws with the exception of his laws on homicide; for how could Dracon's law against tyranny be in force in Peisistratus's day if Solon had dismissed it?[51]

If the *Athenaion politeia* is referring principally (though not precisely) to Solon's law against tyranny when it describes the measures in effect in Peisistratus's day, we must find puzzling Aristotle's remark that the law was mild. The declaration of *atimia* (outlawry) deprived the aspiring tyrant and his family not merely of citizen rights but of all rights due to citizens, aliens, or even slaves. The *atimos* was a virtual nonperson, who could be killed by anyone without legal penalty.[52] Yet if the punishment is the harshest that

---

τὴν τῆς τυραννίδος κατάστασιν. νόμος γὰρ αὐτοῖς ἦν ὅδε· "θέσμια τάδε 'Αθηναίων καὶ πάτρια, ἐάν τινες τυραννεῖν ἐπανιστῶνται [ἐπὶ τυραννίδι] ἢ συγκαθιστῇ τὴν τυραννίδα ἄτιμον εἶναι αὐτὸν καὶ γένος."

49. See Wallace 1985, 23 with n. 73.
50. See Ostwald 1955, 106, and, for objections, Wallace 1985, 23–24.
51. It is probable that Solon's legislation incorporated many elements of earlier law codes, including Dracon's, and only Dracon's homicide law was recognized as pre-Solonian. But even if Solon's law against tyranny preserves much of some earlier law, it survived because of its place in Solon's legislative package.
52. I take Solon's *atimia* as the older, harsher variety. Recently, Manville (1980 and 1990, 147–48) has argued that Solon initiated the younger and milder form of *atimia* (loss of political rights) as a logical consequence of the new and much more significant form of citizenship for which Manville gives Solon credit. I agree that

the city could give, the law is indeed mild in one very crucial sense. Solon clearly wanted to criminalize tyranny in the same sense in which he sought to criminalize virtually all forms of injustice: to render it an offense in such a way that its correction was a matter of legal procedure. An individual suspected of aspiring to tyranny was protected by the law until he was convicted. Plutarch (*Comp. Sol. et Publ.* 2.2) is explicit about this: "If someone should undertake to establish a tyranny, [Solon] imposed a penalty on him after he was prosecuted."

This marks the main difference between Solon's law and later Athenian laws against tyranny, that proposed by Demophantus in the fifth century and a second by Eucrates in the next century.[53] Both describe penalties consistent with those noted in Solon's law. But while Solon gave responsibility for the prosecution of tyranny to the Areopagus, the later laws mention no legal procedure. Indeed both call for actions against the aspiring tyrant extending beyond the procedural boundary that Solon established by according every citizen an implicit right to prosecute and punish the "dissolution of the democracy." In the fifth-century decree, "the man who kills him who does these things [dissolves the democracy] and whoever counsels him shall be holy and blameless" (ὁ δὲ ἀποκτείνας τὸν ταῦτα ποιήσαντα καὶ συμβουλεύσας ὅσιος καὶ εὐαγής: Andoc. 1.96).

Plutarch took the legal protection that Solon's law gave the prospective tyrant as proof that Solon did not hate tyranny as much as he should have. For this reason, the Roman Publicola offers Plutarch a better model of antityrannical behavior than Solon; for, like the Athenians, who made laws against tyranny in the fifth and fourth centuries, "Publicola made it legal to punish the tyrant before trial" (*Comp. Sol. et Publ.* 2.2). Plutarch's criticism is essentially correct. As an extrapolitical form of power, tyranny could not be eliminated by political means, since a man whose success proved

Solon was likely responsible for changes in the nature of criminal justice in Athens, but I think those changes lay primarily in the procedural safeguards that Solon imposed, not in the softening of the punishments themselves.

53. On the decree of Demophantus, see Andoc. 1.96–98, where the law is quoted; for Eucrates', which was found in excavations in the Athenian Agora, see *SEG* xii 87. Ostwald (1955, 110–28) discusses the two in relation to earlier legislation against tyranny. On the Athenian legislation against tyranny, see also Rhodes 1981, 220–22.

him guilty of the charge of tyranny was not likely to allow the Areopagus to prosecute him. Solon's law therefore undercuts itself. It follows from Plutarch's analysis that since the failure of Solon's law against tyranny meant the collapse of his entire legislative package, the Athenians cannot alone be faulted for Peisistratus's rise. Trusting in his new laws to protect Athens, Solon seems to have thought it unnecessary and unwise for anyone to possess sufficient power to protect the laws themselves.

But Plutarch's judgment of Solon was based in the political conceptions of a very different period, which were greatly influenced by the political developments of the later sixth and fifth centuries. Solon should not be blamed for failing to anticipate these developments, particularly since he wished to avoid the most important of them, the Athenians' actual experience with tyranny. We can be sure, however, that Solon did not leave his laws without adequate defense because of mere oversight or overconfidence. To appreciate (as Plutarch does not) Solon's determination to force his laws to stand alone, we may turn to the second law Solon seems to have designed as a defense against tyranny, his law against neutrality in periods of *stasis*.

In the paraphrase presented at *Athenaion politeia* 8.5, Solon decreed that "when the city is in conflict, whoever takes up arms with neither side shall be disenfranchised and have no share in the city" (ὃς ἂν στασιαζούης τῆς πόλεως μὴ θῆται τὰ ὅπλα μηδὲ μεθ' ἑτέρων ἄτιμον εἶναι καὶ τῆς πόλεως μὴ μετέχειν). Ancient scholars were baffled by the law. The *Athenaion politeia* believes that it was intended to encourage civic involvement, but Plutarch (*Sol.* 20.1), labeling it "peculiar" (ἴδιος) and "paradoxical" (παράδοξος), thought it was more likely to promote *stasis*. Diogenes Laertius noted that the law was not at all in keeping with Solon's own behavior. Repeating the basic construction of the law as the *Athenaion politeia* records it, he noted that "when there was *stasis* in the city, Solon sided neither with those of the town nor those of the plain nor, again, with those of the coast."[54]

---

54. D.L. 1.58: ἀλλὰ καὶ τῆς στάσεως γενομένης οὔτε μετὰ τῶν ἐξ ἄστεως οὔτε μετὰ τῶν πεδιέων ἀλλ' οὐδὲ μετὰ τῶν παράλων ἐτάχθη. The three regional factions appear also at Plut. *Sol.* 13.1, but they are not discussed as part of the Athenian political landscape before Peisistratus in Solon's own poetry or in the *Athenaion politeia*.

Modern scholars until recently have exonerated Solon of sedition and inconsistency by rejecting the law as inauthentic. The strongest arguments have been based on Lysias 31,[55] which the orator wrote to dispute the eligibility for political office of a certain Philon, who had avoided the civil war that shook Athens in 404/403 by moving across the northern border of Attica to Oropus. This would seem to violate Solon's law against neutrality. But Lysias does not mention Solon's law; in fact, he remarks (31.27) that lawgivers of Athens never imagined a crime as enormous as Philon's. Scholars have therefore concluded that the law that the *Athenaion politeia* in the fourth century attributes to Solon was invented sometime after the end of the fifth. Recent studies,[56] however, have neutralized this argument by noting that the special circumstances of the speech (as a δοκιμασία) did not require Lysias to prove that Philon violated specific laws, and that the political circumstances (the amnesty proclaimed for crimes committed during the civil war of 404/403) made it unwise for Lysias to make the attempt.[57]

But if Lysias's failure to mention the law at 31.27 does not cast doubt on the authenticity of Solon's law, how is Solon to be saved from the crime of inciting the sedition, or, at the very least, of violating his own law? Common opinion now reconciles Solon's law against neutrality with his determination to avoid *stasis* and tyranny by construing it as a political expedient that Solon drafted at a moment when his popularity and the appeal of his laws were at a particularly low ebb.[58] In this view, the law was to attract the political support of the Athenian "middle," who, by the same view, "immediately profited" from Solon's reforms and whom Solon

55. See Hignett 1952, 27, and Masaracchia 1958, 174, with the extensive bibliography supplied in Goldstein 1972, 538–45.

56. See Goldstein 1972 and Bers 1975, 493–98.

57. Goldstein (1972, 542–43) argues that the similarity between Lysias's description of Philon's crime and the language of the law argues for the law's existence (even though Lysias pretends to know no such law). The argument is interesting (though not conclusive) and deserves more credit than Bers (1975) gives it.

58. See Bers 1975 and von Fritz 1977. Goldstein (1972) is more concerned to defend the law than to explain it. But in arguing that "Solon could well have hoped to force the non-militant 'decent citizens' to take a stand against militant subversives" (538), he seems to share the view of Bers and von Fritz that the law was intended to create or support a politically engaged new faction in Athenian politics.

would naturally expect to "support him expressly."[59] This inter-pretation saves Solon from the embarrassment of inconsistency, but it is speculative: rendered as a temporary expedient, the law is made to occupy a unique status among Solon's laws, which, according to Herodotus (1.29), the Athenians swore to obey for ten years, and, according to the *Athenaion politeia* (7.2) and Plutarch (*Sol.* 25.1), were intended to be valid for a century. It is no wonder that one proponent of this view suggests that the law was not inscribed on the official record of Solon's legislation but was drafted later and published elsewhere.[60]

There is a still more pressing objection. The *Athenaion politeia*'s rendition of the law ("When the city is in conflict, whoever takes up arms with neither side shall be disenfranchised and have no share in the city") makes it very difficult to interpret the law as an attempt to politicize the Athenian "middle." In castigating the citizen who allies himself "with neither side" (μηδὲ μεθ' ἑτέρων), the *Athenaion politeia*'s version acknowledges just two factions with opposing interests, presumably the aristocracy and the demos. We cannot circumvent the problem by treating the *Athenaion politeia*'s wording as inexact; every other mention of the law in antiquity similarly implies that Solon meant the law to force the Athenians to partici-pate in one of two factions.[61] It is possible that the *Athenaion politeia*

59. Von Fritz (1977, 247) believes that Solon saw the need for such a drastic measure to increase his support at the end of his period as a reformer.

60. See von Fritz (1977), who finds some support (which he wrongly takes as absolute proof) in the fact that the *Athenaion politeia* considers the measure near the end of its discussion of Solon's political reforms. Plutarch insists (*Sol.* 25.1) that all of Solon's laws were published on the triangular and wooden tablets (*kurbeis* and *axones*) which made up the official record—a statement, however, that is not confirmed by the *Ath. pol.*

61. Cf. Plut. *Sol.* 20.1: ἄτιμον εἶναι τὸν ἐν στάσει μηδετέρας μερίδος γενό-μενον; *Mor.* 550c: παραλογώτατον δὲ τὸ τοῦ Σόλωνος, ἄτιμον εἶναι τὸν ἐν στάσει πόλεως μηδετέρᾳ μερίδι προσθέμενον μηδὲ συστασιάσαντα; *Mor.* 823f: ἄτιμον εἶναι τὸν ἐν στάσει πόλεως μηδετέροις προσθέμενον; and the Latin translation of Gell. *NA* 2.12.1. Admittedly *heteros* may be used of many alternatives (see LSJ s.v. ἕτερος II), but it is difficult to believe that every other mention of the law would repeat the *Ath. pol.*'s imprecision. Eder (1986, 293) is alone in taking the *Athenaion politeia* as referring to just two factions. It is obvious that Athens and other archaic poleis experienced relatively constant discord among various aristocratic groups; but the law seems to reflect a particular concern with the political consequences of civil discord that bifurcated the city and invited, therefore, the sort of mediation that Solon himself was asked to perform.

completely misrecorded the law, and that other accounts repeated the mistake. But believing (as did his alter ego, Aristotle) that Solon had a close relationship with the Athenian "middle," the author of the *Athenaion politeia* would not make the suggestion lightly that Solon had suddenly discarded his political base. As he records it, the law allows no place either for Solon's own political activity or for a middle faction that he might lead. To make sense of the law, scholars have proposed that Solon intended, like some ancient version of Richard Nixon, to discover and politicize a "silent majority" as ballast against extremists. But this is just what the law seems to have been designed to prevent.

The force of "whoever does not take up arms" (ὃς ἂν . . . μὴ τιθῆται τὰ ὅπλα) presents further complications for the common view of Solon's law. Some have thought its military language must have been intended as a metaphor for conventional political support.[62] But for this it is a very unsuitable metaphor. *Stasis* results when civic conflict turns brutal; by employing the language of warfare, Solon seems to communicate a belief that political struggles naturally follow a path to violence. If Solon had wanted the law to garner him conventional political support, he would surely have found more appropriate language.

So the best efforts of contemporary scholars have done little to dispel the sense that Solon's law against neutrality stands at odds with his own political position. Condemning the citizen who fights "with neither faction" (μηδὲ μεθ' ἑτέρων), the law implicates Solon himself, who refused to offer unconditional political support, let alone his arms, to either rich or poor. But the law's rigorous exclusion of a mediating faction in a time of crisis, which ancient authors condemned as inconsistent and modern scholars have tried to render harmless, may provide the key to Solon's intention. That Solon acted in violation of his law does not mean that he wished to

62. So Develin 1977, 507–8: "What Solon's law says is that each man should take a stance in a state of στάσις; there is no reference to actual military or paramilitary involvement, but the setting up of one's position is a borrowing from the military." Goldstein (1972, 543–44) tries to neutralize Solon's military language by explaining the phrase "whoever does not take up arms" as a sort of technical term for political activity. But his arguments are also unconvincing. I follow Eder (1986, 293), who takes Solon's military language literally.

promote *stasis* or to radicalize the Athenians by pressing them to the extremes of the political spectrum. It does not seem that the law was ever enforced;[63] and it is hard to believe that it was intended to be enforced. Indeed, Solon's law makes more sense if we understand it as offering an image of political disharmony rather than proscribing a particular activity as illegal. On this view, although the law speaks of military support in times of internecine strife and pretends to invent a new form of criminal behavior, it was more concerned with Athenian political vocabulary. If this is correct, the law could have only one purpose: to upset the Athenians' conviction that mediation was a solution of political crisis. It belongs to the law's rhetorical strategy to prescribe what Solon saw as fact and to criminalize what he judged to be impossible. The Athenians were wrong to trust to mediators in Solon's view, because that very hope accelerated the chain of events linking political conflict with *stasis* and tyranny. Solon did not therefore wish to force the Athenians to fight to the death, as Aesop's whales and dolphins chose to do, but like Aesop's creatures, they should learn to distrust upstarts who offer themselves as mediators. That Solon should wish to purge the idea of mediation from the political vocabulary of the Athenians is consistent with his frequent warnings (cf. 30.21–5 and 31.6–10 GP) that the Athenians were very fortunate to have chosen a mediator as impartial as himself and with his determination to force the Athenians to look to laws rather than to mediators to solve their problems. This resolves the question of Solon's inconsistency: that the law contradicts his status as *diallaktēs* is explained by the fact that he took the redefinition of this status as his principal task—that is, he undertook to draft stable laws that would render his job unnecessary. In effect, then, the law against neutrality was aimed to realize in legal form Solon's view that sovereignty must rest with law.

With his measures against tyranny and political mediation, Solon marked the firm boundaries of his political geography. In the middle of the city, serving effectively as sovereign, were the laws, which were obligated to protect the city from injustice and themselves from usurpation. No one individual, no political faction, should occupy this place. If the laws fail to prevent the rise of *stasis*,

63. See Goldstein 1972, 538, and Bers 1975, 493.

the *politeia* itself must fail. It is obvious that Athens's political history followed a very different course than that outlined by Solon. With Cleisthenes, who reformed Athens neither as a tyrant nor as a lawgiver, the middle was occupied not by laws but by the demos itself, and Athens began to eliminate opposition to the demos's power. But the different course Athens followed was the result, not the cause, of Solon's failure.

The cause, as Plutarch implies in his *Comparison of Solon and Publicola*, lay in the personal character of Solon's achievement. Solon's method was by necessity consistent with his aim: determined to define laws as uniquely autocratic in the same way that he was autocratic, he enacted Athens's reform in his own person, transforming and alienating the power that the Athenians entrusted to him by writing laws, by retiring from Athens, and (tragically) by both acknowledging his laws as supreme and allowing them to fail when he refused to use force against Peisistratus. In all this Solon acted alone; his politics implicitly gave the Athenians the same role as audience that his poetry assigned to them explicitly. The Athenians became spectators of a drama that they seem to have appreciated very little. And since they were not centrally involved in the creation of Solon's laws, the Athenians seem to have perceived little interest in their survival. The *Athenaion politeia* (13.2–5) demonstrates this in its sketch of the years following Solon's archonship: the year of *anarchia* (i.e., the failure to elect an archon) after Solon's laws had been in force for a mere five years and, after another five years, Damasias's attempt to retain the archonship indefinitely; following these signs of incipient demise, the rapid emergence of new political factions and the gradual failure of Solon's *politeia* to respond to reemerging economic disputes. No account of this period gives any indication that the Athenians put much faith in the ability of Solon's laws to circumvent political conflict. Plutarch suggests (*Sol.* 29.2) that "though the city still made use of [Solon's] laws, all were looking forward to revolution and anxious for a new constitution, not hoping for equality, but rather to gain through the change and make themselves masters over their opponents." It was only much later that the Athenians began to value Solon's laws, and then they were not recognized as *thesmoi* that owed their authority to their archaic maker but as *nomoi* that were revalidated by the decree of the sovereign demos.

Solon's problem was not merely to make laws but to make the Athenians obey them. The former was a great challenge; the latter proved impossible. Of course, other cities (e.g., Sparta) remained faithful for decades and even centuries to the laws they attributed to their archaic lawgivers. But precisely because his laws and his story were the product not of memory but of history, Solon was less fortunate. Both Solon's story and the legends of other lawgivers constructed the sovereignty of their cities' laws by dramatizing their makers' voluntary alienation of autocratic power, but Solon's story was a product of his self-representation, not of popular legend. A Lycurgus could succeed where Solon failed because Lycurgus existed in the collective imagination of the Spartans, who celebrated the reality of their own political achievement, their collective alienation of personal and immediate control of their affairs, when they remembered Lycurgus's essentially fictional story. In this sense, Delphi was literally correct that Lycurgus was more than a mortal man. If he had been anything less than a god—that is, if he were not the imaginative construction of the entire city—his task would have proved impossible. Any political figure could write his own story, as Solon did more deliberately than most, but none could himself make that story into a collective possession.

The collapse of Solon's personal venture to devise a legal sovereignty explains the rapid replacement of his *politeia* by tyranny, the form of government Solon most wanted to avoid. As a personal success and a political failure, by avoiding tyranny but not replacing it, Solon created a political system oriented around a sovereign who did not exist; and the very failure of Solon's laws announced the need for an autocratic center. It is therefore more accurate (albeit less sympathetic) to say that Solon *prepared* Peisistratus's road to tyranny than to say that he merely foresaw it. In fact, Peisistratus could find a script for the successful establishment of tyranny by reading between the lines of Solon's legislation for what the lawgiver most feared. As though following such a script, Peisistratus demolished Solon's fragile political edifice story by story. He first obscured the lawgiver's political vision of two balanced factions by establishing a third, which, though it had a regional origin, attracted the support of the Athenian demos (which was indifferent to the limits Solon had placed on it).[64] Then, with the demos as his accomplice, he effectively replaced the legal mechanism Solon had established for punishing (and politically neutralizing) injustice with his own more personal and remystified form of *dikē*. It would seem that Peisistratus understood Solon's reforms even better than Solon knew tyranny.

Yet in Plutarch, Solon also understands Peisistratus; indeed, the lawgiver completes his personal tragedy by providing a commentary on the tyrant's rise. Plutarch's Solon was the only Athenian able to perceive Peisistratus's thirst for power beneath his magnanimous persona (*Sol.* 29.3). And Solon alone recognized the request for a bodyguard of club-bearers for what it was, a first step toward tyranny (*Sol.* 30.1–2). Solon upbraided Peisistratus for his avarice, and the Athenians for their stupidity and cowardice.[65] But only when he was too old and the tyranny was too well established did he admit that Peisistratus should be met with force. In fact Solon gradually lost his interest in criticizing political events along with his ability to change them. Remaining in Athens after Peisistratus had secured the tyranny, Solon was swayed by the attentions the tyrant paid him and impressed by his show of obedience to those laws that he did not, as tyrant, implicitly violate. According to Plutarch, Solon voluntarily served the new master of Athens as a confidential advisor in the last years of his life (*Sol.* 30.4–31.2).

Plutarch probably shaped his description of Solon's last years to strengthen his view that Solon was not quite the enemy of tyranny that he should have been, and thereby to explain Solon's political failings by reference to his personal character. But if he is right that Solon eventually accepted tyranny, it may be that Solon did so not because his vanity proved stronger than his hatred of tyranny. Perhaps Solon learned from his experience as a lawgiver and as a subject of a tyrant that a city could profit more from the tyrant's political self-indulgence—if it could eventually overthrow him—than from the lawgiver's selfless alienation of power in the form of

64. On the significance of the Peisistratid bodyguard of club-bearers as a sign of the Athenian demos's support for his rule, see chap. 2.

65. See also *Ath. pol.* 14.2.

laws. This seems to be suggested by Solon's remark after Peisistratus made himself tyrant of Athens: "It is relatively easy to avoid
tyranny, but more glorious and illustrious to destroy it once it is
established and formed" (Plut. *Sol.* 30.5). The glories that belonged
to cities that overcame established tyrannies are the subject of the
next chapter.

CHAPTER FOUR

Master and Slave:
The Fall of Tyranny

Ad generum Cereris sine caede et vulnere pauci
descendunt reges et sicca morte tyranni.

Few kings descend to the son-in-law of Ceres
except by slaughter and wounds, and few
tyrants die bloodless deaths

Juvenal 10.111–12

In the third book of the *Histories*, Herodotus narrates at great length the story of the Samian Maeandrius, who was the *grammatistēs* (secretary) and, after 522, the successor of Polycrates, the illustrious tyrant of Samos. Herodotus apparently found Maeandrius interesting because he struggled against an overpowering fate; Maeandrius, Herodotus says, "wished to be the most just of men," but "it did not turn out so" (3.142). This makes him a peripheral member of a significant group of figures in Herodotus—Croesus, Astyages, and Cambyses are among the more prominent—who vainly resist unfortunate fates. But Maeandrius was a distinctive member of this group, for, unlike the others, he struggled vainly not to hold on to his power, but to renounce it. Maeandrius's unsuccessful attempt to divest himself of the Samian tyranny, which he claimed he did not want, elucidates a principal characteristic of archaic Greek tyranny: when a tyranny came to an end, it was not, as a rule, the tyrant's peaceful return to private life that ended it, but his murder or banishment at the hands of his former subjects. This

rule was significant both for tyrants and for the collective governments that replaced them. In fact, liberation—the forced removal of
a tyrant by his own city, by another city, or sometimes by another
tyrant—was a political action that both destroyed and preserved the
tyrant's distinctive power.

According to Herodotus, Polycrates was lured to Asia Minor
by the Persians, then summarily murdered.[1] When Maeandrius
heard that Polycrates was dead, he marked out the boundaries of a
sacred precinct (τέμενος) on the outskirts of the city of Samos and
placed an altar in the middle of it to Zeus Eleutherius. When he was
finished with this task, he called an assembly of all the Samians and
made a formal end to tyranny in Samos. There he announced that
he could rule Samos as a tyrant but did not in fact approve of
Polycrates' behavior and had no intention of doing what he did not
think another man should do. Therefore, he proclaimed, he would
establish political equality (ἰσονομία) in Samos and give the Samians their freedom (ἐλευθερία). But he wanted something in
return for his sacrifice: six talents of Polycrates' great wealth and a
hereditary priesthood of the new sanctuary of Zeus Eleutherius that
he had himself established.[2]

The offer, Herodotus goes on, did not appeal to the Samians.
An aristocrat named Telesarchus rejected the offer on behalf of the
entire city: "You are certainly unworthy to rule over us, for you are
lowborn and a bane; you make sure you can account for the money
you have handled."[3] Maeandrius determined to do the exact oppo-

1. See Roisman 1985, 257–77. Shipley (1987, 103) speculates that Polycrates fell
to a conspiracy in which Maeandrius was involved. This is certainly possible;
Maeandrius's claim to be Samos's liberator seems to suggest that he played some
part in Polycrates' death.

2. In his words (Hdt. 3.142.3–4): ἐμοί, ὡς ἴστε καὶ ὑμεῖς, σκῆπτρον καὶ
δύναμις πᾶσα ἡ Πολυκράτεος ἐπιτέτραπται, καί μοι παρέχει νῦν ὑμέων ἄρ-
χειν· ἐγὼ δὲ τὰ τῷ πέλας ἐπιπλήσσω, αὐτὸς κατὰ δύναμιν οὐ ποιήσω· οὔτε γάρ
μοι Πολυκράτης ἤρεσκε δεσπόζων ἀνδρῶν ὁμοίων ἑωυτῷ οὔτε ἄλλος ὅστις
τοιαῦτα ποιέει. Πολυκράτης μέν νυν ἐξέπλησε μοῖραν τὴν ἑωυτοῦ, ἐγὼ δὲ ἐς
μέσον τὴν ἀρχὴν τιθεὶς ἰσονομίην ὑμῖν προαγορεύω. τοσάδε μέντοι δικαιῶ
γέρεα ἐμεωυτῷ, ἐκ μέν γε τῶν Πολυκράτεος χρημάτων ἐξαίρετα ἓξ τάλαντά μοι
γενέσθαι, ἱερωσύνην δὲ πρὸς τούτοισι αἱρεῦμαι ἐμοί τε αὐτῷ καὶ τοῖσι ἀπ' ἐμεῦ
αἰεὶ γινομένοισι τοῦ Διὸς τοῦ Ἐλευθερίου, τῷ αὐτός τε ἱρὸν ἱδρυσάμην καὶ τὴν
ἐλευθερίην ὑμῖν περιτίθημι.

3. Hdt. 3.142.5: ἀλλ' οὐδ' ἄξιος εἰς σύ γε ἡμέων ἄρχειν, γεγονώς τε κακῶς
καὶ ἐὼν ὄλεθρος, ἀλλὰ μᾶλλον ὅκως λόγον δώσεις τῶν μετεχείρισας χρημάτων.

site. Frustrated in his attempt to give away the tyranny on his own terms, Maeandrius decided to keep it. He did this by summoning Samos's leaders to him one by one on the pretext of presenting an account of Polycrates' funds, and putting them in chains. A little later when Maeandrius fell ill, and his brother Lycaretus, who had sights on the tyranny himself, took charge, the imprisoned aristocrats were all put to death.

Maeandrius, in Herodotus's account, is clearly surprised when his offer is not accepted. From his perspective, the offer benefits the city as well as himself. He would be delighted to avoid the animosity and danger that tyrants typically faced without losing all the wealth and fame that tyranny offered; the Samians, he seems to have thought, would consider six talents to be a small price to pay for their liberty. But there is nothing simple about the arrangement Maeandrius proposes. Maeandrius's declaration begins by making three related points: Polycrates possessed the scepter at Samos, which is a somewhat antiquated and unpolitical symbol of legitimate power;[4] the scepter has passed to Maeandrius; and (therefore) Maeandrius can claim power in Samos. But Maeandrius takes an abrupt turn when he asserts that Polycrates deserves blame for ruling as an equal over equals and that he will do nothing that he finds blameworthy in others. The contradiction is striking: if Polycrates had a real claim to his power, if he had a scepter (a sign of power that came from the gods), he surely was not an "equal lording it over equals." And if Maeandrius is Polycrates' heir, he can do what others should not do: exercise autocratic rule at Samos.

So Maeandrius seems confused. He claims both that he has a right to tyranny and that no man has such a right. His actions appear likewise muddled. Before Maeandrius calls the assembly, he dedicates a sanctuary and altar to Zeus Eleutherius, who would later be known on the mainland in connection with the deliverance of

4. There is no other evidence of a tyrannical scepter at Samos; and scepters are rare as symbols of royal power in archaic Greece (although Cleomenes may have had one: see Hdt. 6.75.1). But if Maeandrius was not speaking metaphorically (as Xerxes must be at Hdt. 7.52), it would seem most possible that Polycrates was the first to import this ancient image of divinely commissioned power to Samos. For the scepter as a sign of divine favor in Herodotus's time, see Aesch. *Eum.* 626 (διόσδοτα σκῆπτρα); for the image of a tyrannical scepter, *Aesch. PV* 761.

Greece from the Persians. Maeandrius clearly meant Zeus Eleutherius to be a divine patron for the city's new liberty and autonomy. The dedication was a striking piece of persuasion, for it
implied that the gods had already approved Maeandrius's proposal,
and the religious celebration of Samian liberty was ready to begin.
But this sort of dedication was unusual for private individuals in
Maeandrius's day: tyrants often dedicated sanctuaries; common citizens apparently did so only very rarely.[5] If there were any doubts
about Maeandrius's actions, his attempt to install himself in a position as hereditary priest would have erased them. This too was an
occasional practice of tyrants,[6] but hardly de rigueur for private
citizens. In effect, Maeandrius was crossing the border to tyranny at
the very moment that he was offering Samos *isonomia* and *eleutheria*.

Telesarchus, in his brief response, seems no less confused than
Maeandrius.[7] His "You are not worthy to rule over us" prefers to
ignore Maeandrius's proposal in order to counter what Maeandrius
had already rejected. Moreover, Telesarchus's remark that Maeandrius was ill-born and ruinous for Samos was neither constructive
nor particularly accurate: Maeandrius's family was almost certainly
beyond reproach.[8] In his defense, Telesarchus's contempt is directed
primarily against Maeandrius's occupation, rather than his character
or birth. Before Polycrates was killed, Maeandrius had served a

5. Themistocles built a temple to Artemis Aristobule at Melite that, according
to Plutarch (*Them.* 22.1–2), annoyed many of his fellow citizens; the new epithet
that Themistocles' temple imposed on Artemis boasts of his good counsel to the
Greeks; see Garland 1992, 64–81. At some time after Polycrates' death, Maeandrius
also gave the decorations in Polycrates' dining hall (ἀνδρεών) to the Hereion (Hdt.
3.123.1).

According to Plutarch's *Life of Pericles* (14), Pericles answered the Athenians'
reluctance to finance the restoration of the Acropolis by offering to pay for the job
himself. The offer was disingenuous but clever. The Athenians could no more allow
any single individual to pay for the restoration than any single individual could
actually afford it.

6. See Burkert 1985, 96. On the Deinomenids' priesthood of Demeter, see van
Compernolle 1957, 474–79. For Cyrene, see Chamoux 1953, 136–59. The priesthood must have had a particular attraction for Maeandrius; the position would
certainly have protected him from reprisals at the hands of his political enemies.

7. See also Roisman 1985, 266–67.

8. For the epigraphical record of its accomplishments, see Shipley 1987, 104–5.
Roisman (1985, 258) is right to doubt the veracity of Telesarchus's remark, but he
undervalues its significance in treating it as "hostile political propaganda."

tyrant, and, as Sophocles wrote (873 P), "Whoever approached a tyrant, even as a free man, became his slave." That the job of secretary gave Maeandrius great power and made him Polycrates' successor (in default of sons) meant nothing to the Samians. For them, it lay in the nature of his position as Polycrates' secretary that he was responsible for his actions; and the Samians, as Telesarchus makes clear in his response, had every intention of holding him responsible, as had Polycrates, his former master. This is the substance of Telesarchus's rejection of Maeandrius's offer: the Samians believed that no private individual could stake a claim to the whole or any part of Polycrates' legacy. The Samians were Polycrates' heirs; Maeandrius was not. As a result, Maeandrius did not even have the right to dissolve the tyranny. This may explain why Telesarchus does not dispute the first, logically more dubious part of Maeandrius's implicit argument: that Polycrates possessed a valid claim to tyranny in Samos. Telesarchus does not reject Polycrates' credentials perhaps because he needs them to reject Maeandrius's.

The substance of Telesarchus's response helps uncover the considerable subtlety beneath Maeandrius's apparently illogical proposal. Maeandrius did not want to see tyranny end at Samos quite as much as he wanted to be the person who ended it. His speech constructs a neat opposition between Polycrates, Samos's tyrant, and himself, its liberator. Polycrates was unjust; Maeandrius is just. Polycrates had his moment but has now fulfilled his destiny, and it is Maeandrius's turn. Polycrates had a right to the tyranny; Maeandrius has the same right but will free Samos instead. Yet in opposing the tyrant and the liberator, Polycrates and himself, Maeandrius also construes them as close parallels. The liberation from tyranny, in Maeandrius's view, belongs to someone, as the tyranny once belonged to someone: Polycrates had the tyranny; the liberation will be his own. So it becomes clear that tyrant and liberator are both positions of wealth and privilege. The tyrant is far richer, but the liberator profits from the respect of his fellow citizens. His speech locates Maeandrius at a personal crossroads between tyranny and liberation. Samos would no doubt benefit from his decision to free it rather than possess it as a tyrant, but all of the credit and a healthy portion of the profit would go to Maeandrius himself.

Some recent scholars find evidence in Telesarchus's remarks

that the Samians rejected Maeandrius's offer for its aristocratic spirit.[9] But Herodotus's account does not support this interpretation. There is nothing particularly aristocratic in his account of Maeandrius's proposed *isonomia*, while there is obvious aristocratic pride in Telesarchus's insulting accusation that Maeandrius is "lowborn" (3.142.4). In fact the Samians seem to respond on a less obvious, but more important level: how Maeandrius characterizes himself when he makes his proposal. Telesarchus counters Maeandrius's choice of liberation or tyranny with a very different one: Maeandrius, he implies, may plead that he acted as a mere servant to Polycrates and obey the Samians as he obeyed his former master (presumably buying his life but certainly relinquishing all claims to Polycrates' wealth and the priesthood of Zeus Eleutherius), or he can claim the tyranny as his own and risk his life to enjoy it. In either case the liberty and equal rights of the city—if and when it achieved them—would be its own, not a tyrant's gift. In short, Telesarchus insists that a tyrant by any other name is still a tyrant.

But if the Samians reject Maeandrius's plan as a spurious form of freedom, what does one make of Herodotus's remark that the Samians "were not interested in freedom" (3.143.2)? Graham Shipley argues that Herodotus blamed the Samians for not accepting Maeandrius's offer and taking advantage of him to unite against the threat posed by the Persians.[10] There may be some truth in this. Herodotus could not help but be exasperated with the Samians, who, at the moment of Polycrates' death, had their one good opportunity to gain control of their political destiny. Not only was the end of tyranny in sight, but just then Samos (thanks to Polycrates' efforts) commanded the economic and military presence and the political unity necessary to maintain its independence. It never did

9. See Mitchell (1975, 86), whose position is taken over by Shipley (1987, 103–5), for whom Maeandrius is "a factional aristocrat." Yet other scholars, such as Ostwald (1969, 107–9), who pronounces Maeandrius's *isonomia* "a democratic form of government," and La Bua (1975), who sees Maeandrius as a man from the lower classes (55–56) determined to introduce social and political reform (61–62), are no closer to the truth.
10. Shipley (1987, 104), who elsewhere (105) attributes Herodotus's remark that Maeandrius wanted to be just to the "bias of his informants." But Maeandrius's action is certainly just in seeking to resolve an inequity and imbalance in his city (on this notion, see chap. 2).

again. While Maeandrius was making his extraordinary proposal, the Persians were preparing an attack on the island and, when it materialized, the Samians were so absorbed in their internal problems that they hardly noticed that the Persians had come. When Samos finally escaped tyranny and Persian domination forty-five years after Maeandrius had attempted to put an end to tyranny,[11] Samos's freedom was due more to the efforts of the mainland Greeks than to the Samians themselves, whose great contribution to the Greek effort was to give the Persians unreliable help.[12] From that moment of Samos's liberation, it became a fixed element of the growing Athenian hegemony in the Aegean, a hegemony that the Athenians justified by claiming to be both the founders and the liberators of the Samians and their Ionian neighbors.[13]

Yet if Herodotus was exasperated by the Samians, it was not their refusal of Maeandrius's offer that most annoyed him. Rather their mistake was doing nothing to keep Maeandrius from taking up the tyranny himself. Rebuffed but still powerful, Maeandrius found it easy to rationalize a revision in his original proposal: he would become a tyrant rather than a liberator, for, as Herodotus says, he realized that "if he resigned power, someone else would rise up as tyrant in his place" (3.143.1), which would have negated the value of his persona as Samos's liberator. Herodotus apparently agreed with Maeandrius, and although no friend to tyrants, he seemed to think that the Samians got what they deserved: if they had been "willing to be free," they would have come together to the Acropolis as soldiers determined to expel Maeandrius or kill him, not singly, like accountants intending to liberate Samos with ledgers and pens. In the end, the Samians accomplished nothing more than to make Maeandrius honest.

11. I am passing over the short interruption of the Samian tyranny brought about by the Ionian revolt; see below.

12. According to Herodotus (9.99.1), Leotychides, who was the Spartan commander of the joint expedition at Mycale, neutralized the Ionians' value for the Persian side. Borrowing a trick from Themistocles' repertoire, he exhorted the Ionians to betray the Persian cause and fight for their liberty. The Persians' fear that the Ionians would mutiny compelled them to disarm the Samians and send the Milesians elsewhere, which weakened their forces considerably.

13. The Athenians made their first explicit claim to hegemony over the Ionian cities as their founder at the council held at Samos after the close of the first campaign against the Persians in Ionia. On this, see Hdt. 9.106.3 and Meiggs 1972, 413–14.

We may wonder what kind of metal might be mined from Herodotus's story. It is clearly one of his many political essays. That Herodotus or his Samian sources could have known the details of an assembly that took place over two generations earlier is easy to doubt. But the story has been questioned in a more serious way. Kurt Raaflaub has suggested that Herodotus was misinformed— perhaps by a surviving member of Maeandrius's family—about the sanctuary of Zeus Eleutherius, which, in Raaflaub's view was dedicated not by Maeandrius in the late 520s but by the Samians after 479, when their city was liberated from the Persians.[14] Raaflaub's objection to the dedication stems from his conviction that the conceptual opposition between freedom and tyranny emerged from the Greeks' experience in the Persian Wars, long after Maeandrius's day. There are, however, serious objections to the redating of Maeandrius's sanctuary that is required by Raaflaub's view of the development of Greek political language. Herodotus knew Samos and its monuments particularly well,[15] and not, in all probability, from a single, interested source. Even if Herodotus had been a virtual stranger in Samos, it is difficult to believe that he could be persuaded to disassociate an important Samian monument from a major recent chapter of Samos's history and link it to a rather obscure and thoroughly unhappy event that had taken place over forty years earlier. The difficulties in redating the sanctuary of Zeus Eleutherius require us to reexamine the larger question implied by Maeandrius's dedication and elaborated in the exchange between Maeandrius and Telesarchus: Does the language of political liberation characteristic of the classical polis first emerge not from the experience with Persia but out of the death throes of tyranny, when the tyrant's pretense to justice was exhausted and when his subjects focused on wresting his extraordinary power from him?

There are clear parallels for the sort of behavior Herodotus expected of the Samians in response to Maeandrius. The most famous was the destruction of the tyranny of the Cypselids at Corinth. According to Nicolaus of Damascus (*FGH* 90 F 60.1), who borrowed from Ephorus, the tyranny fell in a wave of general resentment and revenge. Nicolaus does not report the immediate

---

14. Raaflaub 1985, 139–40; Raaflaub 1981, 259.
15. This was shown long ago by Cole (1912).

cause of the Corinthians' anger, or what end Psammetichus met, but he is clear about its course: the Corinthians joined together to "destroy the houses of the tyrants, confiscate their goods, destroy their tombs, and eject the bones of Cypselus and his ancestors."[16]

The fall of the Deinomenids in Sicily at the end of the archaic period presents a much elaborated version of the same picture. According to Diodorus, who borrowed from Timaeus,[17] the last of the Deinomenids was Thrasybulus, who came to power when Hieron died in 467 and stayed there for eleven months. Thrasybulus earned the wrath of the Syracusans for his policy of random banishments, executions, and confiscations, which were undertaken to raise funds for his mercenaries. Getting rid of Thrasybulus was not very difficult. His own family had given him up as a lost cause, and while a good many Sicilian cities were anxious to see the Deinomenids fall, Thrasybulus had, besides his mercenaries, the support of only the small city of Aetna, which his brother Hieron had founded and where he was buried with civic honors. Seeing that his plight was hopeless, Thrasybulus negotiated a quick exile into southern Italy. Thrasybulus's departure did not, however, completely exhaust the Sicilians' rage against the Deinomenids and their legacy. The returning inhabitants of Catana, whom Hieron had exiled when he founded his Aetna on the same spot, retook the city and destroyed Hieron's grave much as the Corinthians destroyed the Cypselids' graves at Corinth (Diod. 11.76.3; Strab. 6.2.3).

A much greater challenge faced the Syracusans after Thrasybulus's exile, for a large portion of Thrasybulus's mercenaries (some seven thousand) remained in Syracuse, having been invested with citizenship by the Deinomenids. To drive them out and purify the city of all traces of the tyranny, the Syracusans decreed that public office was limited to citizens who predated Deinomenid rule. This was courageous, for the Syracusans had sent home the armies of

16. Plutarch (*De Herod. mal.* 21 = *Mor.* 859c–d) maintains that the Spartans were involved in bringing tyranny to an end in Corinth. The notice is difficult to accept for several reasons, not least of all because Herodotus was apparently unaware of it (if he had been, he would surely have included it in the speech of Sosicles at 5.92, which has the very purpose of convincing the Spartans that their reputation as a force against tyrants prohibits them from reinstalling a tyrant in Athens). So also Salmon 1984, 229–30, and Cartledge 1979, 139–40.

17. Diod. 11.67.5–68.7, 72, 73, 76.1–2. On the Sicilian historical traditions, see Pearson 1987, 125–56.

their neighbors who had come to help, and the action could only bring about open revolt. The mercenaries acted as expected and were vanquished only after costly battles both on land and at sea. The Syracusans celebrated their revolution with the dedication of a colossal statue of Zeus Eleutherius and established a yearly festival, the Eleutheria, which included sacrifices of thanksgiving and games.[18]

But tyrants were not killed or banished every day. Most important tyrannies of archaic Greece, including the Cypselids of Corinth, the Orthagorids of Sicyon, and the Peisistratids of Athens, lasted longer than a single generation and survived without great difficulty a transference of power from the tyranny's founder to his successor. Theagenes, tyrant of Megara in the late seventh century B.C., and Lygdamis of Naxos, a contemporary of Peisistratus, are exceptions, although Lygdamis did not apparently fall victim to internal pressures alone.[19] Yet if strong tyrannies could as a rule endure safely the transfer of power from father to son, or from brother to brother, nonetheless no tyranny, with the possible exception of the Orthagorids of Sicyon (whose chronology is very confused),[20] made it safely through a second such transference. Those unfortunate individuals who undertook to assume a tyranny after two predecessors—Psammetichus of Corinth and Thrasybulus of Syracuse are examples—were besieged from the very outset of their reigns. Even strong tyrants of the second generation seem to have felt some anxiety about their position. It was said in antiquity that second generation tyrants were harsher than their predecessors.[21] It

18. Diodorus does not say that the Syracusans, after overthrowing Thrasybulus, founded the sanctuary and the worship of Zeus Eleutherius, and it must be considered possible that the Deinomenids (or pre-Deinomenid Syracuse) established the cult, and the Syracusans later redefined it in celebrating their liberation from tyranny.

19. Plutarch's assertion (*De Herod. mal.* 21 = *Mor.* 859c–d) that Sparta deposed Lygdamis of Naxos is usually accepted: see Bernhardt 1987, 263.

20. For a recent attempt to make some sense of Orthagorid chronology, see Leahy 1968.

21. Cf. Arist. *Pol.* 1312b21–25: so Periander; Hippias; Thrasydaeus, son of Theron; Hieron, brother and successor of Gelon; and Dionysius the Younger. On Periander's cruelty, see Nic. Dam. *FGH* 90 F 58.1; for Hippias, see Hdt. 5.62.2–3; Thuc. 6.53.3, 6.59.2; *Ath. pol.* 19.1; for Thrasydaeus, Diod. 11.53.2; for the escalating cruelty of the Deinomenids after Gelon, see Diod. 11.67.3–5; and on Dionysius the Younger, see Pl. *Ep.* 348a–49b.

is certainly likely that tyrants found it necessary to use larger and larger doses of violence to pacify their subjects. It is also probable that the Greeks saw the violence of tyrants as gradually less justified as the dynasties became older.

But if most individuals bold enough to assume a tyranny were confident they could overcome their subjects' resentment, Maeandrius was not the only tyrant to try to change the character of his power. In fact, a substantial number of tyrants, particularly in the later archaic period, pretended to resign or concealed their tyranny in one of several ways. Although none seem to have returned to private life, the striking changes that later tyrants underwent in their elaborate efforts to disguise themselves provide perhaps the best indication of the increasingly sophisticated responses of the tyrants' cities to their rule.

Tyranny and Liberation

Maeandrius's closest parallel is perhaps Cadmus, the tyrant of Cos. According to Herodotus, Cadmus received the tyranny of Cos as a gift from his father, Scythes, who gave it up after 500 to venture west to southern Italy, where he ruled for a time over Zancle as the agent of the ambitious Hippocrates, tyrant of the city of Gela. After a time, Cadmus "put the power in the middle out of his own volition, there being no pressing need but his own sense of justice."[22] Cadmus, like Maeandrius, wanted to be just; the desire expressed itself, as did Maeandrius's, in his perception that there was an imbalance in the state—namely, his own tyranny—that he needed to correct.[23] There was, however, this difference between the two: while Maeandrius promised a transition between tyranny and freedom that would play itself out in his own soul, Cadmus seemed to understand that the end to tyranny required the tyrant's

22. Hdt. 7.164: ὁ δὲ Κάδμος οὗτος πρότερον τούτων παραδεξάμενος παρὰ πατρὸς τυραννίδα Κώων εὖ βεβηκυῖαν, ἑκών τε εἶναι καὶ δεινοῦ ἐπιόντος οὐδε-νὸς ἀλλ᾽ ὑπὸ δικαιοσύνης ἐς μέσον Κῴοισι καταθεὶς τὴν ἀρχὴν οἴχετο ἐς Σικελίην ἔνθα παρὰ Σαμίων ἔσχε τε καὶ κατοίκησε πόλιν Ζάγκλην τὴν ἐς Μεσσήνην μεταβαλοῦσαν τὸ οὔνομα.
23. On this, see chap. 2 passim.

removal. Herodotus indicates this when he notes that shortly after he put "the power in the middle [τὴν ἀρχὴν ἐς μέσον]," Cadmus left Cos for Sicily. It is perhaps better to attribute to Cadmus an acute sense of self-preservation than the altruism of lawgivers, who removed themselves after drafting their law codes.[24] In any case, Cadmus did not end his career as a tyrant when he made his escape from Cos. When he arrived in Italy, Cadmus took possession of the city of Zancle, which his father had also governed for a time, and ruled it as a tyrant.[25] Yet he could still impress for his justice and integrity: it was this that recommended him to Gelon, who sent him to Delphi with a large sum of gold to hand over to Xerxes in the event that the Persians defeated the mainland Greeks (Hdt. 7.163–64).

Perhaps the most important member of the distinctive class of tyrants who pretended to resign was the ingenious Aristagoras, who, together with Histiaeus, orchestrated the unsuccessful Ionian revolt of 499–494. According to Herodotus, one of Aristagoras's first moves in preparing his revolt was to give up his formal power in Miletus as Histiaeus's regent and set up a government based on equal rights (ἰσονομία), a procedure he followed in the other Ionian cities as well.[26] Herodotus does not treat Aristagoras very fairly. He oversimplifies in painting Aristagoras as an adventurer (ψυχὴν οὐκ ἄκρος) who initiated the revolt to further his own personal ambitions and abandoned it when he perceived that he could not win.[27] And it seems arbitrary of Herodotus to dismiss Aristagoras's resignation as a mere pretense,[28] when he is quite willing to credit Cadmus and Maeandrius with a genuine interest in justice. Yet

24. On the self-elimination of the lawgiver, see chap. 3.

25. See Vallet 1958, 341.

26. Hdt. 5.37.2: καὶ πρῶτα μὲν λόγῳ μετεὶς τὴν τυραννίδα ἰσονομίην ἐποίεε τῇ Μιλήτῳ, ὡς ἂν ἑκόντες αὐτῷ οἱ Μιλήσιοι συναπισταίατο, μετὰ δὲ καὶ ἐν τῇ ἄλλῃ Ἰωνίῃ τὠυτὸ τοῦτο ἐποίεε.

27. Hdt. 5.30.3, 124.1. On the episode, see Tozzi 1978, Lateiner 1982, and Wallinga 1984; and on Aristagoras's motivation, Manville 1977. On the patterning that went into Herodotus's presentation of the Ionian revolt, see Lang 1968, 24–36. Herodotus was not so troubled by Maeandrius's cowardice (3.146), but Maeandrius, to his credit, was not responsible for directing Persia's attention toward Samos.

28. Ostwald (1969, 110) forces Herodotus's language when he insists that λόγῳ is to be taken with μετεὶς τὴν τυραννίδα but not with ἰσονομίην ἐποίεε.

Herodotus is certainly correct that Aristagoras dissolved the tyranny of Miletus in such a way that he remained supreme in the city. Aristagoras's revolt created a situation in which his new position as *stratēgos* (general) closely paralleled his earlier position as tyrant. The revolt from the Persians was Miletus's primary concern as long as it lasted, as Persia's domination had been primary before the revolt. As a tyrant before the revolt, Aristagoras was identified with the Persians, and as a general during it, he identified himself with their overthrow. Though we may question Herodotus on Aristagoras's motives, we can see his logic in continuing to call Aristagoras "tyrant of Miletus" (ὁ Μιλήτου τύραννος: e.g., 5.49) even after his nominal resignation.

Although Aristagoras's resignation as tyrant hardly signaled an end to his power, there is little doubt that it deserves to be considered—as Herodotus himself seems to consider it—as a crucial first step of the revolt. Aristagoras ventured from his city in search of allies more freely than other tyrants, for, unlike other tyrants, he did not fear leaving his army unsupervised at home—in fact he departed on his diplomatic missions to Athens and Sparta immediately after liberating Miletus and the other Ionian allies (5.38.2). The second element of Aristagoras's suppression of tyranny in other Ionian cities was likewise fundamental for the Ionian revolt. Aristagoras united the Ionians by expelling the tyrants by means of whom the Persians kept them fragmented. Yet Herodotus might have reason to regard this act too as a nominal change; for, having rid them of their tyrants, Aristagoras had each of the Ionian cities select a general to replace the tyrant he had suppressed (5.38.2). The new generals must have exercised many of the powers that the exiled tyrants had held. More important still, the allegiance that the new *stratēgoi* felt to the war (and to Aristagoras, who had initiated it) preserved, while it redirected, the loyalty felt by their predecessors to Persia. Aristagoras seems therefore to have reduplicated in each of the allied Ionian cities the transformation that took place in his own person at Miletus. The Ionian city-states were permitted to select their own generals, perhaps by popular vote, but *isonomia* meant something more in archaic Greece than the right to select one's autocrat.

Aristagoras's resignation therefore was a step in his self-transformation from tyrant to autocratic general. Yet a public resignation could also mark the transformation of a military into a civilian tyranny. This was the achievement of Gelon, the first of the Deinomenids, tyrants of Syracuse. In Diodorus's detailed account (11.26.5–6),[29] Gelon called an assembly of the Syracusan demos after his extraordinary victory over the Carthaginians in 479. Appearing before this assembly unarmed, he rendered an account of his achievements (ἀπελογίσατο μὲν περὶ παντὸς τοῦ βίου καὶ τῶν πεπραγμένων αὐτῷ πρὸς τοὺς Συρακοσίους) and offered himself to anyone who wished to exact vengeance from him. To be sure, Gelon's offer to quit was not quite so sincere as Cadmus's or even Maeandrius's—perhaps a better comparison is Tiberius's pretense of refusing the principate of Rome (Tac. *Ann.* 1.11). Gelon certainly intended to be shouted down, and the Syracusans did not disappoint him: in response to his offer to quit, they proclaimed him in a single voice their "benefactor, savior, and king" (εὐεργέτης, σωτήρ, βασιλεύς).[30]

It was not beyond the talents of Gelon, whom Diodorus called "preeminent in both generalship and cleverness" (11.20.3), to plan this entire scene. But it is also not inconceivable that the affection was genuine; everyone knew the significance of his victory over Carthage, and many at the assembly were also indebted to Gelon for their Syracusan citizenship.[31] Even those whose enthusiasm was not entirely genuine may still have agreed to play Gelon's game, thinking it better to give away the control of their city voluntarily than to lose it by force. In any case, it would be difficult for Gelon's most implacable enemy to take advantage of the opportunity Gelon pretended to offer. Unarmed and, as Diodorus says, nearly naked, he was not at that moment a tyrant but a servant, who by rendering accounts was implicitly conceding his responsibility to his master. Gelon was clever with disguises: before the assembly began, he was

29. See also Ael. *VH* 6.11.13.27; Polyaen. 1.27.1. On the credibility of the story, which is usually traced to Timaeus, see Berve 1967, 1:147; Berve 1953, 546–48.

30. Εὐεργέτης and σωτήρ have a clear place in the language of Hellenistic kingship (see Habicht 1970, 156–59). Diodorus (or rather, Timaeus) perhaps applied them anachronistically, as Pearson (1987, 139) has recently argued. But there is no reason to doubt the historicity of the assembly itself.

31. See Hdt. 7.155–56. The older segment of the Syracusan citizen body probably remained the majority, but Gelon's supporters may have crowded the assembly.

Syracuse's tyrant; in the course of it, he transformed himself into Syracuse's subordinate; and he left it as Syracuse's king.[32]

Gelon was not merely seeking to confound the Syracusans; rather, he was attempting to avoid the distinctive danger that always accompanied tyranny. In the *Politics* (1312b17–21), Aristotle makes the hatred that arises from the ruler's hubris and the *kataphronēsis* (contempt) instilled by his self-indulgence the principal causes of the single ruler's fall. A city, Aristotle seems to suggest, overthrew its tyrant by gaining control of his reception. The city felt *kataphronēsis* when it was able to measure the disparity between its tyrant's acts and standards of legitimate behavior. By that measurement, the tyrant's actions were labeled as hubris, and the city understood itself as his victim. Alcaeus may have intended to promote this sort of political criticism in Mytilene when he attacked Pittacus as "ill-born" (κακόπατρις);[33] the insult tells Mytilene that Pittacus was unworthy of its regard or fear. This is likewise what Maeandrius implied in blasting Polycrates "for ruling over his equals," or, again, what Telesarchus meant to accomplish in insulting Maeandrius as a fraud: he was unworthy to rule because he was lowborn.[34] In a remarkable move, Gelon's announcement in the Syracusan assembly anticipated this sort of insult in the hope of neutralizing it. Perceiving, like Antilochus after the chariot race in *Iliad* 23 (570–611), that he might lose the prize he wanted, Gelon "voluntarily" gave up his autocratic power in Syracuse (as Antilochus gave up his prize), insisting that the Syracusan demos was his superior. The demos, like Menelaus in the famous Iliadic scene, when it heard· Gelon disingenuously proclaim it to be his superior, was undone by its desire to play the benefactor and handed Gelon what he most desired, lifelong autocratic power in Syracuse. To be sure, the Syracusans deserve some credit for their behavior in the assembly. Like the Samians who rejected Maeandrius's offer, they seem to

32. Even this is too simple; Gelon seems also to have cultivated the persona of Syracuse's second founder (οἰκιστής), a honor to which his repopulation of the city after transferring his tyranny to Syracuse perhaps entitled him in the eyes of the Syracusans (Hdt. 7.155–56). On the Sicilian tyrants' self-representation as the founders of the cities they dominated, see chap. 5.

33. Alc. 75.12 LP; cf. 348 and 72.

34. Herodotus (see chap. 2) relates the extraordinary lengths to which Deioces went to keep his people from seeing that he was no different than they. On the significance that fear had for tyranny, see chap. 2.

have understood that their *eleutheria* would be meaningless if it came as a tyrant's gift. Unlike the Samians, they also recognized some value in subtle differences. If Gelon's offer did not give them a real chance to gain their freedom, it nonetheless presented an opportunity to make their tyrant into a mild and beneficent ruler. By all indications, this is what Gelon became.[35]

Hieron, Gelon's brother and successor, also occupies a chair in the gallery of tyrants who toyed with the image of the liberator, although he did not pretend to liberate Syracuse, the seat of Deinomenid power, but two cities that were oppressed by a rival tyrant. Diodorus notes (11.53.4–5) that in the latter half of the 470s, Hieron was attacked by Thrasydaeus, tyrant of Acragas and Himera. The unprovoked and unexpected attack caused Hieron some difficulty, but it was in the end repulsed, and Thrasydaeus himself was forced into exile to Megara. As soon as their tyrant was exiled, the citizens of Acragas (and, presumably, the Himerans as well) established a democracy in the place of Thrasydaeus's tyranny and sent an embassy to Hieron, who accepted their terms for peace.[36]

Hieron's benevolence is surprising. Diodorus (11.53.4) points out that Thrasydaeus's force consisted not only of mercenaries but also of citizen armies from Acragas and Himera. To punish the two cities might yield long-term rewards. If Hieron captured Acragas and Himera, he could establish faithful dependents as local tyrants in place of the newly established democracy and secure their place in Deinomenid Sicily. This was the method the Deinomenids used to control Gela, which Gelon entrusted to Hieron when he took over Syracuse and which Hieron, when he assumed the tyranny in Syracuse, left to Polyzalus. Hieron's decision to accept the terms offered by Acragas, rather than take the cities by force, was a virtual concession of liberty to the city. Hieron's respect for the freedom and autonomy of other states might seem odd. Moses Finley certainly thought so: "The notion of Hieron as a protector of democracy," he commented doubtfully, "is pretty remarkable."[37] But Hieron's attitude toward Himera and Acragas does seem consistent

35. On the benevolent character of Gelon's rule, see Diod. 11.67.3 and Plut. *Mor.* 552a.
36. On this important episode in Himera's short but dramatic history, see Meier-Welcker 1980, 59–60, and Wilamowitz 1922, 304–6.
37. Finley 1979, 59.

with the achievements Pindar celebrates in his magnificent *Pythian* 1: Hieron's foundation of Aetna and establishment in it of "god-made freedom" according to the ancestral laws,[38] and his splendid defeat of the Etruscans at Cyme in 474. About the latter Pindar wrote:

λίσσομαι νεῦσον, Κρονίων, ἥμερον
ὄφρα κατ᾽ οἶκον ὁ Φοίνιξ ὁ Τυρσανῶν τ᾽ ἀλαλατὸς ἔχῃ,
ναυσίστονον ὕβριν ἰδὼν τὰν πρὸ Κύμας.
οἶα Συρακοσίων ἀρχῷ δαμασθέντες πάθον,
ὠκυπόρων ἀπὸ ναῶν ὅ σφιν ἐν πόντῳ βάλεθ᾽ ἁλικίαν,
Ἑλλάδ᾽ ἐξέλκων βαρείας δουλίας.

(*Pyth.* 1.71–75)

I beg you, son of Cronus, make a sign
so that the Carthaginian and the war cry of the Etruscan
remain quiet at home,
having seen at Cyme that hubris is ruinous for ships;
such great things they suffered, tamed by the leader
of the Syracusans
who threw their youth from quick ships into the sea,
delivering Greece from burdensome slavery.

Scholars have also raised questions about this language. It was usual for tyranny to be represented as a struggle against hubris,[39] though here the hubris belongs to the barbarians, not, as the mainlanders said,[40] to the city's former leaders. And Pindar's claim that Hieron "saved Greece from slavery" has not always seemed fitting language for the praise of tyrants. In fact, to explain the prominence of *eleutheria* in *Pythian* 1 Wilamowitz felt it necessary to postulate that the poet and his patron were not quite getting along.[41] But the sugges-

---

38. Pind. *Pyth.* 1.60–62: ἄγ᾽ ἔπειτ᾽ Αἴτνας Βασιλεῖ φίλιον ἐξεύρωμεν ὕμνον· / τῷ πόλιν κείναν θεοδμάτῳ σὺν ἐλευθερίᾳ / Ὑλλίδος στάθμας Ἱέρων ἐν νόμοις ἔκτισσ᾽. It is, admittedly, a strange idea of freedom on which Hieron modeled Aetna: he made his son, Deinomenes, king.

39. The struggle is usually commissioned by a divine patron. Hieron's is no exception: so at Pind. *Pyth.* 1.56: "May the god be the preserver of Hieron for the coming time."

40. See chap. 2 (Hesiod) and chap. 3 (Solon).

41. Wilamowitz 1922, 304.

tion is unwarranted: tyrants were hardly allergic to the language of *eleutheria*. *Eleutheria*, according to Aristotle's *Politics* (1310a32–33), "the ability to do what one wishes," does not entail the recognition of anyone else's rights. Needing to acknowledge no human authority beyond himself, the tyrant, from his own viewpoint, would be very pleased to regard himself as uniquely *eleutherios*;[42] and he could best prove that he possessed freedom by bestowing it conspicuously on others. Freedom thus fits tyranny much as the theme of clemency pervades the opera seria of eighteenth-century Europe: the monarch proves his power most convincingly when he uses it sparingly.[43] This may help explain Pindar's advice to Hieron in *Pythian* 2 to use his wealth "with a free mind" (ἐλευθέρᾳ φρενί: 57), which is praise thinly disguised as admonition. In the same spirit, Pindar compared Hieron's victory over the Etruscans in *Pythian* 1 (76–80) to the Athenians' victory at Salamis and the Spartans' at Plataea, and even to the achievements of Philoctetes, "who defeated Troy and put an end to the woes of the Danaans" (50–55), thus likening Hieron, the liberator, to great cities and heroes. In sending their appeal to Hieron, the citizens of Himera and Acragas probably hoped for nothing more than to deflect his anger by disassociating themselves from Thrasydaeus. But whatever their intentions, their request seems to have dovetailed exactly with Hieron's interest in representing himself as the liberator of the politically suppressed cities of Sicily.[44]

42. By the same logic, "no one is free except Zeus" (Aesch. *PV* 52). See Hdt. 3.80, where, in the famous debate on government, Otanes defines monarchy as the government that "can do what it wishes without rendering an account." See also chap. 1.

43. On the theme of clemency in classical representations of tyrants, see above p. 43 n. 54.

44. It is possible that Hieron was particularly interested in granting liberty to Himera as a political monument to the Deinomenids' glorious victory over Carthage, which had taken place near Himera in 480. Unfortunately we know less about Hieron's intervention in Italian affairs a few years on behalf of Locri: Hieron apparently sent Chromius, his brother-in-law and agent, to Rhegion to warn off Anaxilas, who had designs on Locri (cf. schol. ad Pind. *Pyth.* 2.36–38; Just. 21.3.2; and Stauffenberg 1963, 215). Pind. *Pyth.* 2.18–20 gives some idea of the terms in which he wished the event to be known. At 2.20 (διὰ τεὰν δύναμιν δρακεῖσ᾽ ἀσφαλές), the scholiast glosses δρακεῖσ᾽ ἀσφαλές with ἐλεύθερον βλέπουσα; the freedom of the Locrian maiden is therefore made to seem consistent with the power of the tyrant. If the scholium to *Pyth.* 1.99 is correct, the event was dramatized by Epicharmus in his comedy *Islands*, which may have been intended to make Anaxilas look like a fool.

It is a rare piece of good luck that we can look at the newly won liberty of Himera and Acragas through Pindar's short *Olympian* 12, which was written about this time for a certain Ergoteles, who was a new citizen of Himera. This little ode begins with a hymn to the patron of the recently liberated city of Himera:

λίσσομαι, παῖ Ζηνὸς Ἐλευθερίου,
Ἱμέραν εὐρυσθενέ᾽ ἀμφιπόλει, σώτειρα Τύχα.
τὶν γὰρ ἐν πόντῳ κυβερνῶται θοαί
νᾶες, ἐν χέρσῳ τε λαιψηροὶ πόλεμοι
κἀγοραὶ βουλαφόροι. αἵ γε μὲν ἀνδρῶν
πόλλ᾽ ἄνω, τὰ δ᾽ αὖ κάτω
ψεύδη μεταμώνια τάμνοισαι κυλίνδοντ᾽ ἐλπίδες·
σύμβολον δ᾽ οὔ πώ τις ἐπιχθονίων
πιστὸν ἀμφὶ πράξιος ἐσσομένας εὗρεν θεόθεν·
τῶν δὲ μελλόντων τετύφλωνται φραδαί.

(*Ol.* 12.1–9)

I beg you, Tyche Soteira, daughter of Zeus
Eleutherius, take charge of wide-ruling Himera,
for, with your help, swift ships are steered in
the sea, and on land quick war and council-bearing
assemblies. For the hopes of men are tossed at one moment
high, at another low, cleaving through false vanities.
For no mortal has yet found a sure sign
from the gods of coming events;
for intimations of the future are dim.

The ode makes use of the popular archaic metaphor of the ship of state. Tyche Soteira is taken from her usual province as the patron deity of sailors at sea and set into place as the guardian of the city's maiden voyage on the sea of political autonomy. With her new role comes a new parentage: once the daughter of the remote sea-god Oceanus (Hes. *Th.* 360), she is now introduced as the offspring of Zeus Eleutherius, the universal patron of political liberty.[45] As she

45. See Aesch. *Ag.* 664 for her more conventional persona. In Soph. *OT* 80–81, she is more loosely associated with good luck. Ziegler (1948, 1649, 1652–53) argues that Pindar invented the connection he makes between Tyche Soteira and Zeus Eleutherius.

guides ships, so she is asked to help the Himerans navigate the straits of "council-bearing assemblies."[46] Men and cities can never be utterly sure of their success, so it is natural, perhaps even necessary, for Pindar to warn his audience of the vanity of human hopes while celebrating Himera's political autonomy. But Pindar takes this cliché to greater lengths than convention requires, encasing it in an extended image of a troubled sea that tosses a helpless ship up and down with utter abandon. To strengthen his point that human hopes are vain, Pindar thereby contorts the metaphor of the ship of state into an image of a threatening sea, which from Homer symbolized social and political chaos.[47] Pindar's audience, if it followed his kaleidoscope of poetic images, might now remember that Tyche Soteira, before her recent adoption into the house of Zeus Eleutherius, was the daughter of Oceanus, a faceless and unpredictable deity who was virtually indistinguishable from the vast watery expanse he ruled.[48] Is political freedom, Pindar seems to ask, a mere whim of fortune, like the momentary calm of the sea?[49]

Pindar cannot be blamed for suggesting that Himera's new political situation was tenuous; after all, Himera and Acragas owed their liberty to Hieron's generosity, and Hieron surely had no intention of allowing them any real say in Sicilian politics. But the practical limits on their autonomy did not completely prevent Acragas and Himera from acting in their self-interest, and they found a chance to validate their liberty only six years later. When news came to

46. "Council-bearing assemblies" (ἀγοραὶ βουλαφόραι) recalls (probably by intention) *Od.* 9.112, where they are among the deficiencies of the uncivilized and unpolitical Cyclopes.

47. The metaphor reemerges at *Ol.* 12.11–12 (ἀνιαραῖς ἀντικύρσαντες ζάλαις). On Homer's use of sea similes, see McGlew 1989, 290. On the related notion of the ship of state, see chap. 2.

48. The name of Fortuna, Tyche's Roman double, was later virtually synonymous with storms at sea: see Patch 1974, 107.

49. The discomfort caused by making Tyche Soteira patron of the new liberated city would have been heightened if the Deinomenids anticipated the Himerans as devotees of Tyche. Diodorus names the Syracusan suburb Tyche in the context of the revolutionary overthrow of Thrasybulus (11.68.1 with the accepted emendation of the manuscripts' ἰτύκην to Τύχην), and Cicero (*Verr.* 4.119) remarks that the suburb had an ancient temple of Fortuna (= Tyche); hence it is commonly accepted that the suburb was established at the time of Gelon's refoundation and expansion of Syracuse in 484. So Herzog-Hauser 1948, 1689–93. See, however, the skeptical remarks by Drögemüller (1973, 835–36), who insists (to my mind unconvincingly) that Tyche was not honored with a cult before the fourth century.

them that the Deinomenids were in trouble, they joined forces and marched together on Syracuse to help the Syracusans to expel Thrasybulus, Hieron's successor (Diod. 11.68.1). Thus, although Himera and Acragas missed their chance to kill Thrasydaeus, they did the next best thing: they helped destroy their liberators.

This striking ingratitude on the part of the Deinomenids' client states gives further support to the simple rule that Juvenal cites in the epigram, "Few tyrants die bloodless deaths" (10.111–12), or, rendered more exactly, that tyrants did not leave power voluntarily; rather, they were banished or killed. There was no mystery in this to the Greeks; tyranny, as we have heard from Solon, "was a great place to be, but a hard place to get out of" (Plut. Sol. 14.5). A popular tyrant like Gelon could vary at will the face of his tyranny and prolong his family's rule for several years, but even he could not change himself into a private citizen, nor could he pass on to his successor the cloak of legitimacy that the Syracusans gave him. As Periander, reincarnated as a sage, noted in Diogenes Laertius (1.97), there was great danger for the tyrant both in being deposed and in resigning voluntarily. Cadmus got rid of the Coan tyranny by getting out of Cos. In this respect, his retreat differs little from Thrasybulus's escape from Syracuse or Hippias's from Athens. Of course, Cadmus decided when and how he would leave; but that he had to go came with the job.

If tyranny, for the tyrant, was the greatest form of happiness, his fellow citizens viewed it from the first as subjugation.[50] This is implied in the first occurrence of the word *tyrannos* in Greek, when Archilochus compares a man's all-consuming passion for a woman to the tyrant's power over his city.[51] The personal character of the tyrant's power made him as much the city's master as its ruler. It follows that removing a tyrant was a matter of taking his mastery over the city away from him. The city might win its power over itself—its *isonomia* and *eleutheria*—from the tyrant, even if it could not accept its freedom as his gift. The argument confirms the close relationship between liberator and tyrant that is evident in Hero-

---

50. See chap. 1 for Aristotle's views. For earlier sources, see Raaflaub 1985, 5–68; Raaflaub 1981, 193.

51. 23.18 W; see above in chap. 1.

dotus's story of Maeandrius: that the city that liberated itself from tyranny or the individual who liberated a city retained essential elements of the tyrant's position and power. The Samians might permit Maeandrius to throw himself on their mercy; but they were no more willing to accept him as their liberator than to adopt him as their tyrant. Hieron, if had he lived so long, might have been shocked by the ingratitude of Himeras and Acragas, as Maeandrius was surprised by the Samians' reaction to his proposal. But he should not have been. Hieron granted Acragas and Himera peace and autonomy as the most efficient way to control them in the way he needed to—as allies in his Sicilian ventures. That the liberator and tyrant were unstable metals was also the experience of those who genuinely wished to keep them apart. Consider the unfortunate experience of Dion, who freed Syracuse from the younger Dionysius in the hope of replacing him with a just and stable oligarchy (à la Plato). But he failed. However pure his intentions and great his integrity and sense of justice, Plato's friend found it impossible to avoid taking up the tyranny that he had devoted a good part of his life to put down.[52]

The close link between tyranny and liberation was understood and exploited not only by isolated individuals. Cities used the connection as well. Fifth-century Athens is the obvious example of a state that created allies by "liberating" them. But Sparta may have anticipated Athens in this respect. Admittedly, Sparta did not deserve its great reputation in antiquity for deposing tyrants.[53] Yet some part of it must be true. There is no doubt that Sparta undertook to liberate Samos from Polycrates and Athens from Hippias. There can also be little doubt about the Spartans' conviction that liberating Athens from tyranny gave them the right to determine Athens's political future.[54] Sparta returned to this policy, with vari-

52. See Plutarch's *Life of Dion* and Westlake 1969.

53. See the recent examination by Bernhardt (1987, 257–89), who explains Sparta's reputation as the enemy of tyrants as a justification for the power that Sparta acquired in the fifth and fourth centuries by less subtle means.

54. There may be some historical basis for Sparta's role in deposing the Orthagorids at Sicyon: see Griffen 1982, 58–59, and Cartledge 1979, 140. Bernhardt (1987, 269) seems right to doubt that the Spartans were motivated by a simple desire to eliminate tyranny but wrong to insist that the Spartans gained no influence over Sicyon as a result of their actions. Sicyon's virtual disappearance from the historical

ations, in its long war with Athens in the fifth century. With fewer economic resources than the Athenians, the Spartans had a correspondingly stronger need to secure the goodwill of both old and potential allies. This need makes sense of the third and final ultimatum that the Spartans sent to Athens before the commencement of open hostilities in 431, that the Athenians should "free Hellas" (Thuc. 1.139), a demand that was not a desperate last attempt to bring the Athenians to abandon their imperialistic ways but a first salvo in the ideological war that would accompany the inevitable military conflict. Thucydides (2.8) notes the success the Spartans had claiming that they were fighting to liberate the Greeks from the slavery imposed by the Athenians (they need not have questioned this themselves). But the best evidence comes from the remarkable campaign Brasidas waged against Athenian territories in northern Greece in the late 420s with a tiny army but a huge understanding of the language and behavior befitting a liberator.[55]

Greeks were not alone in liberating their neighbors with the intention of dominating them. Herodotus (6.43.3) notes that the Persians, after the Ionian revolt, deposed the tyrants of Asia Minor and replaced them with democracies, much as Aristagoras had done at the outset of the revolt. The change in the Persians' policy toward the Greeks may reflect a new distrust of individuals like Aristagoras, who used a tyranny to liberate himself from Persia, but they perhaps also learned from him that at times a more effective control is exerted over a city by liberating it than by imposing a tyrant over it.

The political principle linking the destruction and preservation of tyranny is perhaps best confirmed by the behavior of those cities, such as Corinth and Syracuse, who owed their liberty to their own efforts. Cities that liberated themselves, like individuals that liberated cities, gained considerably more than the satisfaction of seeing

limelight after the fall of the Orthagorids suggests that by liberating Sicyon, Sparta rendered it impotent as an independent force in the Peloponnese. Sicyon's eventual incorporation into the Peloponnesian League (when it actually took place is not known) was already determined from that moment.

55. On Brasidas's remarkable diplomacy, see especially his speech to the Acanthians: Thuc. 4.85–88.

free citizens; they also retained much that the tyranny had achieved. This is obvious in the case of the most conspicuous benefits of tyranny, its economic and military gains. The Corinthians maintained the *diolkos*, the device attributed to Periander that carried ships and cargo between the Saronic and Corinthian gulfs, and they apparently reasserted claims to the northern colonies, most notably, Ambracia and Potidaea, that Cypselus and Periander had established, even allowing the provincial members of the Cypselid family to remain in power as Corinth's agents.[56] The city's preservation of the gains of tyranny, as Eduard Will remarked, made it very difficult to draw a distinction between the tyrant's and the city's financial affairs.[57] Corinth was likely an example of a city that so consistently followed the financial policies of its fallen tyrant that, as Aristotle implies in the *Politics* (1276a10–13), it assumed his debts. But the Corinthians' interest in preserving the Cypselid legacy was not limited to military and financial matters. The Corinthians wanted to take over Cypselus's treasury at Delphi and the golden statue that his family had dedicated at Olympia, and asked permission at the sanctuaries to rewrite dedications.[58] Most important, the Corinthians had no intention of negating the greatest achievement of the Cypselids, the effective elimination of the Bacchiads as a political force. It has long been thought (though evidence is not

56. On the date, function, and purpose of the Corinthian *diolkos*, see Salmon 1984, 136–39. On the Cypselid colonies and continued Corinthian domination in them, see Graham 1983, 30–31, 118–53), and Werner 1971, 19–73. On the foundation of these colonies, see chap. 5. It is possible that the ejection of the Cypselids from Corinth brought about a temporary end to Corinth's relations with the Cypselid colonies, but we have no evidence of this nor any trace of a reestablishment of relations before Plataea, when the Cypselid colonies fought against the Persians very possibly on Corinth's behalf (on this, see the next chapter).

57. Will 1955, 488 n.1: "Il ne nous paraît pas possible de distinguer rigoureusement les finances des tyrans de celles de la *polis*."

58. Plut. *De Pyth. or.* 13 = *Mor.* 400e. The Delphians granted the Corinthians' request; the official at Olympia did not (which deeply offended Corinth). An archaic inscription found on the site of the Corinthian treasury at Delphi may belong to the rededication; see Daux and Salač 1932, no. 153. It is probable that the Cypselids' responsibility for the Corinthian treasury at Delphi (where the Corinthians' attempt to have the treasury rededicated in their name was accepted) was generally forgotten; Herodotus seems to want to remind his audience of this at 1.14.1.

abundant) that the tribal constitution of classical Corinth was put into place under the tyranny.[59] If there was such reform, it was perhaps intended to suppress the Bacchiads or to promote other Corinthian tribes. To continue these innovations was only reasonable and expedient: it would certainly be more remarkable if the Corinthians had rejected the benefits of tyranny. But what made it possible for the Corinthians to preserve the legacy of Cypselids without fear of compromising the integrity of Corinth's collective government was surely their conviction that they were themselves responsible for the Cypselids' demise.

Events at Syracuse present a similar picture. When the Syracusans threw out the Deinomenids, they began, much like revolutionary France, to export their newfound success against tyranny to the neighboring cities that were still under the dominion of tyrants.[60] This was the basis of Syracuse's quick recovery from its tyranny; transformed from an oppressed city to a liberator, Syracuse was able to maintain the political and military prestige it held under the Deinomenids. There is no doubt that the Syracusans sincerely hated tyranny. Yet it is difficult to distinguish their behavior from that of the tyrants they displaced: both saw Sicily as their sphere of interest, and both expressed this interest by assuming a paternalistic role among Sicily's Greek cities. So the Syracusans paradoxically realized their new resistance to the Deinomenids most fully as they were establishing themselves as the Deinomenids' political and rhetorical heirs.

Classical Corinth, Syracuse, and Athens all linked *eleutheria* and *autonomia* (the autonomous action of a community in realizing its own interests)[61] in a way that exhibits the continuity between tyrannies and the collective governments that followed them.[62] The

59. For the traditional view, see Dunbabin 1948, 55. New epigraphical evidence has complicated the issue of Corinth's tribal structure without clarifying its origins. See now Jones 1980 and Salmon 1984, 413–19.

60. On Syracuse's actions, see Diod. 11.68.5.

61. *Eleutheria* and its cognates are commonly applied to cities in the classical period; and when they are, they are virtually synonymous with *autonomia* and its cognates. *Eleutheria* and *autonomia* are also frequently linked in a sort of pleonasm; in Thucydides, see, for example, 2.71.3, 3.10.6, 3.46.5, 6.77, and 8.64.5.

62. Raaflaub's (1981, 258) disagreement is based partly on Solon: "Die Untersuchung der Begriffsverwendung bei Solon hatte ergeben, daß man mit einiger Wahrscheinlichkeit im ersten Drittel des 6. Jh. in Athen zwar einen mit der Tyrannis

collective destruction of the tyrant marked the crucial first step in the assumption of a collective identity based on the ability to act in pursuit of a single goal, to make the polis, in Gernet's words, into "un pouvoir sui generis."[63] Both the establishment and the destruction of tyranny are crucial moments in the political history of the Greek city-state. The rise of tyranny signaled the demise of the simple aristocratic polis of archaic Greece (even when the *aristoi* remained politically powerful); the elimination of the tyrant gave the polis the political equipment to rule itself. Despite its violence and spontaneity, the overthrow of tyranny was a politically creative moment. What it created was the autocratic polis, in whose name citizens acted and to whom they were accountable. This gives a particular political sense to Solon's remark that it was "more glorious and illustrious" to destroy a tyranny "once it is established and formed" (Plut. *Sol.* 30.5).

We know this best at Athens. The Athenians institutionalized the overthrow of tyranny by making their own constitution the principal object of their collective energy. Insisting (logically) that power could remain in the middle (ἐν μέσῳ) only if citizens were true political equals and if the polis were formally identified with the demos, the Athenians maximized the numbers involved in all state actions and subjected magistrates to the scrutiny of the popular courts. Inclusive and univocal by nature, the assembly and popular courts demonstrated and justified the definition of the polis as a collective will whenever they exercised the powers that that definition gave them.[64] For the Athenians, the process of radicalizing democracy was closely related to the possession of an empire.[65] Empire and democracy seem to have been bound in a process of

---

verbundenen politischen Knechtschaftsbegriff, aber noch nicht den entsprechenden Freiheitsbegriff verwendete." But what is true of Solon is not necessarily true of the Athenians or of the Greeks generally, for Solon acted to escape and replace tyranny, not to effect a liberation from it—which he likely feared as much as he feared tyranny itself. See the treatment of Solon in chap. 3.

63. Gernet 1968, 344.

64. On the sense of democracy at Athens, see especially Meier 1980 and Farrar 1988.

65. The criticism that Bdelycleon makes in Aristophanes' *Wasps* (656–70) of Athenian state expenditures of funds that come to Athens in great part from its empire (that less than 10 percent goes to jurors) may reflect a common Athenian sense that the empire was intended to help achieve economic equality in Athens.

political apperception; the polis defined itself as a subject as it re-made the world into its objective field. So the Corinthians thought when they complained to fellow Peloponnesians that a "tyrant city has established itself in Greece against every city alike, ruling already some, intending to rule others."[66] The empire gave Athens, as a tyranny gave an individual ruler, a source of great power and also of great danger. The Athenians themselves made the comparison in just these terms; as Pericles told the Athenians, "You now possess something like a tyranny, which was perhaps unjust to take on but is dangerous to give up."[67] Athens was certainly not immune to the excesses that plagued tyrants. Thucydides traced the self-destruction of Athens in part at least to its ruthless exploitation of allied cities in pursuit of its self-interest. He was perhaps right. Yet fifth-century Athens realized, more than it perverted, the promise offered by liberation from tyranny.

But were the Athenians responsible for their liberation? The fall of the Peisistratids, which in the fifth century was a subject of serious historical controversy, seems to offer an exception to the rule that liberty was real only if it was won. Yet this is, as we will see, an exception that proves the rule, for the Athenians rewrote their own history to believe that they, like the Corinthians and Syracusans, liberated themselves from tyranny.

Athens and Its Tyrannicides

According to the historical tradition represented (with some variations) by Herodotus, Thucydides, and the Aristotelian tradition, the Athenian tyranny was assumed after Peisistratus's death by his

---

66. Thuc. 1.124.3: καὶ τὴν καθεστηκυῖαν ἐν τῇ Ἑλλάδι πόλιν τύραννον . . . ἐπὶ πᾶσιν ὁμοίως καθεστάναι, ὥστε τῶν μὲν ἤδη ἄρχειν, τῶν δὲ διανοεῖσθαι. We cannot know to what extent the conclusion the Corinthians draw from their observations about the nature of Athenian power (παραστησώμεθα ἐπελθόντες, καὶ αὐτοί τε ἀκινδύνως τὸ λοιπὸν οἰκῶμεν καὶ τοὺς νῦν δεδουλωμένους Ἕλληνας ἐλευθερώσωμεν)—so redolent of Athenian imperial language—shows that they wished to imitate the Athenians. On the meaning of the tyrant city, see Connor 1977.

67. Thuc. 2.63.2: ὡς τυραννίδα γὰρ ἤδη ἔχετε αὐτήν, ἣν λαβεῖν μὲν ἄδικον δοκεῖ εἶναι, ἀφεῖναι δὲ ἐπικίνδυνον. Compare Periander's remark (D.L. 1.97; cf. the discussion above) that there was danger for the tyrant both in being deposed and in resigning voluntarily.

sons, Hippias and Hipparchus. After a time Hipparchus was killed by Harmodius and Aristogeiton in retribution for a personal act of hubris, while Hippias continued to rule until he was deposed by the Spartans on orders from Delphi, which was influenced by the Alcmaeonids. Thucydides makes it clear (1.20.1; 6.53–59) that the majority (τὸ πλῆθος) of Athenians had a very different story; Athenian popular tradition ignored the role of Sparta and the Alcmaeonids and gave honor for the liberation of Athens solely to Harmodius and Aristogeiton.

Herodotus (6.123.2) makes the point that Harmodius and Aristogeiton left the job of freeing Athens half finished: "By killing Hipparchus, they roused up the rest of the Peisistratids and did not at all stop them from ruling as tyrants." The Athenians, from this perspective, share the faults of the Samians, who refused Maeandrius's gift of liberty but allowed him to reestablish the tyranny. This commentary agrees with Herodotus's observations elsewhere concerning the Athenians' timidity toward the Peisistratids—for example, their attempt to auction off Peisistratus's property during his exile. If it had worked, Peisistratus would have had nothing in Athens to return to, but the Athenians were not equal to it: only Callias offered bids when Peisistratus's goods came on the block (6.121.2).[68]

Thucydides treatment is more detailed. He argues at length that Hippias, not Hipparchus, was the tyrant of Athens in 514. Moreover, he explains the tyrannicides' motivation as entirely personal: Hipparchus, unable to win Harmodius's attentions, was killed after he insulted his rival, Aristogeiton.[69] The deed itself Thucydides

68. The *Athenaion politeia* seconds Herodotus when it states (16.8–9) that the Athenians' timidity made it easy for the Peisistratids to rule for a long time and to return to power from exile. Solon in Plutarch (*Sol.* 30.2–5) notes the Athenians' inability to enforce their natural wisdom with decisive action in resisting Peisistratus's tyrannical aspirations. To Herodotus's account of the timid Athenians, it is worth comparing Livy's account of the Senate's decision, after the failed plot of the disgruntled Roman youth, not to confiscate the property of the kings but to offer it to the plebs to plunder. Livy pragmatically explains this as an attempt on the Senate's part to alienate the plebs permanently from the Tarquins (*ut contacta regia praeda spem in perpetuum cum eis pacis amitteret*: 2.5). However, the Senate at the same time ensured that the first collective act of the Republic would appear to take place not only at its center but also at its peripheries.

69. Aristotle (*Pol.* 1311a37–b39) agrees, though he tells the story somewhat differently. On the various versions, see the recent account by Thomas (1989, 238–82).

sees as nothing more than an act of reckless stupidity (ἀλόγιστος τόλμα) that invited Hippias to implement a far crueler tyranny until he was deposed by the Spartans, who came to Athens through the machinations of the exiled Alcmaeonids. The Athenians, Thucydides seems to have thought, tried to persuade themselves that Harmodius and Aristogeiton liberated Athens, but they knew deep in their hearts that they owed their liberty to Sparta. They were so sure that they had failed the test of tyranny that they were suspicious of strong leadership even when they most desperately needed it—the pertinent example being their treatment of Alcibiades in 415.

Thucydides' treatment of the killing of Hipparchus exaggerates and oversimplifies the distinctions between personal and political motivation and interest. When Pausanias in Plato's *Symposium* (182c) praises the love of Harmodius and Aristogeiton for the part it played in the demise of the Athenian tyranny, he presents a position that was more sophisticated and probably more widely believed. Although they responded to a personal insult, Harmodius and Aristogeiton almost certainly intended to depose the Peisistratids; their quest for vengeance could end with nothing less. But what Thucydides says otherwise about the conspiracy could hardly have shocked the average Athenian, who must have known that Hipparchus was less powerful than Hippias and that the tyranny was far worse for Athens after Hipparchus's death than before it. Thucydides clearly wanted to correct the Athenians' confusion about their history. Yet the status that Harmodius and Aristogeiton enjoyed as the liberators of Athens was based not on confusion but on a deliberate rejection of history.

In this sense, the tyrannicides are creatures of political and religious myth rather than of history. The historical facts that Thucydides somewhat pedantically revives had been neutralized already long before by the powers of such myth. The Athenians celebrated the deed of Harmodius and Aristogeiton with a cult supervised by the state and with a statue that had been commissioned by the city and was placed in the agora (an unheard-of honor). Popular songs of the fifth century compared Harmodius and Aristogeiton to Achilles and Diomedes and proclaimed that their great achievement ("killing the tyrant and establishing *isonomia* in Athens") would win them eternal glory and the immortality of heroes. The Athenians also decreed special privileges to the descendants of Harmodius and Aristogeiton, such as meals at the city's expense in the Athenian Prytaneion.[70]

The honors paid to Harmodius and Aristogeiton made them into civic heroes much as founders were regarded as heroes in cities of relatively recent origin.[71] Like founders, the tyrannicides were symbols of civic identity. The celebration of their glorious achievement was also implicitly a celebration of *isonomia*. The symbolic significance of the cult of the tyrannicides may explain Xerxes' decision to take the first statue of the tyrannicides with him when he left Athens: he satisfied his wrath by stealing the image of Athenian *eleutheria* and *isonomia*.[72] And Alexander (or a successor) probably for the same reason returned the group to Athens a century and half later, thereby establishing his credentials as a guardian of Athenian liberty.

Thucydides is obviously sensitive to the misrepresentation of history, and the popular story of Harmodius and Aristogeiton, as he makes clear at the outset of his history (1.20), is a particularly egregious example. But Thucydides' own report of Amphipolis in 422 (5.11.1) shows the serious political significance that might come from rewriting history, as the Athenians did with their tyrannicides. Amphipolis, as we noted earlier, was a city that Athens had founded a decade and a half earlier under the leadership of Hagnon, whom the Amphipolitans honored as their founder until they tired of their obligations to Athens. Then they simply tore down all monuments honoring Hagnon and established a new founder in his place, the Spartan general Brasidas, who had recently died fighting the Athenians for control of Amphipolis. That Sparta and Brasidas

70. On the cult, statue, and popular songs celebrating the Athenian tyrannicides, see Fornara 1970, Brunnsåker 1971, Taylor 1981, and Garland 1992, 94–96, 199.

71. The usual interpretation makes the tyrannicides a special case of the Athenians' honors to their war dead, but Clairmont (1983, 1:14–15) is probably right to make the cult of the tyrannicides an antecedent of the Athenian custom of public honors for the war dead. On the cult of founders, see chap. 5 passim.

72. So Taylor 1981, 46. In much the same spirit the Carthaginians destroyed the monument of Gelon at Syracuse (Diod. 11.38.5), and L. Lucullus removed the statue of Autolycus, founder of Sinope, which had been made by Sthennis of Olynthus from Sinope: see Pape 1975 and Waurick 1975. To be sure, Xerxes probably took the Water-Bearer that Themistocles dedicated in Athens (Plut. *Them.* 31.1) out of pure spite.

had had absolutely nothing to do with Amphipolis's foundation did not bother the Amphipolitans in the least. The most expedient way to change their international allegiance was to name a new founder.[73]

History is malleable, and the Athenians had a serious reason to alter it. They could hardly give credit for their liberation to the Spartans, who had, after all, made it clear that they believed that expelling Hippias gave them the right to install a Spartan puppet in his place. Of course, even in the popular tale, the Athenian demos played no part in the conspiracy that killed Hipparchus, and the tyrannicides' motives were obviously personal. But this probably did not bother the Athenians any more than the fact that the conspiracy failed. When they treated Harmodius and Aristogeiton as civic heroes, the Athenians embraced the private actions of the tyrannicides as public and secured themselves from the contradictions revealed by the historian's logic. Much like Brutus in Rome or the heroes of Greek foundation lore whom we will meet in the next chapter, Harmodius and Aristogeiton acted in Athens's collective memory both to exact a personal revenge and to free all Athenians.

It is not likely that the heroizing of Harmodius and Aristogeiton detracted from the political aspirations of the Alcmaeonids, who persuaded the priestess of Apollo to incite the Spartans to depose Hippias.[74] The Alcmaeonids were interested in political office, not in free meals; they presumably knew that the political climate of fifth-century Athens did not permit them to flaunt the title of Athens's liberators. Cleisthenes, Athens's greatest democratic reformer, was himself neither a liberator in the manner of Maeandrius nor a lawgiver like Solon. Instead, he introduced changes to the Athenian political system by "befriending the demos" (προσεται-ρίζεται τὸν δῆμον: Hdt. 5.66.2), that is, by winning political support—the method required by the character of his reforms and by

73. On Amphipolis, see also chap. 1. The parallel with founders may also explain why the Athenians were not much bothered by the stories that Harmodius and Aristogeiton acted as the consequence of a love affair; many young cities happily linked their origins to the domestic troubles (often thoroughly sordid—incest and parricide) of their beloved founders (see chap. 5 passim).

74. So also Fornara 1970.

the model of political leadership in the fifth century.[75] Perhaps more attention should be given to the suggestion made years ago by Victor Ehrenberg, that the Alcmaeonids themselves introduced the cult of Harmodius and Aristogeiton.[76] Cleisthenes' great idea, to reinvent Athens's tribes, employs the same suspension of historical disbelief that is involved in crediting Harmodius and Aristogeiton with the liberation of Athens. Some evidence puts the identification of Harmodius and Aristogeiton as the liberators of Athens very soon after Hippias's expulsion: Pliny the Elder (*HN* 34.16–17) makes the first statue group contemporary with the liberation of Rome from the Etruscans, an event traditionally dated to 509. If we can take this seriously, the heroization of Harmodius and Aristogeiton seems to belong to the same historical moment as the rejection of the Spartan puppet Isagoras and the military victory over Cleomenes' forces and seems to function, like the celebration of a cult of Zeus Eleutherius at Syracuse, as a symbolic corollary to these events.

Athens thus gained from cult what history did not quite allow it—the conviction that it held full control over its own *eleutheria* and *isonomia*. The Athenian heroization of Harmodius and Aristogeiton itself answered Herodotus's criticism of the Athenians' passivity toward the Peisistratids, for it completed the Peisistratids' destruction no less thoroughly than if the Athenians had indeed deposed the tyranny themselves. Thucydides' analysis of the liberation of Athens in the context of fifth-century Athenian politics should also be reversed: it is hardly true that the Athenians made poor use of leaders such as Alcibiades (whose case brought the tyrannicides to Thucydides' mind) because they knew that they had been unable to rid themselves of tyranny; it is more probable that the designation

75. Cleisthenes, like Solon, left Athens after making his reforms (Hdt. 5.72), but he did so in response to the Spartans' insistence that the pollution of the Alcmaeonids be expelled, not in order to allow his reforms to assume an independent force. It follows that the difference between the demagogue and the tyrant lay not in the amount of power but in the character of its expression: the demagogue concealed his power; the tyrant exaggerated his—or, from a political perspective, the demos tolerated the demagogue as an advisor but viewed and accepted the tyrant (and the lawgiver) as essentially separate from itself.

76. Ehrenberg 1956.

of Harmodius and Aristogeiton as the liberators of Athens gave the Athenians the confidence to trust their leaders. Thucydides' own account of the Athenians' suspicion of Alcibiades, the exception to the rule, actually supports this. When Alcibiades was summoned to trial in 415, he was not accused of forming personal alliances with foreign states or of arming his supporters for an attack on the Acropolis, the methods for establishing tyranny that Peisistratus had used a century and a half earlier. What sparked the Athenians to recall Alcibiades were far more serious fears that he had ridiculed the cults and religious symbols of Athens—that, in other words, he threatened the Athenians' collective possession of the very focused kind of power that they inherited from their tyrants.

CHAPTER FIVE

Narratives of Autonomy:
Greek Founders

Nach dem "Vatermord" an seinem Vorgänger Ulbricht im Jahre 1971 machte sich SED-Chef Honecker unabsetzbar. So sorgte er dafür, daß sein System seine eigene politische Existenz nicht überleben konnte.

After his "patricide" of his predecessor Ulbricht in 1971, Honecker, leader of the SED, secured that he could not be succeeded. Thereby, he made it impossible for his government to survive his own political existence.

Die Zeit, 11 October 1991

In crediting the tyrannicides' killing of Hipparchus for Athens's liberation from tyranny, the Athenians followed the Corinthians and anticipated the Syracusans in linking civic violence and political autonomy. The nature of this link is elucidated in Greek foundation legends. The interest these legends take in the passions, crimes, and sordid origins of founders may seem incongruous among the treasured political memories of Greek cities, but the legends actually translate into narrative form the same political lessons and imagery that Greek cities learned from their difficult experiences with tyrants, and, in particular, the need Greek cities came to feel both to destroy and to preserve the power and freedom of their autocratic origins. In fact, foundation legends served much the same purpose as the popular Athenian tale of Harmodius and Aristogeiton: by inventing and retelling foundation stories, cities helped secure their collective and autonomous political existence.

The founders of Greek legend were creatures of political beginnings; their stories belonged to the popular history of the polis and its public life and political interaction.[1] As political inventors and innovators, the *prōtoi heuretai* (discoverers) of Greek cities,[2] legendary founders reflect an interest in attaching the names and individuality of particular makers to institutions and cities. Their force, in the words of Paul Veyne, is the "affirmation of the personality of each city": they construct the rudiments of the new city's history from the personal quest and achievements of its founder.[3]

In this sense, the foundation legends preserved by historians, geographers, and poets since the fifth century narrate local history as analogy: the history of the city is rendered in the personal trials and achievements of its single founder. The analogy is often complex. The political achievements of founders are characteristically represented as the result of personal and domestic crises in which founders are intimately involved. In rare instances the founder is an innocent victim: Croton's founder, Myscellus, went to Delphi to ask about his childlessness and left with orders to depart for Italy (Diod. 8.17). More often his own crime against his family or his illegitimate social status forces his departure. The urgency of the founder's quest reflects the seriousness of its cause; at its conclusion, the founder discovers not only a new city but also a new personal existence: a position of power and prestige that erases the crime or bastardy that stained his former life.

Quests for Purification and Legitimacy

The most famous act of domestic crime in ancient foundation legend is Romulus's killing of his brother Remus, a story that the Romans were careful to preserve along with Romulus's name and

1. See chap. 1. Despite their popularity in antiquity, foundation legends have interested few modern scholars. Exceptions include Prinz (1979) and three dissertations: Schmid (1947), Strosetzki (1954), and Gierth (1971). A new direction is taken by Veyne (1988), who includes foundation stories in his essay on Greek myth.

2. On the Greek attribution of ideas and institutions to the achievements of single individuals, see Kleingünther 1933.

3. Veyne 1988, 80.

the memory of his divine origins. But even a partial list of crimes against brothers, sisters, mothers, and fathers in Greek foundation legend suggests that the Romans did not invent this feature. Perhaps the most productive fratricide in Greek foundation legend was the work of the Heliadae, sons of Helios and Rhodes. According to a legend preserved by Diodorus (5.56–57, 61), the seven brothers were the best men in their time, but they were not all alike; for his outstanding cleverness, Tenages, the youngest, was hated by his brothers. Macar (sometimes Macareus), Triopus, Candalus, and Actis joined to kill him, and when their crime was discovered, they were forced to flee Rhodes. Macar became the founder of Lesbos, Triopus of Triopium in Caria, Candalus of Cos, and Actis went south to Egypt, where he established Heliopolis.[4] This is not the only account of Macar; others make him a son of Aeolus or Crinacus. These accounts also sometimes include domestic crime: in one, Aeolus's son is guilty of incest with his sister, Canace (Hyg. *Fab.* 242).

The story of the Carian Leucippus, who comes also from Asia Minor, combines the two most serious domestic crimes, incest and patricide. Having angered Aphrodite, Leucippus is made to conceive an uncontrollable passion for his sister, and when he threatens to kill himself, his mother allows him to gratify his desire. But his father (Xanthius) discovers the two, kills his daughter, and is immediately killed by his son. Having compounded incest with patricide, Leucippus flees, wandering in his search for atonement to Delphi, where, for his punishment, he is instructed to serve as the leader of a band of uprooted Magnesians. With these he returns to Asia Minor and establishes Magnesia on the Menander.[5]

Patricide figures as well in the story of Althaemenes, the founder of Cameirus in Rhodes. Althaemenes, who is the son of Catreus, hears of oracles foretelling his father's death at the hands of one of

4. Fratricide likewise plays a role in the legends of Telamon and Peleus, who flee after killing their brother, Phocus. As it turns out, they do not become founders but instead marry the daughters of the kings in their new homes (Apollod. 3.12.6–7; Diod. 4.72.6).

5. Parth. 5; the source is Hermesianax. Leucippus's crimes against his family are left out of the official record of the foundation of Magnesia on the Menander; see Kern 1894. On the political significance of incest and patricide, see Detienne 1977, 144, and Moreau 1979.

his children and escapes Crete to ensure that he does not unwittingly fulfill the oracle. But Catreus longs for his son and travels to Rhodes to find him. There Althaemenes mistakes him for an enemy and kills him. When the error comes to light, Althaemenes is overwhelmed with grief, and, in one version, he prays for the earth to envelop him, while, in another, he spends the rest of his life hiding from mankind. The Cameirians did not forget him; Althaemenes was honored as a civic hero in the city he founded (Apollod. 3.2.1–2; Diod. 5.59).

A few founders are guilty of matricide. Orestes was regarded by some as the leader of the Aeolic colonization of Asia Minor from Amyclae (Pind. *Nem.* 11.34) or from Arcadia (Tzetz. ad Lycoph. 1374), and by others (Strab. 7.7.8) as the founder of Argos Oresticum in the rugged northwest.[6] Alcmaeon, in one version of his tale, kills his treacherous mother, Eriphyle, and consequently is pursued by the Erinyes; when he reaches Acarnania, he founds a new Argos (Strab. 7.7.8, 10.2.26). In another version, presented by Apollodorus (3.7.5) and Pausanias (8.24.8–10), Phegeus, king of Psophis, purifies Alcmaeon, who then marries the king's daughter. But the stain of his act continues to plague Alcmaeon; he flees the Erinyes to Achelous, who purifies him a second time and gives him his daughter in marriage. At this second wife's bidding, Alcmaeon returns to Psophis to recover the necklace that Eriphyle accepted as a bribe to betray Amphiaraus, but is killed by Phegeus's sons. Alcmaeon's own sons by Achelous's daughter avenge their father's murder by killing Phegeus and his family. From Psophis's perspective, these are bastard offspring, and their act is a domestic crime. They follow their crime by fleeing; one, Acarnan, becomes the eponymous hero of Acarnania.

Founders are sometimes accused falsely of crimes against their families. Tenes, the son of Cycnus of Colonae, was wrongly accused of seducing his stepmother, Philonome. Acting on false information, Tenes' father packed him in a box, which he dropped into the sea. With the help of the gods, Tenes drifted alive to an island,

6. That Orestes was believed to be buried at Tegea not Lesbos (Hdt. 1.67–68) suggests that these stories were not widely accepted. In fact, there are other versions of the Aeolic colonization of Lesbos. In one that must have been more popular, Orestes sends his bastard son, Penthilus, instead of himself (see below).

which he named Tenedos and where he established a city. There, according to Diodorus, he was honored with a cult long after his death.[7]

Other founders committed domestic crimes of yet different varieties. Elephenor, founder of Amantia, murdered a grandfather (Lycoph. 1034–46; Tzetz. ad Lycoph. 1034); Althaemenes in Apollodorus (3.2.1–2) killed his sister; and Poimandrus, although he managed to reach Poimandria without incident, soon corrected his omission when, while building the walls of his new city, he inadvertently killed his son Leucippus (Plut. *Mor.* 299c).

Domestic conflict of a different sort is involved in the departure of Archias, the Corinthian founder of Syracuse. According to Plutarch, Archias was banished from Bacchiad Corinth for murdering his lover, Actaeon.[8] We do not know what crime Archias's fellow Corinthian Chersicrates committed. But he must have done something wrong, and after the Corinthians stripped him of his political rights, he ventured north and established Corcyra (Timaeus *FGH* 566 F 80). Better explained is the exile of Miletus, who was loved simultaneously by the three sons of Zeus and Europa—Sarpedon, Minos, and Rhadamanthys. Offered a choice among the three, Miletus took Sarpedon; in revenge, Minos exiled him from Crete. His flight took him to Caria, where he founded the city that bore his name.[9] A version mentioned by Apollodorus (3.1.2) makes the story about Atymnius, who suffered the same fate to become the founder of Tymnius. A free variation on the theme of domestic crime involves Diomedes, whom Aphrodite punished for wounding her at Troy by alienating the affections of his wife, Aegileia. Aegileia plotted to kill Diomedes soon after his return, and he was

7. Diod. 5.83. Paus. 10.14.2–4 (who writes Tennes) tells the same story but does not mention the cult. Cf. schol. ad Lycoph. 232 and Apollod. *Epit.* 3.23–25.

8. See Plut. *Mor.* 772e–773b and, for different versions, Andrewes 1949 and Zörner 1971, 68–70. The story has been variously interpreted; see Malkin (1987, 42–43), who believes it must be separated from the account of Archias's consultation of Delphi, which he sees as historical.

9. As the son of Apollo and a mortal woman, Miletus also falls into the category of bastard founders; on these, see below. In Herodotus (1.173.2), Sarpedon, forced out by Minos (without mention of sexual intrigue), lives as an exile in Lycia; according to Ephorus (*FGH* 70 F 127), he founded Miletus. On Minos's various infatuations, see Sergent 1984, 227–31.

forced to flee to save himself. In Italy Diomedes founded Argyrippa (Arpi: Strab. 6.3.9; Lycoph. 592–613).

There is no reason to treat the themes of crime and punishment in foundation legends as reflective of early Greek colonization. As far as we know, founders, as Irad Malkin puts it, "came from the highest orders of society and usually acted as the representatives of their states."[10] Foundation legends are myth. They narrate a single hero's movements from the center to the margin, from a secure city surrounded by Greek neighbors to the wilds and dangers of an often unknown and uncivilized hinterland. It is therefore appropriate that the individual whose journey foundation tales narrate is himself an outcast, whose story often begins with an account of his social alienation and follows his quest—often by way of Delphi, the earth's geographical center—to establish a new city on the margins of the physical world.

This applies as well to bastard founders, who are almost as common in Greek foundation legends as criminals.[11] Half noble but also often half slave, the *nothos* (bastard) of Greek legend often harbored ambitions that were inconsistent with his social position. When this happened, he usually found himself at odds with his half brothers, the legitimate heirs, or with their mother, who undertook to protect their interests. As an internal threat to his own family, the *nothos* was often expelled and forced to find a home elsewhere. But, like the criminal founder, the *nothos* founder is not a simple victim; his social marginality defines a distinct political potential.

Homer tells us much about the bastard's social position. In *Iliad* 2, he reports that Philoctetes, the rightful ruler of Methone, Thaumacia, Meliboea, and Olizon, was still on Lemnos, and that Medon, the bastard son of Oeleus and half brother of Ajax the Lesser, was leading (κόσμησεν) the troops in Philoctetes' stead (726–29). *Kosmein* stresses the function of commanding independently of the commander's inherent superiority and his right to command (ἄρχειν or ἡγεμονεύειν); in this case, *kosmein* is used instead of *archein*

10. Malkin 1987, 30.

11. The familial and civic status of the Athenian bastards has received considerable attention in recent years. For a careful treatment and full bibliography, see Patterson 1990. There is as yet no comprehensive study of *nothoi* outside Athens. For indications in this direction, see Hannick 1976, Latte 1936, and Vernant 1974.

to imply that Medon is a temporary substitute.[12] Homer explains Medon's exile when he narrates his death in a duel with Aeneas in book 15 (335–37): Medon was compelled to leave his home after he killed the kinsman (probably the brother) of Eriopis, Oeleus's legitimate wife. The cause of the dispute is not noted, but there was undoubtedly a potential for conflict between Oeleus's bastard son and a man whose position in Oeleus's household was directly related to his sister's status as the legitimate wife.[13]

The elaborate story that Odysseus invents for Eumaeus in *Odyssey* 14 (192–359) brings into closer focus the potential for conflict between the legitimate and illegitimate sides of a single family. To explain his presence on Ithaca, Odysseus relates that he was born the bastard of a wealthy Cretan, who honored him no less than his legitimate sons, although his mother was a slave (*Od.* 14.203). But when the father died, the legitimate sons divided up the family wealth among themselves and gave their half brother only a little land and a hut (14.208–10). Reduced to poverty and to the status of a servant, he resolved to test his fate in exile.[14]

The respect that the Cretan bastard in Odysseus's story enjoyed in his father's household was not unusual. Antenor loved his bastard

12. *Kosmein* has a similar sense a few lines earlier (*Il.* 2.704), when Homer remarks that Podarces stands at the head of the contingent from the neighborhood of Phylace instead of the recently deceased Protesilaus. Protesilaus was clearly more suited for command (he was "older and better": *Il.* 2.707), although Podarces is Protesilaus's full brother (αὐτοκασίγνητος: *Il.* 2.706) and not, like Medon, a bastard. Elsewhere *kosmein* describes the activity involved in commanding, when that activity is something separate from the right to command; see *Il.* 2.554, where the poet notes that Menestheus was not only the (rightful) commander of the Athenians but was also extremely good at the actual job involved in leading troops.

13. Prinz (1979, 59–60) explains the similarity between Medon and Teucer as a case of reduplication and suggests that either Teucer or Medon was originally a bastard, but not both.

14. The noble bastard's treatment at the hands of his legitimate half brothers resembles the reward Eumaeus receives for his loyalty at the end of the *Odyssey*: a wife and a small house near Odysseus's own (21.214–15). It is worth noting that Odysseus promises to treat Eumaeus as Telemachus's brother (κασίγνητος: 21.216), which recalls Odysseus's claim that he was treated like the legitimate sons (ἶσον ἰθαγενέεσσιν: 14.203) in the Cretan family he invents for Eumaeus. In Homer and probably also in early Greek society, the status of the *nothos* was squeezed between that of the legitimate son and the servant; the treatment the illegitimate son could hope to receive represented a real improvement for the domestic slave.

son, Pedaeus; and Theano, Antenor's legitimate wife, honored her husband by raising Pedaeus as though he were legitimate (*Il.* 5.69–71). Megapenthes, the illegitimate son of Menelaus, is likewise treated with considerable honor in the *Odyssey* when his father marries him to the daughter of a local man of some standing (*Od.* 4.10–12). Yet the Cretan should not have been surprised at his change in fortune when his father died. The legitimate wife in Homer might well disapprove of her husband's philandering and its results; sometimes she was able to restrain him: Anticlea, for example, kept Laertes from sexual relations with Euryclea (*Od.* 1.431–43). Post-Homeric legend is full of legitimate wives attempting to prevent the illegitimate elements of the family from arrogating their own and their children's rights.[15] This concern stands behind the commonplace of the hostile stepmother represented in tragedy by the Sophoclean Idaea, who was the wife of the Thracian Phineus and stepmother of Plexippus and Pandion (704 P), and the Euripidean Creusa, Phaedra, and Ino (Hyg. *Fab.* 4). Even Penelope, whom Greek myth offers as the ideal image of the faithful wife, could be thought capable of contriving to bring about the death of her husband's illegitimate progeny.[16]

The bastard's troubles might well begin before his father's death gave the legitimate wife and children free rein to enforce the prerogatives of their status. While his father lived, the bastard was often pressed into service as the personal attendant for his more fortunate brothers. *Nothoi* in the *Iliad* conduct their more illustrious brothers to and from battle in chariots: Isus drives Antiphus to battle (*Il.* 11.101–3), and Cebriones conducts Hector (*Il.* 16.738).[17]

15. How important the wife considers this is evident from Euripides' *Hippolytus* (305–10), where the lovesick Phaedra is dissuaded from suicide by the nurse's warning that if she dies, her children will be ruled by Theseus's bastard son, Hippolytus.

16. This is the subject of Sophocles' lost *Euryalus*. The legendary *nothos* did not apparently have an automatic right to his father's property and social position even when there were no legitimate male heirs. Menelaus's bastard sons, Megapenthes and Nicostratus, drove out Helen in a futile attempt to control Sparta. The Spartans resisted the *nothoi* and gave the kingdom to Orestes (Paus. 2.18.6, 3.19.9).

17. Chryses, the son of Chryseis by Agamemnon, served this role for his legitimate half brother Orestes, when Orestes killed Thoas (Hyg. *Fab.* 121: the story may have been told in Sophocles' *Chryses*), and Jason presumably had something similar in mind for his children by Medea, when he tried to persuade her that his new marriage served their common interests (Eur. *Med.* 596–97, 620).

The importance of the bastard's services for his legitimate half brother is underscored by the story of Teucer, the illegitimate son of Telamon and half brother of Ajax the Greater. For failing to avenge his brother by killing Odysseus, Teucer was driven into exile by his father, Telamon (Pind. *Nem.* 4.46).

Whether bastard or legitimate, the aristocrat was temperamentally unsuited to the life of a *therapon* (servant); consequently, exile was a common fate of *nothoi* whose natural virtue outreached their social position. Some of these followed the leads of the disguised Odysseus and Archilochus,[18] leaving their homes in search of gain; others, like Teucer and Medon, were banished by their fathers for the mess they made of their family duties. The fate of the exiled varied. Some found new homes in neighboring kingdoms. The bastard sons of divine fathers and mortal mothers (e.g., Heracles and Perseus) were frequently accepted as members of their hosts' families and given daughters to be their wives. The same happy fate sometimes fell to those exiled for crimes, such as Odysseus (according to some versions of his story), Telamon, and Bellerophon, who eventually inherited their father-in-laws' kingdoms.[19] But those whose sordid past made them universally unwelcome,[20] or who simply refused to live again as domestically inferior, ended their wandering only when they established their own cities where their illegitimacy and their crimes were neutralized. Thus *nothoi* easily found their way into the ranks of legendary founders. Indeed Homer's tale of the colonization of Rhodes (*Il.* 2.653–70), which is the earliest surviving oecist legend, features a bastard son of Heracles and Astyocheia, Tlepolemus, who flees Argos for Rhodes after killing Licymnius, his father's uncle and the brother of Alcmene.

18. On Archilochus's poetic persona and its relation to that of the Cretan Odysseus, see Seidensticker 1978. The relation seems to weaken Anne Burnett's (1983, 27–28) argument that Archilochus would not even have pretended to be a bastard and that Critias (B44 DK = Ael. *VH* 10.13), who explicitly states that his information derives from Archilochus's own poetry, simply misunderstood the poet.

19. Similar good fortune was also occasionally enjoyed by historical figures such as the exiled Bacchiads, Damaratus (who migrated to Etruria and whose Italian progeny included Roman kings: Strab. 8.6.20; Livy 1.34.2), and Philolaus (who became a lawgiver for the Thebans: Arist. *Pol.* 1274a33–b6).

20. Hippolytus when banished asks, "Where will I turn, wretched as I am? Into whose house will I be received, fleeing there for such a cause?" Theseus answers that he will be welcomed by "whatever man likes to entertain strangers who corrupt his women" (Eur. *Hipp.* 1066–69).

Perhaps of a similar vintage is Teucer's role as a founder; driven out of Salamis by his father, Teucer likewise wanders eastward and, eventually reaching Cyprus, establishes a new Salamis (Pind. *Nem.* 4.46).

Sons of a divine and a mortal parent are especially common as founders in Greek foundation lore. Among these are some founders encountered above, such as Miletus, Atymnius, Macar, and Tenes, and others who are not involved in domestic crime, such as Meliteus, the founder of Milete in Thessaly (Ant. Lib. 13), and Endymion, founder of Elis (Apollod. 1.7.5), who appear in some stories as sons of Zeus. Foundation legends are also rife with the offspring of mortal men and nymphs: for example, the eponymous hero Aetolus (Apollod. 1.7.6) and the founders of Seriphus, Polydectes and Dictys (Apollod. 1.9.6). Here too belong Odysseus's illegitimate progeny. Even in Homer, where Odysseus never forgets Penelope, he has liaisons with goddesses; and in tales that do not stress his marital devotion, Odysseus reaches great heights as a producer of illegitimate offspring. Nine of the dozen or so sons attributed to him are bastard products of his visits to Circe and Calypso. Six of these nine appear in Italian foundation legends: Latinus, Agrius, Telegonus, Romus, Anteius, and Ardeius.[21]

The offspring of divine-mortal liaisons are always exceptional in *aretē*. For this reason alone they are natural founder figures. Yet their connections to the gods do not protect them from the trials of their illegitimacy. Like conventional *nothoi*, those bastards who count one immortal parent often experience difficulties in the home of their births. So the interesting tale Diodorus (4.67.2–7) relates of Aeolus's family. Aeolus had a daughter, named Arne, who was raped by Poseidon. When Arne's pregnancy showed, Aeolus disbelieved her claim that Poseidon was responsible and handed her over to a Metapontian. This man installed her in his household as a concubine, though he adopted her twin sons from Poseidon, Boeotus and Aeolus (who was named for his grandfather). But this did

---

21. Hes. *Th.* 1011–16; Dion. Hal. 1.72. Telegonus's inclusion in the *Theogony* (1014) may be an interpolation. Odysseus himself is in some legends a founder: after slaughtering the suitors, he flees, as if a criminal, and travels to Italy, where he becomes involved before or with Aeneas in the foundation of Rome (Dion. Hal. 1.72).

not end their troubles. When the boys grew older, Arne quarreled with Autolyte, the Metapontian's legitimate wife, and Boeotus and Aeolus killed Autolyte. Banished by their adopted father, the boys separated; Boeotus became Boeotia's eponymous hero, while Aeolus traveled to the Tyrrhenian Sea and established Lipara.[22]

There is also no shortage of *nothoi* sons of mortal men and women in Greek foundation legends. Bastards are particularly conspicuous among the founders of Ionian cities in the Athenian accounts of the Ionian migration. Canopus, founder of Erythrae, Cydrelus, founder of Myus, and Nauclus, who founded Teos, were all illegitimate sons of the Athenian king Codrus.[23] From *nostoi* legends, the accounts of the trials of the Achaeans returning from Troy, comes the story of the Lesbian founder, Penthilus, the bastard son of Orestes and Erigone, the daughter of Aegisthus and Clytemnestra.[24] The Minyae, who were the bastard sons of the wandering Argonauts, derive also from the annals of Spartan colonization (Hdt. 4.145–48). Abandoned as infants, they appear at Sparta in search of their delinquent fathers. The Spartans first welcome them, offering their daughters as wives. But gradually they find them a nuisance and eagerly give them to Theras, the uncle of the first Spartan kings,

22. In his lost tragedy *Melanippe desmōtēs*, Euripides makes Melanippe the mother of Boeotus and Aeolus. Apollodorus's story (1.9.8–9) of Poseidon's sons by the mortal Tyro, Pelias and Neleus, founder of Pylos, follows similar lines. Heracles was a bastard (not, albeit, by the conventional definition, but rather according to Athenian usage: since his mother was a foreigner, he could not qualify as an Athenian citizen) and is so lampooned by Aristophanes (*Av.* 1650–52). He was also a prodigious founder of cities: at least two dozen cities from Saguntum in Spain to Palibothra on the Ganges were attributed to him. For a list, see Leschhorn 1984, 367–72.

23. Not all the founders of Ionian cities in the Athenian versions were illegitimate. Androclus was not (Strab. 14.1.3), and his legitimacy gave Ephesus a basis to present itself as the predominant city of Ionia. Euripides makes Ion, the eponymous hero of the Ionians, the bastard son of Apollo and Creusa. The genealogy was apparently new and politically motivated. When Apollo, rather than Xuthus, is Ion's father, Athens and the gods become exclusive partners in the Ionian migration. Euripides borrows the familiar pattern of the bastard's traditional ambivalence in his father's household and the threat he poses to the legitimate wife in the course of transforming Ion from a foundling into a *nothos* and from a *nothos* into a *parthenias* (son of a maiden).

24. The source is Cinaethon. Orestes' legitimate wife was Hermione, who bore him Tisamenus. The ruling family of the Penthilidae at Lesbos claimed descent from Penthilus (Paus. 2.18.6; Strab. 13.1.3).

Procles and Eurysthenes, to colonize Thera. The Partheniae, the illegitimate offspring of Spartan women and their slaves during the First Messenian War, provide a variation on the same theme. Unlike *nothoi*, who challenge the status of the legitimate wife's children, the Partheniae run afoul of the male element of their families and city. When the Spartan men return from the Messenian War, the Partheniae rebelled and later left Sparta under Phalanthus for Italy, where they established Tarentum.[25]

The plethora of bastards and criminals in Greek foundation legends may reflect particular attitudes about colonization, which by its nature was an experience in social liberation. The Greeks did not exile their criminals to colonies, and colonists were not simply "the poor, hungry, and huddled masses,"[26] yet every colony, as a new autonomous polis, required the establishment of a new social order, and in this the first citizens functioned very much as equals. Aristotle expressed this when he noted that it was impossible "to use the criterion of descent from a citizen father or mother [to determine the citizenship qualifications of] a city's first colonists or founders" (*Pol.* 1275b32–33); the definitions of citizenship and class status, which had determined the social and political existence of the departing citizens, were formally canceled as soon as the land on which they were based was lost to sight.

But more certainly, the criminal and bastard share significance as images of liberation and self-legitimation. The criminal and bastard founder both lose all connection with their families—the former, by violating its rules; the latter, by rejecting its restrictions. Both, whether marked as polluted or illegitimate, must face the difficult life of the exile.[27] To erase the stain of his illegitimacy or crime, the bastard or criminal underwent a personal quest, which separated

25. See Antiochus of Syracuse *FGH* 555 F 13; Ephorus *FGH* 70 F 216. On the Partheniae, Minyans, and the colonists of Italian Locris (whose story is similar), see Pembroke 1970.

26. The colonists of Cyrene came from every social group of Therans (5.27–30 ML); on the other hand, Archilochus (102 W) says that the lower classes predominated in Thasos, which seems to have been true in Brea (49.39–42 ML).

27. For the relation of purification and exile, see Seibert (1979, 355–59). On purification in general, see Parker 1983, 114, 118. Pollution certainly could be used to justify political murder; see, for example, the case of the Thirty Tyrants of Athens (Lys. 12.5: see Burkert 1985, 82–84). Empedocles' *Katharmoi* (cf. 115 DK) frames purificatory powers of exile in cosmological terms.

him permanently from the *oikos* and polis of his origins and led him to establish a new society from its domestic roots. Viewed as political analogy, the founder's quest to overcome domestic crime or illegitimacy articulated the colony's own distinct history of autonomy.

It should perhaps be noted that exile did not always work. In particular, the stain of domestic crime could not always be removed. The Furies, who were roused by crimes against blood kin, paid no attention to political boundaries; Alcmaeon was never free of his crime of matricide, and his trials did not end with the establishment of a new city (Apollod. 3.7.5). Archias was likewise unable to escape full punishment for murdering his Corinthian lover. In Syracuse, he was himself killed by a new lover, significantly named Telephus, the "fulfiller" of his destiny (Plut. *Mor.* 772c–773b). But to the extent that the stain of the founder's crime can be obliterated, relief for him and those he leaves seems contingent on permanent exile. Foundation legend seems indifferent to the legal innovations of archaic Greece, or, at least, of Athens since Dracon. While Athenian law punished the intentional killer with death, the unwitting killer could in fact return home after a period of exile if the relatives of his victim permitted it. For founders, however, the unwritten laws of foundation legend imposed the single and universal penalty of exile, no matter how severe their crime and no matter what their intention. Only one legendary founder returned to his original home: Phocus, the bastard son of Aeacus and eponymous hero of Phocis. He would have been wiser to stay away, for his half brothers, Telamon and Peleus, wasted little time in killing him.

The founder's break with his family brings into focus another general principle in foundation legend. Founders only rarely traveled from their homes accompanied by family members.[28] And very few male founders were said to be accompanied to their new homes by a legitimate wife[29]—nor, in the few cases of foundations

---

28. Aeneas, who reached Italy with his son, Ascanius, and Poimandrus, who was accompanied to Poimandria by his son Lycippus, are rare exceptions. Poimandrus's story, however, is self-correcting: Poimandrus kills his son before the new city is completed (Plut. *Mor.* 299c).

29. Phalanthus, founder of Taras, was an exception. Pausanias (10.10.6–8) makes mention of a wife, Aethra, by whom he was accompanied to his new home in southern Italy. But this exception does not completely vitiate the rule. Aethra is

by women (e.g., Locri Epizephrii), do the women who establish the new city take along their legitimate husbands. As a rule, the establishment of a new city went hand in hand with the oecist's remaking of his own family. When his legend follows him this far, the founder usually marries a woman from the local population, thereby committing his own family, in the same way that he commits his new city, to the newly adopted land.[30] The women of foundation legend thus act in a limited capacity. Although they are often involved in the incidents that prompt the founders' exiles, they are typically excluded from their quests and reappear only at their conclusions to signal the familial and political ties to the new land. By incorporating the story of Dido's frustrated love into the *Aeneid*, Vergil made his version of Aeneas's wandering an exception that proves the rule: Dido is present only to be abandoned, because (and as a confirmation of the fact that) Carthage is not the site of the new Troy. It is not arbitrary that Aristophanes' *Birds* concludes with Peisetaerus's marriage, although Basileia, his bride, comes from the neighboring land of the gods rather than from the birds' territory, where the new city is located.

It is no doubt wrong to take these accounts as proof that women actually played no part in historical projects to establish new cities.[31] But foundation legend's predominant interest in domestic disturbances and broken family ties may have some relationship to the actual patterns of colonization. The Therans' decision to select one colonist for Cyrene from each family (5.27–29 ML; Hdt. 4.153) effectively compelled the colony's new citizens, like legendary founders, to commit themselves to new families as well as to a new city.

In the quest of the founder, foundation legend encapsulates the

---

involved in the accidental discovery of Taras' location but plays no other role. For a possible second case where colonization was initiated and led by women, see Jacoby's commentary on *FGH* 390.

30. Herodotus reflects this is his account of the foundation of Miletus, where only Athenian men participated, and they found wives among the daughters of the local Carians they slaughtered (1.146.2–3).

31. So Graham 1980–81. I do not follow Graham in concluding from Herodotus's account of the foundation of Miletus that the historian believed "that it was normal for colonists to take women with them" (295). On the role of women in colonization legend and history, see also Rougé 1970, 307–17; and on contacts between Greek colonists and indigenous women, see van Compernolle 1983.

colony's prehistory in the pains and achievements of its founder. So understood, foundation legend obviously does considerably more than provide a simple narrative justification for the founder's memory and cult. Replete with murder, incest, and exile, the founders' legends invite their audiences to listen to their oecist's story but do not incite them to admire or imitate him. The destructiveness of his crime or the irreconcilable character of his domestic situation focuses and dramatizes the colony's own autonomy; for as it adopted its founder's home as its mother-city, so too the colony celebrated the independence that rendered it a true polis, despite its close relationship with its mother-city, by means of its founder's quest for liberation. Here lies the sense of the colony's considerable investment in the founder's cult and rather painful legend. The new city is both liberated from its mother-city and linked to it by the founder; and the founder offers his city a personal solution to the dilemma of choosing between political autonomy and the loss of political identity.

In this respect, migrating founders bear comparison with the autochthonous heroes of cities whose citizens claimed to be the original inhabitants of their country.[32] The criminal and bastard founders' violent break with their past and commitment to their new land by marriage to indigenous women parallels the autochthonous founder's emergence from the earth in older cities' foundation legends, which, like the legends of criminal and bastard founders, offered narrative images of autonomy. There is, of course, this difference: the autochthonous founder initiates human habitation in a particular area of the world, while criminal and bastard founders establish the political organization of their new lands. For this reason, older cities, like Athens, could have both autochthonous and wandering founders, while colonies, whose political history was conterminous with the history of their inhabitation, usually had a single immigrant founder. The political character of foundation legends frames a more important difference. The legend of the wandering founder translates the religious notion of purification into political language. He establishes a new city as the result of a

32. The Arcadians, Aeginetans, and Thebans all had autochthonous founders (see Hellanicus *FGH* 4 F 161). Megara also had one in Cres (Ephorus *FGH* 70 F 145); the Athenians, never to be outdone in political symbolism, had four. On the political character of the Athenian autochthony myths, see Loraux 1979.

personal quest originating in a domestic disturbance that is usually his making and that he alone can resolve.

From this perspective, criminal and bastard founders show the same distinguishing mark as the early archaic tyrant: they are reformers.[33] Founders, like tyrants, resolve a fundamental infraction in the human order, some act of injustice or some form of pollution. This comparison does not negate the difference between the founder and the tyrant, whose narratives are reversed: the founder follows a *cursus vitae* from pollution to purification, while the tyrant begins as a reformer to end his life as the image of injustice.[34] In fact, it makes that distinction politically concrete. Foundation stories frame the new city's origins in a legendary narrative that focuses on the intensely personal exploits of the city's founder. The city finds itself indebted for its very existence to the achievement, often self-interested, of a single individual. What prevented foundation legend from being exploited as a script for new achievements of personal initiative like the founder's? The answer seems to lie in the very medium by which the founder's story was narrated and preserved. As legend, the founder's quest was firmly sequestered in the city's unrecoverable past, even as it was celebrated as formative.

In this sense, the founder's legend is closely related to his cult. The religious rites that were paid to the founder distinguished him from all men living and dead and honored him with the exclusive and untransferable status of the civic hero. And the founder's cult makes explicit legend's inherent tendency to bracket and distance its own subject matter. The founder's story therefore relates to his cult very much as myth relates to tragedy; the founder's cult shapes legend (as tragedy shapes myth) in order simultaneously to arouse and to limit participants' identification with their founder. Together, cult and legend sustain the impression that the founder's cult and achievements are unique. As he is honored as something past, the single ruler is implicitly represented as unrepeatable, and the colony's experience with autocratic power is defined as completed at the same time that it is commemorated.

The early history of the Greek colonies that remembered and honored wandering founders seems to confirm the political sense of foundation legend and cult: despite their relative youth and unset-

33. See chap. 2 passim.
34. See chap. 1 passim.

tled social circumstances, Greek colonies generally avoided the political instability, *stasis*, and tyranny that plagued older mother-cities. And when tyrannies arose in colonies, they were typically understood as responses to the hubris of external military threats rather than to domestic injustice. The image of the founder might be exploited by his descendants as a basis for special political and religious authority. The family of Battus at Cyrene is the obvious example.[35] But although they enjoyed many privileges, Battus's descendants did not appropriate the distinctive power that popular memory attributed to Battus. Of all his family, Battus alone was buried in the agora and honored with a civic cult.[36] In fact, the memory of Battus seems to have served as a limit on the power of his successors; the closer Battus's descendants came to asserting the power that he wielded legitimately as founder—Arcesilaus III is the prime example—the more their actions were perceived and resisted as tyrannical.

The example of Cyrene points to a general rule. If the great political achievement of tyrants and lawgivers lay in their manipulation of their subjects' political expectations, the image of the founder effectively substituted for the political reality of tyranny. Although founders were largely the products of their cities' collective imagination, they, like the memory of tyranny, enforced a distinction between political power that is sacred and secular, and immediate and delegated. Most important, foundation lore allowed the city to identify itself as the founder's heir and successor in the very act of narrating and celebrating his achievements.

Tyrannical Founders

That the founder and the tyrant—the former a product of collective legend, the latter of his own self-representation—represent alternative images of power and alternative political experiences does not, however, exclude overlap. In fact, the sacredness of the founder's memory (which the fear of tyrants may well have encour-

35. See Chamoux 1953, 128–210.
36. At *Pyth.* 5.95 Pindar calls Battus *laosebēs* (worshipped by the people), implying that he was honored as a hero, and notes that Battus alone was buried in the agora, while the others were interred "far from [Battus] in front of the dwellings."

aged) made it almost inevitable that tyrants should attempt to project themselves into his space, seizing upon and literalizing the very images that remembered his power as past and unrepeatable. Just as the self-representation of tyrants becomes most significant when it is wielded against tyrants themselves, so too we can best measure the political significance of foundation legend by looking to the history of its distortion.

This history, like the history of the tyrant's political language, begins in Corinth. Sometime after establishing his tyranny in Corinth in the middle of the seventh century, Cypselus set his eyes on the region surrounding the Ambracian Gulf, between Epirus and Acarnania. It is not entirely clear whether Cypselus wanted it for its military or commercial advantages. But whatever his expectations of the Ambracian Gulf, Cypselus was clearly interested in establishing a permanent Corinthian presence there. He sent his three illegitimate sons—Gorgus, Pylades, and Echiades—to be the *oikistai* of a trio of new colonies: Ambracia, Leucas, and Anactorium.[37] Cypselus's colonization interests were taken up by his son. After he succeeded Cypselus, and the tyranny's attention was directed more to the northern Aegean, Periander sent his son Euagoras, who was also very likely a bastard, to Pallene in the Chalcidice to establish the Corinthian colony Potidaea.[38]

Nicolaus (*FGH* 90 F 57.7) reports that the colonists who followed Pylades and Echiades were Cypselus's enemies, whom he

37. For Gorgus, see Strab. 7.7.6 (where the name is garbled), 10.2.8; ps.-Scymn. 453–55; on Pylades and Echiades, see Nic. Dam. *FGH* 90 F 57.5, 57.8 (the source is Ephorus). At F 57.7, Nicolaus calls Pylades and Echiades bastards. Gorgus's illegitimacy is supported by Nicolaus's statement at F 57.8 that "Cypselus left four sons; one, Periander, was legitimate, and the rest were bastards." Cypselus's foundation probably was not the beginning of Corinthian interest in the area of the Ambracian Gulf (cf. Salmon 1984, 90–91, for earlier traces of Corinthian involvement). But it was apparently in Cypselus's day that this interest took an imperialist turn.

38. That Euagoras was illegitimate follows from Hdt. 3.50 and D. L. 1.94–95 (whose source is Heraclides of Pontus's *Peri archias*), where it is reported that Periander's legitimate wife, Melissa, bore just two sons. The first was simpleminded, and the second, Lycophron, was killed by the Corcyraeans when Periander was quite old. There is, moreover, no mention of any other marriage in Herodotus, Nicolaus of Damascus (*FGH* 90), or Diogenes Laertius, while Diogenes Laertius's story of Melissa's death specifically mentions Periander's practice of keeping concubines.

was glad to see go "so that he might rule the rest with greater ease." Modern scholars are right to doubt that Cypselus's enemies would willingly play a supporting role in his foreign policy.[39] But Cypselus did not rely on the colonists' benevolence alone. He seems to have been concerned to give the cities the appearance of real colonies and to make his sons seem genuine founders. If there is any truth to Antoninus Liberalis's story (4.4), Cypselus solicited Delphi's support in his sons' selection as the colonies' leaders.[40] That Cypselus wished to regularize the foundation seems to be supported by the appearance of Gorgus's name on later Ambracian coinage[41] and by Nicolaus of Damascus's reference to Pylades and Echiades as *oikistai* (*FGH* 90 F 57.7), the title of properly designated founders.[42] The bastardy of Cypselus's sons clearly did not conflict with their new roles—in fact, it is not improbable that their domestic status recommended them to the colonists, whether these were Cypselus's friends or enemies.

That tyrants wished to rival legendary heroes in acquiring legitimate and illegitimate wives and children was noted by Gernet,[43] for whom the grandeur of the tyrants' domestic affairs both articulated their liberty from the restraints governing their subjects' behavior and satisfied their need for loyal supporters. Tyrants' liberal production of bastards, however, invited the same problem of domestic disharmony that plagued their legendary antecedents. The solution adopted by the Cypselids follows heroic precedents in part. Like the bastard sons of mythical kings, Cypselus's illegitimate offspring

39. See Will 1955, 528, and Salmon 1984, 215.

40. Antoninus Liberalis notes that Ambracia was founded by Gorgus in response to an oracle from Apollo. He gives his sources as Nicander (Schneider 1856, no. 38) and Athanadas (*FGH* 303 F 1). Nicander presumably told the entire story, but how much was in Athanadas is, as Jacoby noted (commentary to *FGH* 303), impossible to know—nor why Antoninus Liberalis makes Gorgus Cypselus's brother rather than his bastard son.

41. See Ravel (1928, no. 127), who recognizes the name on a Corinthian coin. The coin suggests that the colonies did not hate the memory of the Cypselids as much as their Corinthian cousins did. The name Gorgus is likewise found on a Leucadian inscription (*IG* IX, part 1, 575).

42. Leschhorn (1984, 119) oddly attaches no significance to the use of the title by Nicolaus for the Cypselids, although he demonstrates the significance of the title elsewhere.

43. Gernet 1968.

ventured off to establish their own cities. But there was also something very new in the Cypselid solution. Even in exile from Corinth, the Cypselid bastards remained faithful members of the Cypselid family.

Traces of this loyalty are evident in the efforts the colonial Cypselids undertook to save their Corinthian cousins after Periander's death.[44] But the colonies' loyalty also survived the Cypselids' demise at home and in the colonies. While most of their neighbors maintained a cautious neutrality in the war between the Greeks and Persians, Ambracia, Leucas, Anactorium, and Potidaea fought beside Corinth at Plataea. Later the three northwestern colonies supported Corinth's struggles with Corcyra, and all four took Corinth's side against Athens—with very unpleasant results for themselves.[45] The Corinthians took this loyalty as their due. "We founded our colonies to be their leaders and receive the customary honors from them," a Corinthian envoy, as reported by Thucydides, told the Athenians in 435, "and, indeed, all our other colonies honor us"— Corcyra was the obvious exception—"and we are most loved by them" (1.38.2–3). "Love" translates Thucydides' *stergein*, a word suggesting filial piety, which appears only here in his work. The colonies, the envoy is made to suggest, acted with the respect and obedience that a child owes parents. This casts a very good light on the relationship; in fact, the Cypselid colonies acted with the subservience expected of a bastard child.[46]

44. Psammetichus, a son of Gorgus, the founder of Ambracia, went to Corcyra in the family interest after the Corcyraeans killed Periander's last surviving legitimate son, Lycophron (*FGH* 90 F 59.4; cf. Hdt. 3.53). When Periander died, he moved to Corinth, where he assumed control of the tyranny's main branch. The Corinthians did not tolerate Psammetichus and probably disliked the Ambracian Cypselids for their interference, but they did not undertake to remove the Cypselids from power in the colonies. On the status of the colonies, see Graham 1983, 30–31, 118–53, and Werner 1971.

45. On the events, see Salmon 1984, 270–323.

46. Corinth's close relationship with Leucas endured still longer; it has left its mark on a mid-fourth-century Corinthian mirror cover (Louvre 1699; see Züchner 1942, 98), on which the nymph and patron deity, Leucas, is shown crowning a seated and bearded figure identified by inscription as the eponymous hero Corinthus but clearly represented as Zeus (whom the Corinthians believed to be Corinthus's father: Paus. 2.1.1). With Leucas, nymph and city, appearing to place a crown on the head of her divine father, the relationship between the cities is paralleled in the domestic relations of the gods; by analogy, the city of Leucas is represented as Corinth's obedient and, perhaps, since nymphs are Zeus's extramarital offspring, illegitimate child.

Peisistratus apparently also discovered the bastard founder's value as an agent of imperialistic interests. Like Cypselus and Periander, Peisistratus had two sets of offspring. Hippias, Hipparchus, and Thessalus were his sons by an Athenian woman, whose name is lost; and an Argive woman, Timonassa, who had been married to Archinus, a Cypselid tyrant of Ambracia, was the mother of Hegesistratus and Iophon. Herodotus (5.94) calls Hegesistratus a bastard. Unless Herodotus blindly reflects his source's malice or uses *nothos* in the late fifth-century Athenian sense of the child of a marriage between a citizen and a noncitizen (neither of which seems probable), the label argues that something was amiss with Peisistratus's marriage to Timonassa. Gernet has made the intriguing but unlikely suggestion that Peisistratus, like the elder Dionysius in the next century, was simultaneously married to his Athenian and Argive wives.[47] It is unlikely, as Gernet notes, that Peisistratus's attachment to Timonassa was casual: she was not a concubine before, and he would not have squandered the value of her Argive connections by treating her as one. But it is easier to believe that the Athenians would forget the death of Peisistratus's first wife than his conspicuous bigamy. If Peisistratus married Timonassa after his first wife had died, Herodotus's comment that Hegesistratus was a *nothos* might mean, as J. K. Davies noted,[48] that Timonassa's children were never registered in their father's phratry and for that reason shared the political status of the children of concubines.

The cause is a matter of speculation. Perhaps Hegesistratus and Iophon grew up in the household of their maternal grandfather in Argos and were not in Athens when they came of age. The *Athenaion politeia*'s notice (17.3) that Hegesistratus led a contingent of Argives at Pallene suggests, however, that he spent his youth between Argos and Athens, and Peisistratus presumably could have registered his sons by Timonassa when they were in Athens. That he did not do so may have been intentional. We know that Peisistratus's fear of a superabundance of legitimate heirs kept him from consummating his marriage with Megacles' daughter (Hdt. 1.61). That same fear might have prompted him to leave his sons by Timonassa unregistered. Whatever the cause, Timonassa's children

47. Gernet 1968, 346–48.
48. Davies 1971, 446.

were clearly not regarded as legitimate heirs. According to the *Athenaion politeia* (18.1), Hippias and Hipparchus assumed power after Peisistratus "on account of their stature [τὰ ἀχιώματα] and their age." The two were certainly older; *ta axiōmata* (stature) may contain an oblique reference to Hegesistratus's inferior domestic and political standing. In fact, like the Cypselid bastards, Hegesistratus, at least, did not remain at home; he left Athens for the northeastern Aegean, where he helped to consolidate Peisistratid family power in the region of Sigeum. According to Herodotus (5.94), Hegesistratus was a tyrant. But this may reduce form to effect. It is likely that Hegesistratus was sent to Sigeum outfitted as an *oikistēs*.

In their exploitation of the language of foundation, the Cypselids and Peisistratids revived (quite probably with conscious intention) the bastard founder of legend and undertook to shape foundation legend into an ideological tool that could support (and conceal) an imperialistic program. The illegitimacy of the legendary founder implicitly promised forms of social liberation and political autonomy. But the Cypselid and Peisistratid bastards remained fixed within the orbit of their families—tyrannical families clearly indifferent to political boundaries—in the same position of domestic subordination that marked their place before their departure. The Cypselids and Peisistratids seem then to have revived legendary paradigms in order to subvert them, transforming the language of autonomy, which the Greeks understood as autocracy overcome, into a living model of autocratic power.

There are fifth-century Sicilian examples of attempts by tyrants to adopt the persona of founders that might be added to this history of the distortion of foundation imagery. According to Thucydides (6.5.3), Hippocratus, who ruled Gela as tyrant, named himself the new *oikistēs* of Camarina, which he repopulated in 492 after that city's forced evacuation by Syracuse. The Deinomenids followed Hippocratus's lead. Herodotus (7.156) makes the point that Gelon's power waxed as he increased Syracuse's population by mass importation from neighboring cities; it was perhaps this practice that earned him public honors as Syracuse's founder after his death (Diod. 11.38.5). Hieron followed his brother's lead in cultivating the power and honor due to the oecist. He rebuilt Catane after its destruction by a volcanic eruption, renamed it Aetna after the mountain that had so recently caused its demise, and secured his own designation as oecist (Pind. *Pyth.* 1.60–62; Diod. 11.66.4). Diodorus remarks that Hieron founded the city in order to secure heroic honors for himself; modern scholars trace it to a different cause: the Deinomenids' need for military support.[49] In fact Aetna served both purposes. Hieron himself was buried in his new city as a civic hero, and, when almost no one else would help him, Aetna committed troops to Thrasybulus, the founder's brother, at the awesome cost of its own existence. However, the destruction of their city by an army of self-proclaimed liberators did not end the allegiance of the surviving Aetnaeans to the Deinomenids; they continued to honor Hieron as their founder in their new home at Inessa (Diod. 11.67.7; 11.76.3).[50]

Foundation legends and the founder's cult present and support images of autonomy: the autonomy of a new city's territory and its collective activities and political functions. Yet the political language was easily manipulated. It possessed a distinct attraction for both cities and individual rulers, and it served both as a tool of political subjugation and as an image of autonomy. This may help explain the remarkable behavior of the ambitious renegade Dorieus, the second son of the Spartan king Anaxandridas, who deliberately undertook to found a new city without following the usual procedures or invoking the established political language of city foundation.[51] Dorieus was born after years of Anaxandridas's childlessness led the Spartan ephors to compel the king, when he refused to divorce his wife, to take a second wife and establish a second household. But soon after Anaxandridas entered into a state of legitimate bigamy, both of his wives became pregnant. Cleomenes was born to the second wife a little before Dorieus and was there-

---

49. See Stauffenberg 1963, 260–73.

50. It is likely too that Theron, the tyrant of Acragas who shared the fondness of Sicilian tyrants for destroying and remaking cities, was honored after his death as a founder (see Diod. 11.48.6–8; 11.49.4, where it is noted that Theron repopulated Himera after purging it of its large subversive element; and 11.53.2). The elder Miltiades may have anticipated the Silician tyrant-founders, for he was *tyrannos* of the Dolonci while he lived (Hdt. 6.36.1), and was honored after his death "in the customary manner for a founder" (ὡς νόμος οἰκιστῇ: Hdt. 6.38.1).

51. On Dorieus, see Hdt. 5.39–46 and the remarks of Stauffenberg (1960).

fore regarded as his father's heir. Legally Dorieus was a legitimate son, and he would have become king if he had outlived the childless Cleomenes (Hdt. 5.48). But, despite his prospects, Dorieus shared the social problems of legendary bastards: he was the legitimate heir's half brother and a member of the (currently) inferior half of the royal family. He might have felt that he was treated as a bastard; and he certainly resented his family and Sparta. Herodotus notes that Dorieus expected to be made king on account of his superior abilities, and when birth won over virtue, he left Sparta in a fit of anger. Herodotus adds that Dorieus immediately determined to establish a new city, lingering only to collect a group of Spartans willing to undertake the adventure with him.

That he was in a terrific rush is clear from Herodotus: Dorieus did not solicit Delphi's approval or advice, or do "anything customary" for founders who wish to make their venture a success (5.42). For this Herodotus viewed Dorieus as utterly reckless. But another conclusion is possible. Dorieus's disinterest in foundation procedure ensured his new city a de facto autonomy, even if it could not have increased his chances for success. Dorieus clearly wanted to break completely with his family and city, and he did so in such a way that prevented Sparta from interfering in any way with his undertaking. But if the city could not stake any claim to Dorieus's proposed city, it also felt no commitment to protect him or avenge his death, as Gelon found an opportunity to remind the Spartans later (Hdt. 7.158). In addition, if Dorieus's aim was to create a new city that would appreciate his virtues more than Sparta had, his determination to locate it within Carthaginian territory makes a certain grim sense: the precarious international situation of his new city would demand and justify rule by a king/tyrant. Indifferent, therefore, both to the problem of maintaining connections in exile and to the ideal of the Greek polis, whose political formulas had cost him the kingship in Sparta, Dorieus seems to have resorted to a more immediate form of autonomy.[52]

52. That the name of Dorieus's colony is unknown seems to confirm the irregularity of his venture. For his second attempt to establish a colony Dorieus heard oracles that instructed him to establish a Heracleia in Sicily (Hdt. 5.43), but determined instead to return to Libya. According to Herodotus (5.45), Dorieus's death in his second attempt came as a result of this disobedience.

As language and imagery with which political autonomy could be both defined and subverted, foundation lore belongs, like the experience of tyranny, to the political history of the archaic and classical periods, the age of the polis. Yet the language of city foundation and, in particular, bastard and criminal founders also make occasional appearances later, as images of liberation, and hence of power, despite the gradual emergence of new forms of political domination at the spatial and temporal limits of classical Greece.

Consider Archelaus, the bastard son of Perdicaas and king of Macedonia, who was blasted by his critics as a tyrant who had murdered the legitimate successors who stood between him and the Macedonian throne (Pl. *Grg.* 471a–c), but was respected by others as a benevolent maker of cities and roads (cf. Thuc. 2.100.2). However much the two assessments of him diverge, both may well spring from Archelaus's own self-representation. Archelaus resembled archaic tyrants in reviving a legendary precedent for his actions; this precedent was his namesake, the son of Temenos, whose story involved many features common in foundation legends. According to Euripides, who was commissioned to craft the legend into tragedy, Archelaus was driven from Argos by his brothers and came to the kingdom of Cisseus, whom he killed. Ordered then by Apollo to resume his exile, he eventually founded Aegeae (Hyg. *Fab.* 219). The legendary Archelaus's problems with his brothers suggest that he was a bastard as well as a criminal. The real Archelaus perhaps wished to use his legendary model to suggest that his birth and egregious crimes were an inseparable part of his role as Macedonia's second founder.

Worth noting too is the desperado Aristonicus, the illegitimate son of Eumenes II and half brother of Attalus III. When Attalus III died in 133 and left his kingdom to Rome, Aristonicus rose up to resist the legacy and assume the kingship for himself. The rebellion began poorly. Aristonicus counted on support from the aristocratic coastal cities of Asia Minor but was quickly disappointed: the Ephesians attacked and defeated him at sea. Driven to the hills, he changed his tactics and his fortune. With the help of the Stoic philosopher Blossius, who had been a teacher and friend of Tiberius Gracchus, he designed a program aimed at the slaves and disgruntled poor of Asia Minor. Promising them liberty and equality as Heliopolitans, members of a new state that he would himself establish, he molded them into an army that achieved startling, if short-lived, success. Aristonicus regained most of the territory that Pergamum occupied at its peak, and defeated one Roman army commanded by the *pontifex maximus* and killer of Tiberius Gracchus, Scipio Nasica (whose defeat and death must have shaken Blossius's Stoic indifference to changes in fortune). But the Romans recovered quickly; Aristonicus was captured in a second campaign and paraded through the streets of Rome (Just. 36.4; Strab. 14.1.38; Diod. 34.2.26). Aristonicus's Heliopolis was, as a result, never built; we can only guess how he would have realized his quest to establish his political legitimacy.

Archelaus and Aristonicus revived and appropriated the founder's persona, which functioned as a legendary antithesis to historical tyrants in political developments of archaic Greece and became one of the city-state's treasured political symbols. It seems paradoxical that they made use of such images at times and places where political autonomy was a fading memory. But perhaps the polis's decline itself defined the extraordinary promise of power that such paradigms offered them. Greek tyrants were the first to exploit the language of city foundation. But a founder's mask could never fully disguise the nature of the tyrant's power, for the polis itself separated the founder and tyrant and ensured that crossovers were limited and provisional. Archelaus and Aristonicus, while collapsing the distinction between tyrant and founder, undertook also to replace the third term, the polis itself. This aim, which their imitation of Greek political forms conceals, suggests the novelty and significance of their power for the origins of Hellenistic kingship. The tyrant was enthroned as a king when the polis, the audience of his elaborate self-representation, was no longer able to challenge him.

Lovers of the City: Tyranny and Democracy in Classical Athens

ἀλλὰ μᾶλλον τὴν τῆς πόλεως δύναμιν καθ᾽ ἡμέρον
ἔργῳ θεωμένους καὶ ἐραστὰς γιγνομένους αὐτῆς.

Rather I urge you to observe the real power
of the city every day and to become its lovers.

Pericles at Thucydides 2.43.1

This book paints large the roles played by the rise and fall of
tyranny in the political developments that made the polis, by the
end of the archaic age, the free and exclusive arbiter of justice and its
own self-interests. To show that the polis's experience with tyranny
allowed it to link *dikē* and *eleutheria*, I have stressed that the tyrant's
self-representation defined the potential and the limits of his individual power. To continue and focus this argument I look now to
classical Athens, whose memories of tyranny and reactions against
it we know best. The tyrant's role in the political language of the
classical Athenian democracy was rich and complex: tyranny functioned not simply as a liminal construct providing graphic images
of incorrect citizen behavior, but as a defining model of political
freedom and as a bond between individual citizens.

Discussions of the tyrannical elements of classical Athens usually focus on Athens's aggressive foreign policy, which reminded its
enemies and even the Athenians themselves of tyranny. The impression was not accidental: in addition to their military and finan-

cial responsibilities, fifth-century Athens required the states it ruled to adopt its coinage, present legal cases to its juries, and even to honor its deities and make religious contributions to Athens as if its colonies.[1] Athens's most imperialistic leaders, Pericles and Cleon, freely admitted that the Athenian empire was a tyranny (Thuc. 2.63.2; 3.37.2)—an admission meant to convince the Athenians that Athens shared the tyrant's need to act with care and consistency, for it was no freer than he was to abandon its power.[2] Pericles and Cleon seem to have understood, better perhaps than their contemporaries, that the empire gave Athens an economic foundation that the radical democracy of late fifth-century Athens could not do without.[3] Yet there was a fatalistic echo in the words of Pericles and Cleon, as if Thucydides intended to show that even Athens's friends were casting the city in a tragic role. And Athens's tyrannical behavior, like the behavior of tyrants, did in fact invite and direct the resistance of its enemies, most especially the Spartans, who won great support (for a short time) as the liberators of Greece from the Athenian tyranny.[4]

I will not try to describe the process that transformed the Athenian effort to free Greece and punish the Persians into a *tyrannis* (a process that was perhaps less a matter of forgotten ideals and false promises than of realizing the potential that lay within the language and images of punishment and liberation), nor will I focus on the reactions of Athens's great enemy, Sparta, who follows Athenian footsteps first as a liberator and then as a tyrant of Greece. Instead I concentrate on the relation of tyranny and democracy in the definition of citizenship in classical Athens. Plato's harsh accusation against democracy in the *Republic*, that the democratic citizen and the tyrant exercise the same *eleutheria*, will be our guide. Our goal is to see this as praise rather than as criticism of democracy and to find in classical Athens a specific example of the preservation of the

1. For Athens's imperial behavior, Meiggs (1972) remains sound. For brief discussions of Athens's persona as a liberator, see chap. 4, and on the *dēmos tyrannis*, see chap. 2.

2. Like a tyranny, Pericles states in Thucydides, the Athenian empire "was perhaps a mistake to acquire, but it is certainly dangerous to lose" (2.63.2).

3. On the relation between the ideals of the radical Athenian democracy and its empire, see the eloquent essay by Finley (1973).

4. For the language of Sparta's resistance to Athenian domination, see chap. 4.

tyrant's power in the individual and collective possession of freedom.

We can begin to get a sense of the significance of tyranny in democratic conceptions of citizenship by examining tyranny in its most public and official form, namely, in the Athenian democracy's legislation against it. At the end of the fifth, and again in the fourth century, the Athenians passed laws that defined tyrannical acts, made them illegal, and punished them.[5] These laws were briefly discussed above in the context of Solon's legislation against tyranny.[6] As already argued, the two laws most obviously depart from Solon's model in failing to describe specific legal procedures for prosecuting tyranny. While Solon's law refers prosecution for tyranny to the Athenian Areopagus, both later laws call for and sanction immediate personal action by any individual citizen who perceives his fellow citizen's actions as tyrannical. This makes a certain political sense. Tyranny threatens the very existence of the polis; the legal mechanisms of the city become dysfunctional in exact proportion to the seriousness of the threat. Any real solution, it seems to follow, must range as far beyond limits of conventional citizen behavior as tyranny itself. The fifth-century decree, for example, announces that "the man who kills him who does these things and whoever counsels him shall be holy and blameless" (ὁ δὲ ἀποκτείνας τὸν ταῦτα ποιήσαντα καὶ συμβουλεύσας ὅσιος καὶ εὐαγής: Andoc. 1.96). Thus the laws position the tyrannicide outside of law: whoever kills a tyrant is immune to punishment; indeed, as *hosios* (holy), the tyrannicide is protected by the sphere of authority that the law acknowledges as its superior. The tyrant's punishment confirms the laws' intention. They do not define the tyrant as *atimos*, which, in the laws' time, left the criminal with certain legal and procedural rights;[7] rather, they subject the aspiring tyrant to a form of punishment that was as rude and legally peripheral as the power he coveted. Both laws proclaim the aspiring tyrant to be *polemios*, an enemy of the city; he was to be killed according to the

---

5. The first (the decree of Demophantus) is quoted by Andocides (1.96–98); the second (proposed by Eucrates) was found in excavations in the Athenian Agora (*SEG* xii 87).

6. See chap. 3.

7. On *atimia*, see chap. 3.

rules of battle and without reference to the laws and rights of civic society.

But not only their failure to detail a specific form of prosecution distinguishes the fifth- and fourth-century laws against tyranny from Solon's. There is also a clear difference in political tone. Solon's law against tyranny defined and criminalized sedition in an effort to help make law sovereign, the principal goal of his reforms. The later laws seem less high-minded: they transparently serve partisan political interests. The earlier decree was passed in 410, in the wake of, and as a response to, the oligarchic interlude of 411; the later was proposed in 336, probably as a democratic reaction to the disappointing loss to the Macedonians at Chaeroneia.[8] Drafted in times of political emergency, the laws were meant to breathe new ideological life into democratic regimes that were enervated by military failures and internal conflict. By identifying the dissolution of the democracy with tyranny, the laws direct the fear and hate characteristic of democratic attitudes toward tyrants against oligarchical revisions both large and small. This somewhat indiscriminate melting together of oligarchs and tyrants had a special significance when the two laws were proposed; but it was hardly an invention of the moment. Aristophanes knew, and attacked, the sort of ideological project that the laws undertook decades before the first of the two antityrannical decrees was passed. In the *Wasps* (488–91), he parodies the ubiquitous image of the tyrant in Bdelycleon's speech to the chorus of enraged jurors: "Tyranny and conspiracy are everything to you, whatever matter, small or large, is brought to your attention; now that thing [i.e., tyranny] whose name I have not heard for fifty years is far cheaper than salted fish." The fear of tyranny, Aristophanes implies, had become a tool designed to manufacture political hysteria for dubious political purposes. And again in the *Birds* (1074–75), he seems to ridicule legislation against tyranny by incorporating a provision into the *politeia* of Nephelokokkygia that "whoever kills one of the long-dead tyrants shall receive a talent."[9]

8. So Ostwald 1955.

9. Aristophanes' remarks might be taken to suggest that legislation against tyranny was passed earlier in fifth-century Athens. If there was such a law in Athens—and the Erythrae Decree (40 ML) makes it certain that Athens imposed legislation against tyrants on its allies—the oath that is included in Demophantus's decree (discussed immediately below) perhaps explains why the Athenians felt the need for a new one.

Because they equate the weakening of a political regime with the enslavement of the entire city, the laws perhaps deserve our criticism too. But we should not let the tactics of the laws or the partisan interests that fostered them obscure the substantive political ideas from which they drew. The fifth- and fourth-century laws exhibit the fear of a tyranny that emerges not only from the extraordinary acts of extraordinary individuals; instead, tyranny is seen as a potential danger that may lurk undetected in seemingly innocent citizens and everyday political actions. In addition, because tyrannical actions in a democracy might be undertaken by any citizen, all citizens must stand guard against them. From this perspective, the earlier of the two, the decree proposed by Demophantus in 410, may be understood not only as a law but also as a political event. According to Andocides' text, Demophantus's decree required every Athenian citizen to swear to uphold the law, and thereby to articulate his personal commitment to the power that, according to the language of the law, he and all other citizens possessed both to save and to destroy the state. Thus the laws incite political hysteria and serve partisan interests by invoking basic democratic principles: the discovery that the tyrant and the tyrannicide are alternative personas of the same image of citizenship.[10]

The democratic legislation against tyranny suggests that the Athenian democracy did not simply condemn or forget the tyrant's extraordinary freedom but accepted and exploited it; and, moreover, that the tyrant's power passed to his city not as a political abstraction or formula but as an individual possession. But the laws do not explain what makes this power so important in the minds of fifth- and fourth-century Athenians. To come closer to an answer, we might look at Pericles' Funeral Oration, that is, Thucydides' memory and reconstruction of the speech Pericles gave to honor the Athenian casualties of the first year of the Peloponnesian War (2.35–46). In his famous celebration of Athens's war dead, Pericles traces the chief virtues of Athens—the courage, intelligence, and gener-

---

10. The fifth- and fourth-century laws might be compared with ostracism, the procedure employed in Athens after 488 to avert the danger posed to the democracy by distrusted political leaders. Like the laws, ostracism allowed every citizen to cast a vote and any citizen to be selected in a popular election for the position of the most dangerous of citizens. Like the earlier of the two laws, ostracism was public and conspicuous; it restated the principles of democracy, not only protected it. On the

osity of its citizens—to the *eleutheria* that makes them unique. Pericles has in mind a precise notion of freedom. The Athenian is master of himself (2.41.1); he is free to pursue private concerns, and no official can determine how he spends his time or trains his children. Yet this freedom is neither uncultured nor unpolitical. The Athenians, Pericles insists, have a grace and versatility all their own (41.1)—the outward signs of their individual self-mastery. And, most important, the freedom that each individual possesses binds him to his city: no one is fit to be an Athenian who ignores or disdains political matters (40.2). It is for their *eleutheria* that the Athenian war dead celebrated by the oration are worthy of their city, just as the greatness of Athens is proof of the *eleutheria* of citizens like them (41.2). The political character of individual freedom helps explain why Pericles spends little time on the personal qualities of the war dead (42.3), and why he seems to understate the losses suffered by their families (44.1–3).

Pericles eulogizes the war dead by stressing the individual freedom of Athens's citizens: so the deceased appear to have died for Athens freely and willingly, not as victims of chance or necessity. But Pericles' praise of freedom is not simple; it focuses, rather than erases, the question that the fifth- and fourth-century Athenian legislation against tyranny encourages us to ask: What is the relation of citizens, whose freedom allows them to make and destroy tyrants, to their city? Consider the stated purpose of the Funeral Oration. By making an example of Athens's war dead, Pericles says he hopes to incite the Athenians to become lovers of their city (2.43.1). *Erastēs*—the word Thucydides' Pericles uses for lover— hints at a relationship that is not only intimate but active and passionate. The *erastēs* is devoted to his beloved, but also possessive, domineering, and prone to jealousy. He cares for his beloved and is personally interested in her welfare, but he demands exclusive attention. Translated into the realm of politics, the *erastēs'* desire is the passion of the aspiring tyrant, not the loyalty of the honest citizen.

---

origins, purpose, and procedures of ostracism, see Rhodes (1981, 267–71) with his extended bibliography.

In defining citizenship in terms of the individual citizen's theoretical potential for violent action on the city's behalf, the Athenian laws against tyranny have analogues in early modern legal traditions, particularly in John of Salisbury's *Policraticus*; on the tyrant and tyrannicide in the *Policraticus*, see Berman 1983, 276–88.

The implication is not gratuitous: Pericles here employs an established metaphor for tyranny that dates back at least to Archilochus[11] and was still very much current in his own time. When Alcibiades defends himself before the Spartans, after escaping prosecution in Athens, he also describes himself as a lover of Athens:

καὶ χείρων οὐδενὶ ἀξιῶ δοκεῖν ὑμῶν εἶναι, εἰ τῇ ἐμαυτοῦ μετὰ τῶν πολεμιωτάτων, φιλόπολίς ποτε δοκῶν εἶναι νῦν ἐγκρατῶς ἐπέρχομαι. . . . τό τε φιλόπολι οὐκ ἐν ᾧ ἀδικοῦμαι ἔχω, ἀλλ᾽ ἐν ᾧ ἀσφαλῶς ἐπολιτεύθην. οὐδ᾽ ἐπὶ πατρίδα οὖσαν ἔτι ἡγοῦμαι νῦν ἰέναι, πολὺ δὲ μᾶλλον τὴν οὐκ οὖσαν ἀνακτᾶσθαι. καὶ φιλόπολις οὗτος ὀρθῶς, οὐχ ὃς ἂν τὴν ἑαυτοῦ ἀδίκως ἀπολέσας μὴ ἐπίῃ, ἀλλ᾽ ὃς ἂν ἐκ παντὸς τρόπου διὰ τὸ ἐπιθυμεῖν πειραθῇ αὐτὴν ἀναλαβεῖν.

(Thuc. 6.92.2, 4)[12]

And I claim I should not seem worse to any of you if, though once seen as a lover of my country, I now join vigorously with its greatest enemies to attack it. . . . I have love for my country, not when wronged, but when exercising my rights securely. I do not believe that I am now attacking my fatherland but am winning over one that is not now mine. And that man really loves his city who does not refrain from attacking it when he has lost it unjustly, but rather, whose passion brings him to try to win it back by every means.

Alcibiades' behavior is an obvious distortion of Pericles' image of citizenship; Alcibiades is the rejected lover who is determined to force his beloved to take him back. But what is clear even in the caricature is the ideal of the citizen who passionately loves his city and devotes himself entirely to it.

What I mean to suggest is that the city that was labeled by its leaders a *tyrannis polis*—tyrant city—was home to tyrant citizens.

---

11. See Archil. 19.3 W and 23.18–21 W, which are discussed above in chap. 1. For Herodotus's account of Deioces, who is named and acts as a "lover of tyranny," see chap. 2.

12. On Alcibiades and Thucydides' treatment of the Athenian tyrannicides, see chap. 4. For the characterization of Cleon in Aristophanes' *Knights* as an *erastēs* of the Athenian demos, see Connor 1971, 97–102.

The freedom that was once enjoyed exclusively by tyrants was incorporated into the definition of citizenship. This does not mean that classical Athens played a dangerous game when it linked its citizens' political passions and sense of self-mastery. As the fifth- and fourth-century legislation against tyranny suggests, the problem of multiple tyrant citizens provided its own solution: as every citizen could become a tyrant, so all his fellow citizens could act as the city's liberators. In fact, both the problem and the solution were purely theoretical. If Athens was in some ways threatened by those individuals, such as Alcibiades, whose willingness to harm the city overmatched their devotion to it, those threats did not materialize in the form of successful or even attempted tyrannies. Some critics could find other problems in Athens's determination to cultivate its citizens' self-perception as their own masters: the Athenians were reputed to be reluctant to follow directions, overconfident, and precipitous—a characterization that neatly reverses Pericles' eulogy of Athenian freedom in the Funeral Oration.[13] Yet, however evaluated, Athens's interest in *eleutheria* and its incorporation into the Athenian body politic suggests a strong investment in the public memory of tyrants, whose freedom, I argue, functions as a conceptual model for the Athenian idea of citizenship. This investment is reflected in the very public and accessible, yet also politically sophisticated, genre of Attic tragedy. Tragedy invited the Athenians to participate in a memory of tyranny that, in the form of a dramatization of Greek myth, replayed both the demise and the survival of the tyrant's power. In this form tragedy offers an answer to the question posed by Athenian political language: How did Athens make tyranny safe for democracy?

Tyranny and Tragedy

Aeschylus gives a good idea of the place of tyranny in the Athenians' mythical consciousness in the *Oresteia*, a trilogy that subjects

13. So Cleon, a sometime critic of Athenian democracy, speaks at Thuc. 3.37. Plato's similar criticism of democracy in general is discussed below. In Thucydides, the pro-Athenian (i.e., the Periclean Funeral Oration) and anti-Athenian (e.g., the Corinthians' speech at 1.70) treatments of Athenian freedom very nearly overlap.

the notions of *dikē* (justice), crucial for archaic tyranny, to a penetrating and sustained dramatic analysis.[14] In Aeschylus's hands, the account of the fall and restitution of the house of Agamemnon constitutes a narrative progression through distinct images of justice: from an antiquated, unpolitical, and ultimately inhuman notion of *dikē*, which Clytemnestra brandishes and to which she falls victim, toward one that is politically resolvable and firmly confined within precise institutional boundaries and which allows for Orestes' acquittal. This transformation of *dikē* is closely associated with collateral movements through time and space, as the trilogy follows a set of events that begin in Argos in the wake of the Trojan War, progress to Delphi, and find a final resolution in Athens at the time of that city's political birth.

Aeschylus associates the principle of justice and the particular form it takes in the *Oresteia*'s plot with the awful figures of the Erinyes, or Furies:

> κελαι-
> ναὶ δ᾽ Ἐρινύες χρόνῳ
> τυχηρὸν ὄντ᾽ ἄνευ δίκας
> παλιντυχεῖ τριβᾷ βίου
> τιθεῖσ᾽ ἀμαυρόν.
>
> (*Ag.* 462–66)[15]

> In time, black Furies render dark
> that man who is fortunate without justice,
> the fortunes of his life's path reversed.

At first glance, the Furies seem perfect monsters. They bear no resemblance to gods or men (*Eum.* 410–12); they are stern and implacable (385); they haunt the night and dark (386–87, 396); and they acknowledge no authority greater than their own (350). That Aes-

14. On justice in the *Oresteia*, see also Euben 1982. For political interpretation of the *Oresteia*, see also Meier (1980) and Pope (1986, 13–26), who seems wrong to me in interpreting Agamemnon's genuine interest in justice to prove that he was not a tyrant.

15. For the association, see also *Ag.* 1432–33; *Eum.* 511–12.

chylus should associate them with justice at all is neither obvious nor uncomplicated. The Erinyes, particularly keen to exact vengeance for crimes in families, are made by Aeschylus to personify retributive justice in such a way that they implicitly qualify and reshape it as ancient, domestic, and unyielding. It is this justice that "allots learning to those who suffer" (*Ag.* 250; cf. *Eum.* 520–21)[16] and that is objectified in the "net" that is thrown over Troy to punish Paris's crimes (*Ag.* 358), in the "fatal net" of slavery that catches Cassandra (*Ag.* 1048), and in the "tangling nets" that, through the agency of Clytemnestra, cover Troy's avenger, Agamemnon (e.g., *Ag.* 1375, 1581)—as if, as the image itself underscores that *dikē* is inescapable, its many returns are meant to emphasize that *dikē* never appears just once. It is this rigorously reciprocal idea of justice that Clytemnestra has embraced as a dubious ally who will accompany her to her own death (*Ag.* 1432–33).

Yet, for all the implacable harshness and violence of the Furies, Aeschylus's presentation of them and their agents is not purely negative. In the *Eumenides*, the Furies justify the necessity of their work in an extended political discourse remarkable not for its hate but for its goodwill:

> ἔσθ᾽ ὅπου τὸ δεινὸν εὖ
> καὶ φρενῶν ἐπίσκοπον
> δεῖ μένειν καθήμενον·
> ξυμφέρει
> σωφρονεῖν ὑπὸ στένει.
> τίς δὲ μηδὲν ἐν φάει
> καρδίας ἀνὴρ τρέμων
> ἢ πόλις βροτῶν ὁμοί-
> ως ἔτ᾽ ἂν σέβοι δίκαν;
> μήτ᾽ ἄναρκτον βίον
> μήτε δεσποτούμενον
> αἰνέσῃς.
> παντὶ μέσῳ τὸ κράτος θεὸς ὤπασεν, ἀλλ᾽ ἄλλᾳ δ᾽ ἐφορεύει.
>
> (*Eum.* 517–31)

16. Zeus is not indifferent to retributive justice; at *Ag.* 177–78, he is made to stand for the principle that men learn by suffering.

There is a place where fear, a good and
benevolent watchman, must remain
in place: there is advantage in wisdom
won from pain. And what man
fearing nothing in the light of his heart,
or, in the same way, what city of mortals,
would still respect justice?
Praise neither an unruled life
nor one ruled by a despot.
The god granted power to every middle but he oversees them
in different ways.

The Erinyes thus qualify and interpret their own fearsome rhetoric
and posture. Like Solon and Theognis when tyranny was still
relatively young,[17] the Erinyes here focus on the evils of injustice to
persuade men to avoid it. Fear, they claim, protects individuals and
cities from the dangers of injustice, and it is the path of the political
middle between anarchy and tyranny that represents the only safe
course for the city. The validity of this viewpoint is confirmed,
paradoxically, by Athena herself, who a few moments later (*Eum.*
696–703), speaks her own ode to fear, freely borrowing the Erinyes'
words and sentiments.

Confirmation comes too from Aeschylus's portrayal of Clytemnestra, the principal agent of justice in the *Oresteia* and the mother
on whose behalf the Furies are roused to action. No person in the
entire trilogy is drawn with such strong lines as Clytemnestra, who
lives and dies by the ancient idea of *dikē*. And although Clytemnestra is made to suffer for killing Agamemnon, her own arguments for her act are not refuted within the trilogy; by sacrificing
Iphigenia, Aeschylus suggests (*Ag.* 1419–21; cf. 1405–6, 1432–33),
Agamemnon has become a pollution that the city has no choice but
to remove: Clytemnestra does the city's work for it by killing him.

But if Aeschylus grants the behavior of the Erinyes and Clytemnestra a distinct voice and rationale, he also represents their justifi-
cations as limited and flawed. The actions and thought of the Furies
and Clytemnestra clearly belong to a political universe that is de-

17. See chap. 2.

Tyranny and Political Culture in Ancient Greece

fined by two extremes: tyranny and anarchy. If the Furies counsel moderation and balance, they can themselves do nothing more than punish lapses of justice. Their pursuit of Orestes and their words at his trial make it obvious that they understand neither mediation nor purification; in fact, they reject all intervention, whether divine or human, that undertakes to separate injustice and its punishment.

The path of the *Oresteia* eloquently articulates the limits of the Furies' apocalyptic political philosophy: from an impossible choice between uncompromising justice and the terrors of injustice—Agamemnon's decision whether to avenge Troy or to spare his daughter (which is already made before the trilogy even begins)—the *Agamemnon* and *Libation Bearers* tell a story in which anarchy and tyranny alternate as successive and inseparable stages. A furious *dikē* is an implicit ally to the plans and deeds of Clytemnestra and Aegisthus, who team up to correct the appalling record of violence, an impossible tangle of crime and retribution, that the house of Atreus has amassed. As the chorus immediately perceives (*Ag.* 1354–55), to kill Agamemnon is to replace him: revenge and rule are inseparable.[18] Under the banner of *dikē*, Clytemnestra and Aegisthus introduce into Argos a brutal form of political reason (σωφροσύνη), a *tyrannis* (*Ag.* 1355, 1365; *Cho.* 972) that relies on "chains and hunger" to compel the Argives to submit (*Ag.* 1621).[19] But *dikē* also provides the rationale for their destruction, which is suggestively portrayed as an act of tyrannicide. So Orestes' first words to the chorus after completing his act of justice:

ἴδεσθε χώρας τὴν διπλῆν τυραννίδα
πατροκτόνους τε δωμάτων πορθήτορας.
(*Cho.* 973–74)

Behold the double tyranny of the land:
father killers and besiegers of houses.

18. Aeschylus at *Ag.* 844–50 describes Agamemnon's power in tyrannical terms: like an archaic tyrant, he is a surgeon, "burning and cutting benevolently" to eliminate all diseased parts of his city. Personal and political revenge clearly merge, and Clytemnestra and Aegisthus (no less easily than Orestes) can represent themselves as tyrannicides.
19. Cf. *Ag.* 1425, 1620. See Meier 1980, 171–72.

Clytemnestra's extraordinary agency, which contrasts sharply with the passivity of her helpless victims, Agamemnon and Cassandra, may seem politically anomalous. But her transgressions as a woman, wife, and queen do not really detract from her role as tyrant. In Aeschylus, as also in Pindar's *Pythian* 11, Clytemnestra's gender makes her villainy more emphatic. In the *Oresteia*, Clytemnestra's fall is represented in much the same way as her rise, as a momentous act in which brutality and necessity are equally, but unhappily, mixed. Of course Orestes does not imitate his mother in making his act of revenge the foundation of his own rule in Argos; but avoiding tyranny is hardly Orestes' personal achievement. It is paradoxically the quick response of the Furies to his matricide that protects Orestes from polluting his own act of tyrannicide. So Aeschylus suggests that Orestes cannot, either alone or with the help of Apollo, on whose orders he acts, break the cycle of *anarchia* and *tyrannis* from which Argos suffers. The demands of justice must always be met.

Thus Aeschylus's mythical history of Argos provides a commentary on *dikē* itself. His message seems to be that Argos suffers because it lacks a stable political center. There punishment is an independent and divine force, which is indiscriminate and unkind in its employment of human agents. It is obvious that no solution to Argos's dilemma will come from the Furies, who insist that if strict retributive justice is hindered,

> μηδέ τις κικλησκέτω
> ξυμφορᾷ τετυμμένος,
> τοῦτ᾽ ἔπος θροούμενος,
> ῏Ω Δίκα,
> ὦ θρόνοι τ᾽ Ἐρινύων.
> (Eum. 508–12)

> no one may call forth,
> struck by misfortune,
> crying out this word,
> "O Justice! O throne of Erinyes!"

Yet the solution that the *Oresteia* invents is impossible without them. The court Athena creates to decide the case of Orestes exercises little power on its own. And even if it were able to acquit Orestes without Athena's vote, it certainly could not deflect the wrath of the Furies, who announce that they will take his acquittal as a license to exercise vengeance against all mankind. It is therefore not the invention of the Areopagus in the course of the play but the merger Athena engineers between the Furies' power and the Aeropagus's agency at the *Eumenides'* close that gives Athens political control over *dikē*. The *Oresteia*, in this sense, ends with compromise, the union of power and political authority.[20]

In this project, the *Oresteia* does not simply overcome archaic *dikē*; it dramatizes the incorporation of justice within the political order of Athens. As the old gods find a new home under Zeus, the justice they exercise and symbolize is made a principal element of a new political order. The Furies become Eumenides; and although they seem easily bribed by promises of honor (*Eum.* 895), their transformation does not weaken or neutralize them. The *Oresteia* formulates victory as compromise. As Prometheus yields to Zeus, the Furies yield to Athena's city, and retribution is incorporated within a scheme of justice that is genuinely political.

As the *Oresteia*, in this political reading, dramatizes the internal dynamics of archaic *dikē*, Sophocles' *Oedipus Tyrannus* and *Oedipus Colonus* capture, in the figure of Oedipus, the life and remarkable transformations of its principal agent, the tyrant. Oedipus's past actions (both his crimes and achievements) define him as a tyrant. But the narrative paths of the *Oedipus Tyrannus* and *Oedipus Colonus* are concerned less with Oedipus's past than with his present troubles: Oedipus is engaged through the plays in systematically uncovering and destroying his own position and power.

Dikē pervades the *Oedipus Tyrannus* no less than it does Aeschylus's *Agamemnon*, and Oedipus, very much like Aeschylus's Clytemnestra, captures the link between reform and power that is essential in Greek tyranny. At the outset of the play, when his

20. The relation Aeschylus constructs between Athens and a new vision of political justice is perhaps not fortuitous: Athenian homicide law was historically sensitive to mitigating circumstances—to which the Furies are fiercely indifferent (cf. *Eum.* 427).

doorstep is crowded with suppliants, Oedipus proclaims his keen-
ness in matters of justice:

ἀγὼ δικαιῶν μὴ παρ᾽ ἀγγέλλων, τέκνα,
ἄλλων ἀκούειν αὐτὸς ὧδ᾽ ἐλήλυθα,
ὁ πᾶσι κλεινὸς Οἰδίπους καλούμενος.

(OT 6–9)

Holding it right not to learn these things
from others who conduct messages, I have come myself, children,
I who am known to all as famed Oedipus.

So in this first speech, Oedipus announces his determination to
address the troubles of his people personally; thereby he unwittingly accepts the role of the inquisitor of an examination that has
his destruction as its object.

The parodos of the play carries on with this same theme. Oedipus, the chorus says, "redeemed" (ἐξέλυσας: OT 35) the city and
"with the help of a god . . . set right the life" (προσθήκῃ θεοῦ,
ὀρθῶσαι: 38–39) of the Thebans when he answered the Sphinx's
riddle.[21] The chorus continues:

ὡς σὲ νῦν μὲν ἥδε γῆ
σωτῆρα κλῄζει τῆς πάρος προθυμίας.

(OT 47–48)

So now this city praises you as its savior
for your earlier zeal.

And now, when Thebes faces a disastrous plague, Oedipus is urged
again "to set right the city" (ἀνόρθωσον πόλιν: OT 46, 51). Oedipus accepts the obligation for himself, the city, and the gods. "Although you are sick, it is not equal to my sickness" (60–61), he
explains, for while they suffer for themselves, he suffers both for
himself and for the city (62–64). He concludes:

21. Cf. OT 104, where Creon also remembers that Oedipus "set right the city"
(ἀπευθύνειν πόλιν).

197

ὥστ᾽ ἐνδίκως ὄψεσθε κἀμὲ σύμμαχον,
γῇ τῇδε τιμωροῦντα τῷ θεῷ θ᾽ ἅμα.

(OT 135–36)

so justly you will see also me as an ally
avenging this land and the god at the same time.

As a savior and avenger, Oedipus is expected to reform (ἀνορ-θοῦν) and straighten (ἀπευθύνειν) his city; his unique gifts are put to work to remove the pollution in the body politic that is signaled by the plague that opens the play. Like the plague that begins the *Iliad* and the natural disasters feared by Hesiod and Solon,[22] Sophocles' plague proves the existence of injustice but does not itself punish or remove it. What is needed is reported by Creon, who has learned from Apollo that Thebes nourishes "pollution" (μίασμα: OT 96) and that "purification" (καθαρμός: 99), the isolation and expulsion of the transgressor against justice, is necessary to save the city.

The theme of justice in the *Oedipus Tyrannus* is gradually fleshed out as Sophocles borrows more and more heavily from archaic concepts of justice. The first hint of reciprocal justice comes with Apollo's directive that the pollution affecting Thebes requires "banishment [of the guilty party] of expiating murder with murder" (100–101). It becomes clearer as Oedipus gradually identifies himself as the cause of Thebes's plague. Then we learn that the event that has awakened Apollo's anger, much like the overthrow of the Bacchiads and the revenge of Orestes and Clytemnestra, was an acting blending justice and injustice. Directed against a monarch who hubristically dominates the road, as a tyrant controls his city, the murder can be construed as an act of justice: and, as if to underscore that point, Sophocles has Oedipus use his *skēptron* (OT 811), the symbolic and instrumental link between punishment and monarchy, to punish Laius. The hero of the *Oedipus at Colonus* makes this explicit; to justify his crime he says simply: "I was wronged; I retaliated."[23]

22. On these, see chap. 2 (Hesiod) and chap. 3 (Solon).
23. OC 271: ὅστις παθὼν μὲν ἀντέδρων. Oedipus remarks at OT 810 that he "gave me not just an equal penalty" (οὐ μὴν ἴσην γ᾽ ἔτισεν)—the punishment, like that of tyrants (or gods) generally, he admits to have been excessive and brutal—

And as Cypselus replaced the Bacchiads and as Clytemnestra kills Agamemnon and Orestes kills Clytemnestra, Oedipus replaces Laius in an act of justice that invites *dikē*'s return. Sophocles thus hints at the problem that also underlies the *Oresteia* and assumes a commanding role in the historical logic of tyranny: the progression of *dikē* from a small, perhaps forgotten, injustice to a danger that threatens the entire city. But while Aeschylus solves the problems of justice by resorting to divine intervention, as his Orestes appeals to Apollo and Athena to escape the consequences of his matricide, Sophocles presents an answer that is political in its formulation as well as in its result. Although Apollo is active behind Oedipus's crime and punishment and Oedipus sometimes complains that the gods have brought his misfortune on him (*OT* 1329–30), he knows that the curse to which he has fallen is of his own design (819–29, 1290–91), and he is not, like Orestes, a simple, unwitting object of divine machinations. Oedipus acquires power, killing Laius, defeating the Sphinx, and marrying Jocasta, by his own actions. This is also true of his political demise. Throughout the *Oedipus Tyrannus*, Oedipus acts by his own hand (αὐτόχειρ: 1331), and he exercises against himself the very power that defines his position in Thebes.

Sophocles focuses therefore on Oedipus's own distinctive political agency. This is suggested in the first lines of the play, when Oedipus first assumes responsibility to carry out the orders of Apollo. This is a decision that he makes freely and that articulates his extraordinary power. But, like a tyrant, he soon finds that his power is entangled in a greater necessity. Oedipus cannot cease his investigations once he has undertaken them, even when he begins to sense that the results will be personally disastrous. Scholars have found integrity and a desire for truth in Oedipus's character. From the perspective argued here, Oedipus is neither a good nor a bad sovereign; instead, he is a pure monarch, whose destruction is

---

which does not, however, make the killing any less an act of punishment. On the place of scepters and clubs in the language of early Greek tyranny, see chap. 2.

Vernant and Segal find a similar mixture of justice and injustice in Oedipus's act of reforming Thebes and gaining power over it, his victory over the Sphinx. In their view, his remarkable acuity about the span of human life, which allows him to answer the Sphinx, springs from his own ambivalence as a man who has obliterated the difference in generations, by killing his father and replacing him at his mother's side. See Vernant 1982, 24–25, and Segal 1981, 216–17.

entailed by his tyrannical power. In fact, Sophocles tells Oedipus's story, as Greeks often remembered their tyrants, as an account of just two events: the *Oedipus Tyrannus* recalls its hero's rise, and it dramatizes his fall. This is the political side of Sophocles' ironic treatment of Oedipus in the play. Sophocles follows Oedipus's gradual and painful realization that he is himself the object of his own search. Oedipus's demise elaborates his own success, and the dramatic force of his investigation is obviously reflexive. We do not watch in order to learn what happens to Oedipus, but to see what effects Oedipus's painstaking research will have on him.

This brings us to the conspicuous place of *tychē* (fortune) in the *Oedipus Tyrannus*, which, with *dikē*, occupies an outstanding place in the language of Greek tyranny. Oedipus, the "best of mortals" (*OT* 46), victor over the Sphinx, and king in Thebes, prides himself on his good fortune. At a crucial moment of the *Oedipus Tyrannus*, when, paradoxically, the last vestige of his happiness—namely, his ignorance of his own misery—is about to be stripped from him, he announces himself to be Tyche's son:

> ἐγὼ δ᾽ ἐμαυτὸν παῖδα τῆς Τύχης νέμων
> τῆς εὖ διδούσης οὐκ ἀτιμασθήσομαι.
>
> (*OT* 1080–81)

> I believe myself to be the child of Tyche,
> the generous, and I will not be dishonored.

Oedipus's vaunt, though obviously mistaken, articulates an underlying truth. As a statement about his political parentage, his claim is essentially correct: it is by the favor of the gods that he enjoys his great prestige and power. But, Oedipus, like tyrants, underestimates the fickleness of divine favor, which is easily transformed into divine punishment (τιμή). Early in the play, Oedipus prays that the message from Apollo may be "in good saving fortune" (ἐν τύχῃ γέ τῳ σωτῆρι: *OT* 80–81). The prayer works—that is, Apollo's message offers a solution to the Thebans' difficulties. But the prayer also marks the start of Oedipus's demise. So the chorus remarks:

ἐφηῦρέ σ᾽ ἄκονθ᾽ ὁ πάνθ᾽ ὁρῶν χρόνος,
δικάζει τὸν ἄγαμον γάμον πάλαι
τεκνοῦντα καὶ τεκνούμενον.

(OT 1213–15)

Time, which sees all, has discovered you hiding
and punishes a marriage that is no marriage,
the parent that is also the child.

As Oedipus is both parent and child in the same bed, he is also both
the judge and the judged. Thus the rhetorical question with which
Jocasta intends to persuade Oedipus to ignore gloomy oracles—

τί δ᾽ ἂν φοβοῖτ᾽ ἄνθρωπος ᾧ τὰ τῆς τύχης
κρατεῖ, πρόνοια δ᾽ ἐστὶν οὐδενὸς σαφής;

(OT 977–98)

What should man, whom fortune controls, fear,
since no one has clear foreknowledge?

—is in fact an argument to show every concern for the occasional
glimmers of foreknowledge that oracles offer. "This very chance
(τύχη) has destroyed you," Teiresias tells Oedipus at *Oedipus Tyrannus* 442. So Oedipus learned the same lesson as the tyrants of Sicily:
Tyche does not provide a stable foundation for political power.

The point of this political reading is that the *Oedipus Tyrannus* not
only casts Oedipus as a tyrant, it also dramatizes his tyranny.[24] This
is not to comment on Oedipus's behavior toward Creon, Teiresias,
and the herdsmen, who oppose Oedipus either with innocence or
with knowledge. Oedipus's tyrannical power appears only in a
refracted shape in his moral character; it is most apparent in the
play's narrative structure. Dominant in the *Oedipus Tyrannus* are
transformations of reform into crime, divine favor into divine ha-

---

24. On Oedipus as a tyrant, see also Knox (1979, 87–95), who identifies Oedipus
as a symbol of the Athenian state and reads the *OT* as a commentary on the growing
Athenian empire.

tred, and the savior into the damned. Through them, Sophocles imposes on Oedipus a story that captures the political course, as well as the language, of tyranny, its pretensions to divine favor, and its inexorable reversals.

This is not a new discovery: the similarities linking the Sophoclean Oedipus and tyrannical stories, especially Herodotus's portrait of Cypselus, have been noted before, most clearly by Jean-Pierre Vernant.[25] But Vernant traces these similarities to the narrative techniques of Herodotus: for Vernant, "when the father of history recounts as fact the events which installed a line of tyrants at the head of Corinth, quite 'naturally' he mythologizes, and his account lends itself to a type of analysis analogous to that [which] we can apply to the legend of Oedipus."[26] From the perspective argued here, Vernant ignores the elements of Herodotus's story that must certainly antedate him, exaggerates his inventiveness (and underestimates Sophocles'), and dismisses the mythological potential of the tyrant and its relation to his power.

The *Oedipus at Colonus*, Sophocles' account of Oedipus's death and burial, supports a more explicitly political reading. In the *Oedipus at Colonus*, Oedipus appears at the moment of his death as a man on the verge of becoming a hero. In the course of his life, Oedipus has been the man most hated and loved by the gods; Oedipus's great fortune and trials now make him a figure of great significance and lasting power. This power recaptures in part his old life as Thebes's tyrant; when Oedipus is reclaimed in the *Oedipus at Colonus*, he is again called *sōtēr* (savior), as he was at the beginning of the *Oedipus Tyrannus*. Yet Oedipus has lost all interest in political power, and with it all political agency. His power now attaches to his person, but it does not respond to his will—in fact, it is realized only after his death. In this sense, the *Oedipus at Colonus* builds Oedipus's character on established images of political power. As his aggression, achievements, and self-destruction make him a tyrant, his long quest and the power that he holds after his death liken him to city founders.[27]

25. Vernant 1982; see also Jameson 1986, 8–11.
26. Vernant 1982, 33.
27. Of course, Oedipus establishes no new city and is buried far from an urban center. Yet like the tombs of Theseus and Orestes, who were also believed after their

The two sides of Oedipus's complex character define the strange dilemma that Creon faces in the *Oedipus at Colonus*. Creon is trapped between Oedipus's absence and his presence, the *miasma* that clings to his person and the promises of beneficent power that he leaves behind him. Creon desperately wants to control Oedipus's power, but he also fears Oedipus's presence in Thebes. To master Oedipus's power—as Creon and Oedipus both know—is to take control of his burial; to bring him to Thebes is to risk a new plague. Rather than decide for Oedipus's power or against his pollution, Creon wavers. He determines to take Oedipus to Theban territory but not to Thebes; to keep him from the city where he can do the greatest damage but to plant him nearby, where his grave can do the most good. But Oedipus resists this wavering, refuses to cooperate, and insists on staying in Athens. This is all to Athens's good fortune. And although the *Oedipus at Colonus* is less concerned with Theseus's decision to allow Oedipus to die on sacred ground than with Thebes's defeat, the rewards are clearly important. Oedipus hints at his postmortem contributions to Athenian military history (*OC* 459–60, 1518–38, 1764–65); we find these obscure, but Sophocles' audience must have understood them.

This point helps frame the larger problem of the relation between tragedy and its mythical subject matter. Tragedy was the principal narrative, as well as dramatic, art of fifth-century Athens. The heir of epic as much as of dithyramb, tragedy arranged and focused the mythological past and its reception, framing the heroic in the particular posture of yielding itself up, anticipating the postheroic, preparing for its own demise. So the *Oresteia* and Sophocles' Theban plays employed various narrative and dramatic techniques to shape particular myths and connect them with the political and religious institutions, events, and attitudes of contemporary Athens. This, as

---

deaths to protect cities that they had not actually established, Oedipus's grave was a matter of great civic concern. (Since its exact location was secret, the Athenians did not need to be concerned that Oedipus's bones, like Orestes', could be stolen.) The tyrant and founder are not the only images of autocratic power that Oedipus's short but rich political biography seems to invoke. The voluntary self-mutilation he undergoes at the end of the *OT* seems to associate him with legendary lawgivers, who gave sovereignty to their laws at the expense of their own bodies and lives (see chap. 3).

Froma Zeitlin has persuasively shown,[28] explains the intense examination to which Sophocles subjects Thebes. In Sophocles, Thebes is permanently monarchical, dominated by an antiquated and unimproved conception of justice, and unable to control its political destiny: Laius is replaced by Oedipus, the Sphinx by a divine plague; incest begets fratricide. Nor does the impossibility of political power in Thebes end with the demise of Oedipus's own immediate family. In this context, we might remember that the *Oedipus Tyrannus* leaves the political fate of Oedipus's city curiously unresolved. Does Oedipus stay at Thebes? Does the plague end? Caught up in the trials of Oedipus, Sophocles seems indifferent to the dilemma of Laius's murder. This lack of resolution may seem dramatically unsatisfying, but it makes political sense. At the close of the *Oedipus Tyrannus*, Oedipus's home is still Thebes, a city that, according to its Athenian interpreters, was incapable of political resolution. The *Oedipus Tyrannus*, as Cassandra suggests of her own story in the *Agamemnon*,[29] remains without healing: dramatic resolution, like political resolution, characterizes contemporary Athens, but not mythical Thebes.

This relationship between tragedy and myth is particularly evident in tragedy's treatment of tyranny, the political form that the Greeks associated with the real and legendary past. It is a commonplace of scholarship on classical Greece that *tyrannos* is a neutral word in tragedy; Sophocles in particular, who uses the word most often, is believed to have employed the word without thinking, and, apparently, without wanting his audience to think, of Athens's own complex history with tyranny.[30] But Aeschylus's *Oresteia* and the Theban plays of Sophocles suggest that the argument is confused. Political ideas are certainly marked, and tyranny is no exception. Although they almost invariably focused on a world that was dominated by individual rulers, the tragedies of Aeschylus and Sophocles

28. Zeitlin 1986.

29. *Ag.* 1248: "No healer at all presides over the story I tell" (ἀλλ' οὔτι παιὼν τῷδ' ἐπιστατεῖ λόγῳ).

30. See, among historians of tyranny, Andrewes (1956, 20–23) and Berve (1967, 1:194). Euben (1990, 106 n.30), like many scholars of Athenian political culture, reductively assumes the existence of two—and apparently only two—senses of *tyrannos*: one "neutral" and one "pejorative." There are, I think, many senses of *tyrannos*, none of which is entirely neutral or pejorative.

do not endorse the political configurations of mythical time. In fact, rather than offer a dramatic revival of a world in which monarchy was normal, the tragedies replayed and recounted the great divide—framed in remote time and sometimes in remote space—that separated the mythical material of tragedy from the cultural and political setting of its performance. In this sense, the opposition that Sophocles constructs between monarchical Thebes and democratic Athens becomes especially poignant at the end of the *Oedipus at Colonus*. It is Athens, not Thebes, and Theseus, founder of the Athenian democracy, not Creon, who occupies and personifies the Theban monarchy, who can loosen the contradictions that Oedipus, as a kind of *tyrannus fulminatus*,[31] who is equally polluted and sacred, presents. The last chapter—the last in mythical time—of Sophocles' story of Thebes, the *Antigone*, confirms Creon's inability to learn. Unchanged by its successive tragedies, Thebes there witnesses its final disaster, the destruction of Creon's own *oikos*, which, with Antigone herself, becomes a victim of Creon's single rule. Yet, despite the destruction Creon inflicts on Oedipus's family and his own, his kingship and the Theban monarchy remain completely secure. So in Sophocles' Thebes, which, like Aeschylus's Persia, is untouched by history and politics, the agent of the city's destruction survives the disaster he causes.[32]

In its treatment of tyranny and language, tragedy seems to serve a fundamental, if unconventional, political function. The *Oresteia* and *Oedipus at Colonus* describe mythical transformations that lead beyond tragedy, the end of "learning through suffering," and the beginning of political resolutions. Tragedy, which borrows dramatic material from beyond the temporal and (in the case of Aeschylus's *Persians*) beyond the spatial limits of its audience's world, concerns itself with the crossover between the political perspective characteristic of its material and that of its own world. In effect,

---

31. On this figure and the Quintilian declamation in which he appears, see chap. 1 passim. By refusing to decide either to have Oedipus buried in Thebes or to continue to enforce Oedipus's exile, Creon is like a schoolboy who cannot decide which side of the declamation to argue.

32. The distinctive justification for monarchy also survives: no man, as the herald in Euripides' *Suppliants* (412–16) makes clear, is able to escape the penalty for injustice while Creon rules Thebes.

tragedy implicitly celebrates its audience's liberation from the constraints of myth and the tyrannical politics that dominate in myth. Tragedy, by the way that it remembers myth, also rejects the absolute distinctions between myth and the contemporary world, pure and impure political forms, the ideal of the good and its imperfect realizations. Thus Athenian tragedy, by recalling the demise of the old *dikē* and the self-destruction of tyranny, and, in general, by neutralizing myth in the very act of preserving it, reflects a solution for the political problem of how political freedom, once the property of single individuals, could be simultaneously exploited and resisted.

Plato's Republic *and the Extirpation of Tyranny*

Tragedy thus confirms the significant place that tyranny occupies in the political language of Athens, and helps make sense of the Athenians' public position toward tyranny. Tragedy expresses in myth what the Athenians exploited in their legislation against tyranny and in their conception of citizenship: the image of the tyrant as a force that is always present and never resolved, whose freedom is both individual and collective and provides a source for political unity, not divisiveness. In presenting Athens as the end and goal of mythical and legendary history, such memories themselves helped solve the paradox of the Periclean Funeral Oration: How can the *erastēs* of the city function as a citizen? Yet the relationship between democracy and tyranny was certainly not appreciated by all Athenians, and it was disliked particularly by Plato, perhaps classical Athens's greatest critic. In the *Republic*, a dialogue conspicuously set in the political and cultural setting of late fifth-century Athens, Plato attempted to design a very undemocratic state that is just in a sense that Athens was not and stable in ways Athens deliberately shunned. Plato's departure from the political ideas of his home (a move no less radical, perhaps, than his rejection of dramaturgy as a career choice) can be understood as a refusal to appreciate the precarious but vital place of tyranny in the Athenian democracy. This rejection of tyranny and its legacy tied Plato in theoretical and practical knots: his very effort to remove tyranny from his perfect state unwittingly rooted it more deeply, while his attempts to establish a state without the freedom shared by tyrants and democracies forced on him an unhealthy choice between active support of autocratic regimes and philosophical reclusion.

Much like the debate of the Persian leaders in Herodotus (3.80–82), Plato's *Republic* presents a typology of political forms, classified, in the first instance, according to the number of individuals who are able to participate in them. The *Republic* departs from Herodotus, however, in constructing a dynamic relationship among the forms of political power. The various imperfections that Plato finds in the types of government function as catalysts that gradually transform them into still less perfect states. So Plato, more like Hesiod than like his own contemporaries, represented man's collective development as a single process of deterioration that began in the remote past and continued in the cities of his own day, each of which he believed to be in an advanced state of decay.[33] Against extant states, Plato placed his own model of a perfect city, one that has been carefully stripped of every kind of corruption.[34] Plato designed it with a clear hierarchy of political tasks. Socrates imagines a state with an unchanging social structure, a stable economy, little communication with its neighbors, and no navy or empire. Most important, it is a state in which the desire for power always yields to reason, its autocratic ruler. Too great a gulf separates Plato's imaginary city from all others for it to function well as a political model; but Plato perhaps intended his ideal city less as a guide for the imperfect states of his world to imitate than as a standard for determining their relative value. It is certainly easily adapted to this use in the *Republic* itself, where Plato employs it to articulate his great dislike of democracy.

There is therefore a clear political content in Plato's iconoclastic views on power and change in the *Republic* and little doubt that Plato's ideal state shocked many of his contemporaries. Monarchy and democracy, the rule of one and the rule of many, no longer

---

33. On Plato's vision of history, see Vidal-Naquet 1978. Plato's disparagement of the present, as Vidal-Naquet shows, is not without ambivalence: the present witnesses "much wickedness but also much virtue" (πολλὴ μὲν πονηρία, πολλὴ δὲ καὶ ἀρετή: e.g., 678a).

34. On Plato's notion of justice, see Havelock 1969.

frame the extremes of Plato's new political spectrum; that function is now assumed by the two principles, political reason and political desire, which he represents as utterly antagonistic. Tyranny remains situated at the extreme as a political anathema, but its definition is now revised. For Plato, tyranny is a political abomination not because it is the rule of a single individual, but because it represents the domination of the state by its lowest desires. At the other extreme from tyranny, Plato places not democracy, as do the Persian conspirators, but a monarchy of reason, the domination of the city by the individual who is most capable and, therefore (unfortunately for Plato), least interested in political power. Democracy fares badly in this new order; in fact, Plato places it beside tyranny, one step from the complete absence of political reason.

Plato's argument against democracy is long and clever. But his point is simple: he turns democracy against itself. Tyranny, he claims, arises directly from the democracy's greatest good (ἀγαθόν), the *eleutheria* of each citizen (562b).[35] In democracy, Plato has Socrates insist, every citizen does what he wants when he wants: political authority is required of no one; no one needs to obey his superiors; military service is optional; private wars are tolerated; and the exiled and condemned submit to their punishments only if they wish (557e). The pursuit of pleasures, unimpeded by moral or political principles, guides the democratic man in every aspect of his life, including his political activities. When he visits the assembly, he "jumps up, and speaks and acts completely at random" (561d). The unrestrained freedom of the democratic state extends in its most radical form to women (in this respect Plato's visions of the ideal city and the democratic state overlap) and even to slaves and domestic animals, who, as Socrates disingenuously asserts, trot about the streets of democracies fully persuaded of their innate *eleutheria* (563b–c). Of course, Plato here wears the hat of the political satirist. And his satirical tone, even more than his actual remarks, reveals his aim to strip democracy of its pretensions to political rationality.

Plato's annihilation of democracy seems total and unrelenting.

35. The Old Oligarch (1.8) makes a similar move when he attributes the strength of the Athenian democracy to its bad government and its citizens' lack of discipline.

But we get a sense that this is not quite true from Plato's extensive treatment of the problem of realizing the perfect state (471c–502c). The problem is introduced by Glaucon and Adeimantus, whom Socrates answers as if condescending to philosophical novices. In Socrates' hesitation to answer their practical question we may sense Plato's own. The answer is certainly controversial: Socrates concedes that the one chance of establishing a perfectly just state lies in a single individual who has a tyrant's power but is not corrupted by it: this is a philosopher who has acquired political power by chance, or a ruler or his son who possesses a genuine love of wisdom. This transitional philosopher-king balances reason and power; in particular, he knows to search for happiness in wisdom rather than in pleasure. The significance of this figure is perhaps concealed by the *Republic*, which is happy to use him to point out the faults of lesser political creatures. But it is obvious in Plato's own political activities, especially his frustrated attempts to convert the younger Dionysius, tyrant of Syracuse, to the rule of wisdom. In fact, if we assume that Plato's own political aims were shared by his school, it seems probable that the numbers of aspiring tyrants and tyrannicides who came from throughout Greece to Plato's Academy were more interested in breathing the political air than in learning geometry.[36]

In this sense, Plato's ideal form of government is only a small step away from the worst, and tyranny appears no farther from the rule of the wise king than from democracy, the rule of the pleasure-seeking masses. Plato's vision of various political forms thus seems more circular than linear. Although the tyrant and philosopher-king are worlds apart in their understanding of political reason, they are partners as agents of change. It makes some sense then that Plato's hostility to democracy surpassed his hatred of tyranny: from his perspective, a tyranny can be improved, while a democracy only

---

36. On Plato's efforts in Sicily, see below n.37. Diogenes Laertius gives a list of Plato's politically active students at 3.46–47 (cf. 3.23). See also Ael. *VH* 2.42 and Ath. 11.506–8. The Academy prided itself on this tradition. Plutarch, who was a member in his day, asserts at *Adv. Col.* 32 that Plato's "better teachings" (κρείττονες λόγοι) were the lectures presented to his students, which, through them, brought political changes to a significant portion of Greece. On the activities of the Academy and its members, see Schuhl 1946 and Morrow 1962, 143–44.

gets worse. The Athenians might see it very differently; what Plato most despises in democracy is its stability, not its instability: the freedom of its citizens prevents the city's subordination to a single individual, bad or good.

For all its energy, Plato's treatment of democracy does not completely obscure how much he shares with it. For the Athenian legislation against tyranny, the tyrannicide exploits on the city's behalf the extraordinary personal freedom he enjoys as a democratic citizen; similarly, for Plato, true political reform depends on the complete *eleutheria* of the rare philosopher who gains political power. Plato's vision of political reform also shares much with the tyrant. In answering the question of how the ideal state might be realized, Socrates uses language that seems borrowed from the self-representations of tyrants: if "by some extraordinary fortune" (ἐκ τύχης) or "as the consequences of divine providence" (ἔκ τινος θείας ἐπινοίας) the unlimited freedom of the tyrant is conjoined with wisdom (499b), then the political artist possessing both could "wipe" the city and the customs of men clean like a canvas" (ὥσπερ πίνακα πόλιν τε καὶ ἤθη ἀνθρώπων, πρῶτον μὲν καθαρὰν ποιή-σειαν ἄν) and "take possession of it and draft new laws" (501a). We cannot help but be reminded of "*anēr euthuntēr* [reformer] of our hubris" who Theognis feared would rise from the injustice of Megara's political struggles.[37]

Plato certainly did not intend to echo the language and ideas of democracies or tyrants, who, in his mind, drew from no inherent political logic, except that given them by their greed. This indifference to the political character of democracy and tyranny reflects the fundamental bias of the *Republic*: that wisdom is a pure and untainted pursuit of the good that only an act of god can merge with political power. The distinction may underscore the remoteness of his just city even more than Plato intended. It certainly did not

---

37. See chap. 2. For the image of *eleutheria* and *tychē* in the self-representation of the Sicilian tyrants, see also chap. 4 passim, and on the image and function of purification, see chap. 2. The dependence of hopes of political reform on tyranny seems to qualify the rancor between Socrates and Thrasymachus in *Republic* 1 (see especially 498c) as friction generated from closeness. This is not to overlook the disagreement: Thrasymachus's sophist-tyrant wants desperately to rule, while Plato's philosopher-king must be forced out of his contemplative retirement. But in different ways, both find in tyranny a unique potential for political good.

help his own political activities.[38] Plato's inability to convert the younger Dionysius, who toyed with him as one of many literary ornaments of his court, to a rule of political wisdom seems to confirm the practical liability of Plato's radical distinction between power and wisdom. That Dion's efforts to replace Dionysius, after it had proved impossible to reform him, led to a new tyranny should not perhaps be attributed to his political ineptitude or to a misunderstanding of Plato's political philosophy (which he seems to have taken as his guide), but to the inherent limitations of Plato's goal to establish disinterested political rule. Tyranny thus seems to have presented Plato with a virtually inescapable problem: his very attempts to overcome it invariably led him back to it.

Yet the *Republic* does not completely misrepresent democracy; in fact, its goal of replacing the freedom of democracy with a stratified body politic paradoxically highlights the Athenian democracy's great achievements. Plato understood that democratic freedom resembled the freedom of tyranny: it was personal and passionate in nature and directed toward the city as if to a lover. He also saw (albeit, in reverse) a dynamic relationship between democracy and tyranny, driven by *eleutheria*. Most important, Plato understood that democracy was a form of rule that defined itself on the smallest level, the tyrant citizen, whose *eleutheria* pervaded his civic activity. But again Plato's hatred of democracy limited his insight. These free citizens of the democracy, whose political wisdom Pericles idealized in the Funeral Oration and whose ability to follow their political betters even Cleon conceded when blasting their indecision and stupidity (Thuc. 3.37), Plato identifies as creatures who are not just reluctant to apply political wisdom but utterly incapable of it.

In turn, the Athenian democracy highlights what Plato ignores in discussing the relationship between democracy and tyranny (or what, perhaps, in Plato's defense, the Athenian democracy itself had begun to ignore in his time): that the extraordinary personal freedom of tyranny was closely tied to a profound sense of collective interest. The Athenians believed, and continually reminded

38. On Plato's involvement in Sicilian politics, see Finley 1968, 73–88. On the relation between Athens and Syracuse, in which Plato's efforts must be situated, see, most recently, Sanders 1987. On Dion's complex persona as a liberator and tyrant, see chap. 4.

themselves, that they had themselves overthrown their tyrants,[39] and, as has been shown, they were fascinated by accounts of the political transformations that turned the tyrannies of myth into the *isonomia* of their own world. Such memories and stories, however fictional, helped the Athenians preserve the language of *eleutheria*, the source of the tyrant's power, as both an individual and a political possession. Plato wanted nothing of this. It was not justice, which the *Republic* redefines as the harmony of the city's parts under its metaphorical head, but tyranny. From its own perhaps more subtle perspective, democracy improved on tyranny: in particular, it overcame the tyrant's characteristic political instability. Thucydides shows this when, in comparing the imperial fortunes of former cities and nations with those of cities of the present, and particularly Athens, he faults even archaic tyrannies for achieving relatively little (1.17). The reason he gives is simple: tyrants, "providing for their own persons and families, ruled their cities as much as possible in security"—that is, Thucydides seems to suggest, the tyrant's very freedom engendered a fear in him that kept him from any lasting achievement. The *eleutheria* of Athens was not similarly burdened, because all citizens, that is, all political agents, possessed it. Of course, Thucydides' quick dismissal of tyranny ignored the complex history of the *eleutheria* he admired in his own time and his own city; he would perhaps have maintained that no such history exists. My argument is that it does, that the Greeks told it themselves, and that tyranny occupied a large part in it.

39. On the Athenians' memory of their tyrannicides, see chap. 4.

Justice and Liberation

Therefore even the rule of a tyrant, too, is good, although nothing is worse than tyranny.

John of Salisbury, *Policraticus*, 351

The Greeks remembered the rise and fall of their tyrants most diligently; they were far less interested in what tyrants did after their power was secure and before it began to waver. This focus expresses the Greeks' own interests in tyranny, which, when its temporal limits were clearly defined, became a single coherent political event with a clear plot, characters, and a tangible moral lesson. But this focus also makes it very difficult to reconstruct tyranny in other terms than the Greeks did. From a perspective that rigorously distinguishes between the reality and the perception of tyranny, the memories of tyrants are, at their best, politically interested, biased, and partial; at their worst, they are incidental, sensational, and scandalous, full of the fascination tyrants held and virtually devoid of information about what they did. It is impossible to miss the significance of these gaps and biases, and no historian would hesitate to trade a story like Herodotus's tragic account of Polycrates' fall for information about the interactions between tyrants and aristocrats. Nevertheless the evidence that we have does not completely prevent us from understanding tyranny—if we are willing to view the biases and interests underlying the Greeks' memories of tyranny not as impediments but as keys to what the tyrants did and what elements of their works survived them.

It is true that we can never really hope to understand the intentions of Greek tyrants or to reconstruct their political methods. We cannot know whether Cypselus, for example, planned to become Corinth's tyrant, and whether his efforts to promote justice in Corinth and convince the Corinthians to view him as a promoter of justice were merely designed to help him reach this goal. We also know very little about how he consolidated support and eliminated enemies, what titles he possessed, or where he lived. None of these things much interested the Greeks, but that does not discredit what did interest them, that Cypselus emerged as a promoter of justice.

The mythologized accounts of the tyrant's rise do indeed tell us much about his power and appeal. The tyrant's image invited a precise political response. The source of the reformer's power was divine (for, as the Greeks from Hesiod's time believed, the gods were vitally interested in human justice). As divine, the tyrant's power was both necessary and inevitable: resistance was useless; hopes of profiting from him or holding him accountable were futile. The tyrant's power made him uniquely *eleutherios*, and he ruled the city as if it were his personal possession. As an exclusive agent of justice in his city, the tyrant found himself in an increasingly distinct and privileged political position.

Yet, as tyranny matured, the tyrant's discourse acquired and exerted an authority that was independent of his position and greater than his power. Justice was a pendulum that swung back against its own agent. Less secure even than his ambiguous hold on justice was the conflicting and contrary language of *eleutheria*: tyrants inevitably supported the growing sense that, as masters of their city and holders of a full allotment of *eleutheria*, they reduced their fellow citizens to slaves.

To describe this crucial feature of tyranny—the generation of resistance by language that placed the tyrant beyond resistance—I have devoted considerable space to the distinctive political logic of tyranny's demise and, in particular, to the roles played by the lawgiver, liberator, and founder. These are the tyrant's partners in individual power and in the political lore that surrounded it. Yet in different ways, these figures all act as alternatives to tyranny: the liberator replaces the tyrant; the lawgiver and founder render him unnecessary. All possess the *eleutheria* of the tyrant, but they are not tyrants, for they are honored by the cities that their actions benefit, and they avoid the tyrant's unhappy demise, the condemnation that ends his story.

But these are imaginary solutions. Tyranny did not disappear as a result of the actions of lawgivers, founders, or even tyrannicides; in fact, these very images were appropriated by tyrants to revitalize and extend their power. But it is likely that the ideas that these images render in anthropomorphic terms compelled tyrants to resort to such disguises as liberators and founders. What the tyrannicide and his like imply is that power and the judgment of power rest ultimately with the polis. If tyrants presented themselves as liberators or founders, they must have understood the polis's power to judge them, for they were determined to finesse that judgment by appearing to act in the polis's interest, to deserve its honor, and to have passed its scrutiny. Clearly the tyrant's relationship to his subjects was changing.

We can perhaps understand this change only in very general terms. The exclusive possession and conspicuous display of freedom, which the tyrant's power allowed him and which his persona as a reformer required, turned his city into a slave, over which he exercised his power and to which he was not accountable. But the way he exercised political power made it a real and tangible commodity: something that some have and others do not, and something that could change hands. Moreover, the tyrant, in exercising his power over his city, also objectified it and consolidated it into a single political unit. To exhibit power as a form of property was to invite someone to steal it; to unite subjects into a single political body was to concede to them the ability to act as one. The resistance to tyranny was a matter of realizing the political potential that tyrants unwittingly offered their cities.

Yet the resistance to tyranny was as much a program for political action as a political reaction; removing the tyrant was just a beginning (and not always a necessary one). After escaping tyranny, poleis did not return to political innocence. They adopted the tyrant's persona as the agent of justice, took over his political innovations, and assumed his treasury and foreign acquisitions. Most important, they preserved his *eleutheria*, the sense of self-mastery that made tyranny both attractive and dangerous. We have tried to

215

follow closely how this story unfolded at Athens, which rendered the tyrant's power as the individual possession of its citizens. That is a remarkable and perhaps unique story, but the problem to which it responded was certainly not: effective resistance to tyranny required the polis to make itself over in the tyrant's image.

Bibliography

CGF   Kaibel, G. (1899) *Comicorum Graecorum fragmenta*. Berlin.
DK   Diels, H., and W. Kranz. (1951–52) *Die Fragmente der Vorsokratiker*. 6th ed. Berlin.
FGH   Jacoby, F., ed. (1923–58) *Die Fragmente der griechischen Historiker*. Leiden.
GP   Gentili, B., and C. Prato, eds. (1979–85) *Poetae elegiaci: Testimonia et fragmenta*. Leipzig.
IG   *Inscriptiones Graecae*. (1873–) Berlin.
LP   Lobel, E., and D. L. Page. (1974) *Poetarum Lesbiorum fragmenta*. Oxford.
LSJ   Liddle, H., R. Scott, and S. Jones. (1968) *A Greek-English Lexicon*. Oxford.
ML   Meiggs, R., and D. Lewis. (1969) *A Selection of Greek Historical Inscriptions*. Oxford.
OCD   Hammond, N. G. L., and H. H. Scullard, eds. (1970) *The Oxford Classical Dictionary*. 2d ed. Oxford.
P   Pearson, A. C. (1917) *The Fragments of Sophocles*. Cambridge.
Pr   Preisendanz, C. (1912) *Carmina Anacreontea*. Leipzig.
PW   Parke, H. P., and D. E. W. Wormell. (1956) *The Delphic Oracle*. 2 vols. Oxford.
SEG   *Supplementum epigraphicum Graecum*. (1923–) Amsterdam.
SM   Snell, B., and H. Maehler, eds. (1971–75) *Pindarus*. Leipzig.
W   West, M. L., ed. (1971–72) *Iambi et elegi Graeci*. Oxford.

Adam, T. (1970) *Clementia principis*. Stuttgart.
Adkins, A. (1960) *Merit and Responsibility*. Oxford.

Bibliography

Althusser, L. (1971) "Ideology and Ideological State Apparatuses." In *Lenin and Philosophy and Other Essays*, translated by B. Brewster, 127–86. New York.

Andreev, J. V. (1979) "Könige und Königsherrschaft in den Epen Homers." *Klio* 61: 361–84.

Andrewes, A. (1956) *The Greek Tyrants*. London.

———. (1949) "The Corinthian Actaeon and the Pheidon of Argos." *Classical Quarterly* 43: 70–78.

Auden, W. H. (1976) *Collected Poems*. Edited by E. Mendelson. New York.

Benjamin, W. (1977) "Der Erzähler." In *Illuminationen: Ausgewählte Schriften*, 385–410. Frankfurt a.M.

Béranger, J. (1935) "Tyrannus: Notes sur la notion de tyrannie chez les Romains particulièrement à l'époque de César et de Cicéron." *Revue des études latines* 13: 85–94.

Berman, H. (1983) *Law and Revolution: The Formation of the Western Legal Tradition*. Cambridge, Mass.

Bernhardt, R. (1987) "Die Entstehung der Legende von der tyrannenfeindlichen Aussenpolitik Spartas." *Historia* 36:257–89.

Bers, V. (1975) "Solon's Law Forbidding Neutrality and Lysias 31." *Historia* 24: 493–98.

Berve, H. (1967) *Die Tyrannis bei den Griechen*. 2 vols. Munich.

———. (1953) "Zur Herrschaftstellung der Deinomeniden." In *Studies Presented to David M. Robinson*, edited by G. Mylonas and D. Raymond, 2:537–52. St. Louis, Mo.

Bicknell, P. (1982) "Herodotus 5.68 and the Racial Policy of Kleisthenes of Sikyon." *Greek, Roman, and Byzantine Studies* 23: 193–201.

Boardman, J. (1989) "Herakles, Peisistratos, and the Unconvinced." *Journal of Hellenic Studies* 109: 158–59.

———. (1984) "Image and Politics in Sixth-Century Athens." In *Ancient Greek and Related Pottery,* edited by H. Brijder, 239–47. Proceedings of the International Vase Symposium. Amsterdam.

———. (1978) "Herakles, Delphi, and Kleisthenes of Sikyon." *Revue archéologique* 1978: 227–34.

———. (1975) "Herakles, Peisistratos, and Eleusis." *Journal of Hellenic Studies* 95: 1–12.

———. (1972) "Herakles, Peisistratos, and Sons." *Revue archéologique* 1972: 57–72.

Bockisch, G. (1982) "Kypselus und die Bakchiaden." *Klio* 64: 51–66.

Boersma, J. S. (1970) *Athenian Building Policy from 561/0 to 405/4 B.C.* Groningen.

Bonanno, M. G. (1973) "Osservazioni sul tema della 'giusta reciprocita amorosa' da Saffo ai comici." *Quaderni urbinati di cultura classica* 16: 110–20.

Bondenella, P. (1987) *The Eternal City: Roman Images in the Modern World*. Chapel Hill, N.C.

Brooks, P. (1977) "Freud's Masterplot." *Yale French Studies* 55–56: 280–300.

Brunnsåker, S. (1971) *The Tyrant-Slayers of Kritios and Nesiotes*. Stockholm.

Bibliography

Bulman, P. (1992) *Phthonos in Pindar*. University of California Publications: Classical Studies 35. Berkeley.

Burkert, W. (1985) *Greek Religion*. Translated by J. Raffan. Cambridge, Mass. Originally published as *Griechische Religion der archaischen und klassichen Epoche* (Stuttgart, 1977).

Burnett, A. P. (1985) *The Art of Bacchylides*. Cambridge, Mass.

———. (1983) *Three Archaic Poets: Archilochus, Alcaeus, Sappho*. Cambridge, Mass.

Bushnell, R. (1990) *Tragedies of Tyrants*. Ithaca, N.Y.

Carlier, P. (1984) *La royauté en Grèce avant Alexandre*. Paris.

Cartledge, P. (1979) *Sparta and Laconia*. London.

Chamoux, F. (1953) *Cyrène sous la monarchie des Battiades*. Paris.

Chantraine, P. (1968) *Dictionnaire étymologique de la langue grecque*. Paris.

Clairmont, C. (1983) *Patrios nomos: Public Burial in Athens during the Fifth and Fourth Centuries B.C.* Oxford.

Cobet, J. (1981) "König, Anführer, Herr: Monarch, Tyrann." In *Soziale Typenbegriffe im alten Griechenland und ihr Fortleben in den Sprachen der Welt*, edited by E. Welskopf, 3: 47–55. Berlin.

Cole, A. T. (1983) "Archaic Truth." *Quaderni urbinati di cultura classica* 42: 7–28.

Cole, E. E. (1912) *The Samos of Herodotus*. New Haven.

Compernolle, R. van. (1983) "Femmes indigènes et colonisateurs." In *Modes de contacts et processus de transformation dans les sociétés anciennes*, 1033–49. Pisa.

———. (1957) "Les Deinoménides et le culte de Déméter et Koré à Géla." *Latomus* 28: 474–79.

Connor, W. R. (1987) "Tribes, Festivals, and Processions: Civic Ceremonial and Political Manipulation in Archaic Greece." *Journal of Hellenic Studies* 107: 40–50.

———. (1977) "Tyrannis Polis." In *Ancient and Modern: Essays in Honor of Gerald F. Else*, edited by J. D'Arms and J. Eadie, 95–109. Ann Arbor.

———. (1971) *The New Politicians of Fifth-Century Athens*. Princeton.

Cook, R. M. (1987) "Pots and Pisistratan Propaganda." *Journal of Hellenic Studies* 107: 167–69.

Crahay, R. (1956) *La littérature oraculaire chez Hérodote*. Paris.

Daux, G., and A. Salač. (1932) *Inscriptions depuis le Trésor des Athéniens jusqu'aux bases de Gélon, Epigraphie*. Vol. 3, pt. 1, of *Fouilles de Delphes*. Paris.

Davies, J. K. (1971) *Athenian Propertied Families*. Oxford.

Deger, S. (1970) *Herrschaftsformen bei Homer*. Vienna.

Descat, R. (1979) "L'idéologie homérique du pouvoir." *Revue des études anciennes* 81: 229–40.

Detienne, M. (1977) *Dionysos mis à mort*. Paris.

———. (1967) *Les maîtres de vérité dans la Grèce archaïque*. Paris.

Develin, R. (1977) "Solon's Law on Stasis." *Historia* 26: 507–8.

Dihle, E. (1977) "Das Satryspiel 'Sisyphos.'" *Hermes* 105: 28–42.

Drews, R. (1983) *Basileus: The Evidence for Kingship in Geometric Greece*. New Haven.

Bibliography

——. (1972) "The First Tyrants in Greece." *Historia* 21: 129–44.

Drögemüller, H.-P. (1973) "Syrakusai." In *Paulys Realencyclopädie der classischen Altertumswissenschaft,* suppl. 13: 815–36.

Dunbabin, T. J. (1957) *The Greeks and Their Eastern Neighbors.* London.

——. (1948) *The Western Greeks.* Oxford.

Eder, W. (1986) "The Political Significance of the Codification of Law in Archaic Societies: An Unconventional Hypothesis." In *Social Struggles in Archaic Rome,* edited by K. Raaflaub, 262–300. Berkeley.

Edwards, M. (1988) *Homer: Poet of the Iliad.* Baltimore.

Ehrenberg, V. (1956) "Das Harmodiuslied." *Wiener Studien* 69: 56–69.

Euben, J. P. (1990) *The Tragedy of Political Theory.* Princeton.

——. (1982) "Justice and the Oresteia." *American Political Science Review* 76: 22–33.

Evans, J. A. S. (1981) "Notes on the Debate of the Persian Grandees in Herodotus 3.80–82." *Quaderni urbinati di cultura classica* 36: 69–84.

Farenga, V. (1981) "The Paradigmatic Tyrant: Greek Tyranny and the Ideology of the Proper." *Helios* 8: 1–31.

Farrar, C. (1988) *The Origins of Democratic Thinking.* Cambridge.

Ferguson, J. (1970) *Religions of the Roman Empire.* Ithaca, N.Y.

Finley, M. (1979) *Ancient Sicily.* 2d ed. London.

——. (1973) *Democracy Ancient and Modern.* New Brunswick, N.J.

——. (1968) *Aspects of Antiquity.* London.

Flory, S. (1987) *The Archaic Smile of Herodotus.* Detroit.

Fontenrose, J. (1978) *The Delphic Oracle.* Berkeley.

Fornara, C. W. (1970) "The Cult of Harmodius and Aristogeiton." *Philologus* 114: 155–80.

Forrest, W. G. (1966) *Emergence of Greek Democracy, 800–400 B.C.* New York.

——. (1957) "Colonisation and the Rise of Delphi." *Historia* 6: 160–75.

Foucault, M. (1977) *Discipline and Punish.* Translated by A. Sheridan. New York.

Frel, J. (1963) "Dike and Adikia." In ΓΕΡΑΣ: *Studies Presented to George Thomson,* edited by L. Varcl and R. Willetts, 95–98. Prague.

Frisk, H. (1960–72) *Griechisches etymologisches Wörterbuch.* Heidelburg.

Fritz, K. von. (1977) "Nochmals das solonische Gesetz gegen Neutralität im Bürgerzwist." *Historia* 26: 245–47.

Gagarin, M. (1986) *Early Greek Law.* Berkeley.

Gammie, J. G. (1986) "Herodotus on Kings and Tyrants: Objective Historiography or Conventional Portraiture?" *Journal of Near Eastern Studies* 45: 171–95.

Garland, R. (1992) *Introducing New Gods: The Politics of Athenian Religion.* Ithaca, N.Y.

——. (1985) *The Greek Way of Death.* Ithaca, N.Y.

Gelzer, M. (1968) *Caesar: Politician and Statesman.* Translated by P. Needham. Cambridge, Mass.

Gentili, B. (1972) "Il letto insaziato di Medea." *Studi classici e orientali* 21: 60–72.

Bibliography

Gernet, L. (1968) "Mariages de tyrans." In *Athropologie de la Grèce antique*, 344–59. Paris. Originally published in *Hommages à Lucien Febvre* (Paris, 1954), 41–53.

Gierth, L. (1971) "Griechische Gründungsgeschichte als Zeugnisse historischen Denkens vor dem Einsetzen der Geschichtschreibung." Diss., University of Freiburg i.B.

Goldstein, J. (1972) "Solon's Law for an Activist Citizenry." *Historia* 21: 538–45.

Graham, A. J. (1983) *Colony and Mother City*. 2d ed. Chicago.

———. (1980–81) "Religion, Women, and Greek Colonization." *Centro ricerche e documentazione sull' antichietà: Atti* 11, n.s. 1: 293–314.

Griffen, A. (1982) *Sikyon*. Oxford.

Habicht, C. (1970) *Gottmenschentum und griechische Städte*. 2d ed. Munich.

Hannick, J.-M. (1976) "Droit de cité et mariages mixtes dans la Grèce classique: A propos de quelques textes d'Aristote (*Pol.* 1275b, 1278a, 1319b)." *L'antiquité classique* 45: 133–48.

Harrison, A. R. W. (1968–71) *The Law of Athens*. 2 vols. Oxford.

Havelock, E. (1969) "DIKAIOSUNE: An Essay in Greek Intellectual History." *Phoenix* 23: 49–70.

Helm, P. R. (1981) "Herodotus' Mēdikos Logos and Median History." *Iran: Journal of the British Institute of Persian Studies* 19: 85–90.

Herzog-Hauser, G. (1948) "Tyche." In *Paulys Realencyclopädie der classischen Altertumswissenschaft*, 2d ser., 7B: 1643–89.

Hignett, C. (1952) *A History of the Athenian Constitution to the End of the Fifth Century B.C.* Oxford.

Hoffmann, G. (1990) *Le châtiment des amants dans la Grèce classique*. Paris.

How, H. W., and J. Wells. (1912) *A Commentary on Herodotus*. 2 vols. Oxford.

Hurwit, J. (1985) *The Art and Culture of Early Greece, 1100–480 B.C.* Ithaca, N.Y.

Jameson, M. H. (1986) "Labda, Lamda, Labdakos." In *Corinthiaca: Studies in Honor of D. A. Amyx*, edited by M. Del Chiaro, 3–11. Columbia, Mo.

John of Salisbury. (1955) *The Statesman's book of John of Salisbury, being the fourth, fifth, and sixth books, and selections from the seventh and eighth books, of the Policraticus*. Translated by J. Dickenson. New York.

Jones, N. F. (1980) "The Civic Organization of Corinth." *Transactions of the American Philological Association* 110:161–93.

Kahn, C. (1979) *Art and Thought of Heraclitus*. Cambridge.

Kern, O. (1894) *Die Gründungsgeschichte von Magnesia am Menander*. Berlin.

Kleingünther, A. (1933) Πρῶτος εὑρετής: *Aufsuchung zu einer Fragestellung*. Philologus Suppl. 26. Leipzig.

Knox, B. (1979). "Why Is Oedipus Called *Tyrannos*?" In *Word and Action: Essays on the Ancient Theater*. Baltimore.

Kolb, F. (1977) "Die Bau-, Religions- und Kulturpolitik der Peisistratiden." *Jahrbuch des Deutschen Archäologischen Instituts* 92: 99–138.

Kurke, L. (1991) *The Traffic in Praise*. Ithaca, N.Y.

Bibliography

Labarbe, J. (1971) "L'apparition de la notion de tyrannie dans la Grèce archaïque." *L'antiquité classique* 40: 471–504.

La Bua, V. (1975) "Sulla conquists di Samo." *Miscellanea greca e romana* 5: 41–102.

Lamberton, R. (1988) *Hesiod*. New Haven.

Lang, M. (1968) "Herodotus and the Ionian Revolt." *Historia* 17: 24–36.

Lateiner, D. (1984) "Herodotean Historical Patterning: The Constitutional Debate." *Quaderni di storia* 15: 257–84.

———. (1982) "The Failure of the Ionian Revolt." *Historia* 31: 129–60.

Latte, K. (1936) "Νόθοι." In *Paulys Realencyclopädie der classischen Altertumswissenschaft* 17a: 1066–74.

Lavelle, B. M. (1991) "The Compleat Angler: Observations on the Rise of Peisistratos in Herodotus." *Classical Quarterly* n.s. 41: 317–24.

Leahy, D. (1968) "The Dating of the Orthagorid Dynasty." *Historia* 17: 1–23.

Legon, R. P. (1981) *Megara: The Political History of a Greek City-State to 336 B.C.* Ithaca, N.Y.

Leschhorn, W. (1984) *"Gründer der Stadt": Studien zu einem politischen religiösen Phänomen der griechischen Geschichte*. Stuttgart.

Lloyd-Jones, H. (1983) *The Justice of Zeus*. 2d ed. Berkeley.

Loraux, N. (1984) "Solon au milieu de la lice." In *Aux origines de l'hellénisme, la Crète et la Grèce: Hommage à H. van Effenterre*, 199–214. Paris.

———. (1979) "L'autochthonie, une topique athénienne: Le mythe dans d'espace civique." *Annales* 1: 3–26.

MacDowell, D. M. (1978) *The Law in Classical Athens*. Ithaca, N.Y.

McGlew, J. (1989) "Royal Power and the Achaean Assembly at *Iliad* 2.84–393." *Classical Antiquity* 8: 283–95.

Machiavelli, N. (1950) *The Prince and the Discourses*. Translated by L. Ricci. New York.

Malkin, I. (1987) *Religion and Colonization in Ancient Greece*. Leiden.

Manville, P. B. (1990) *The Origins of Citizenship in Ancient Athens*. Princeton.

———. (1980) "Solon's Law of Stasis and *Atimia* in Archaic Athens." *Transactions of the American Philological Association* 110: 213–21.

———. (1977) "Aristagoras and Histiaios: The Leadership Struggle in the Ionian Revolt." *Classical Quarterly* 27: 80–91.

Masaracchia, A. (1958) *Solone*. Florence.

Meier, C. (1980) *Die Entstehung des Politischen*. Frankfurt am Main.

Meier-Welcker, H. (1980) *Himera und die Geschicke des griechischen Siziliens*. Boppard am Rhein.

Meiggs, R. (1972) *The Athenian Empire*. Oxford.

Mitchell, B. M. (1975) "Herodotus and Samos." *Journal of Hellenic Studies* 95: 75–91.

More, T. (1964) *More's Utopia and Its Critics*. Edited by L. Gallagher. Chicago. Reproducing the Robinson translation of 1551.

Moreau, A. (1979) "A propos d'Oedipe: La liaison entre trois crimes: parricide, inceste et cannibalisme." In *Etude de littérature ancienne*, edited by S. Said, 97–127. Paris.

Morrow, G. R. (1962) *Studies on the Platonic Epistles*. New York.

Mossé, C. (1969) *La tyrannie dans la Grèce antique*. Paris.

Mosshammer, A. (1979) *The Chronicle of Eusebius and Greek Chronographic Tradition*. Lewisburg, Pa.

Nagy, G. (1990) *Pindar's Homer: The Lyric Possession of an Epic Past*. Baltimore.

———. (1985) "A Poet's Vision of His City." In *Theognis of Megara: Poetry and the Polis*, edited by R. Figueira and G. Nagy, 22–81. Baltimore.

———. (1983) "Poet and Tyrant: *Theognidea* 39–52, 1081–1082b." *Classical Antiquity* 2: 82–91.

Nietzsche, F. (1969) *Werke*. Edited by K. Schlechta. 6th ed. 5 vols. Frankfurt am Main.

Ober, J. (1989) *Mass and Elite in Democratic Athens*. Princeton.

Oliva, P. (1982) "The Early Tyranny." *Dialogues d'histoire ancienne* 8: 363–80.

Oost, S. (1972) "Cypselus the Bacchiad." *Classical Philology* 67: 10–30.

Ostwald, M. (1969) *NOMOS and the Beginnings of the Athenian Democracy*. Oxford.

———. (1955) "Athenian Legislation against Tyranny and Subversion." *Transactions of the American Philological Association* 86: 110–28.

Pape, M. (1975) "Griechische Kunstwerke aus Kriegsbeute und ihre Öffentliche Aufstellung in Rom—von der Eroberung von Syrakus bis in augusteische Zeit." Diss., University of Hamburg.

Parke, H. W. (1962) "A Note on αὐτοματίζω in Connection with Prophecy." *Journal of Hellenic Studies* 82: 145–46.

Parker, R. (1983) *Miasma: Pollution and Purification in Early Greek Religion*. Cambridge.

Patch, H. (1974) *The Goddess Fortuna in Medieval Literature*. New York.

Patterson, C. (1990) "Those Athenian Bastards." *Classical Antiquity* 9: 40–73.

Pearson, L. (1987) *Greek Historians of the West*. Atlanta.

Pembroke, S. (1970) "Locres et Tarente: Le rule des femmes dans la fondation de deux colonies grecques." *Annales (Economie, Société Civilisations)* 25: 1240–70.

Piccirilli, L. (1973) *Gli arbitrati interstatali greci*. Vol. 1, *Dalle origini al 338 a. C.* Pisa.

Pleket, H. W. (1969) "The Archaic Tyrannis." *Talanta* 1: 19–61.

Pope, M. (1986) "The Democratic Character of Aeschylus's Agamemnon." In *Greek Tragedy and Its Legacy: Essays Presented to D. J. Conacher*, edited by M. Cropp et al., 13–26. Calgary.

Pouilloux, J. (1954) *Recherches sur l'histoire et les cultes de Thasos*. 2 vols. Paris.

Prinz, F. (1979) *Gründungsmythen und Sagenchronologie*. Zetemata 72. Munich.

Raaflaub, K. (1985) *Entdeckung der Freiheit*. Munich.

———. (1981) "Zum Freiheitsbegriff der Griechen: Materialen und Untersuchung zur Bedeutungsentwicklung von ἐλεύθερος/ἐλευθερία in der archaischen und klassischen Zeit." In *Soziale Typenbegriffe*, edited by E. C. Welskopf, 4: 180–405. Berlin.

Race, W. H. (1986) *Pindar*. Boston.

Ravel, O. (1928) *The "Colts" of Ambracia. Numismatic Notes and Monographs* 37. New York.

Rhodes, P. J. (1981) *Commentary on the Athenaion Politeia*. Oxford.

Roebuck, C. (1972) "Some Aspects of Urbanization in Corinth." *Hesperia* 41: 96–127.

Rohde, E. (1925) *Psyche: The Cult of Souls and Belief in Immortality among the Greeks*. New York.

Roisman, J. (1985) "Maeandrius of Samos." *Historia* 34: 257–77.

Romer, F. (1982) "The *Aisymneteia*: A Problem in Aristotle's Historic Method." *American Journal of Philology* 103: 25–46.

Rose, P. (1975) "Class Ambivalence in the *Odyssey*." *Historia* 24: 128–49.

Rougé, J. (1970) "La colonisation grecque et les femmes." *CH* 15: 307–17.

Ruschenbusch, E. (1966) Σόλωνος νόμοι: *Die Fragmente des solonischen Gesetzwerkes mit einer Text- und Überlieferungsgeschichte*. Historia Einzelschriften 9. Wiesbaden.

Salmon, J. B. (1984) *Wealthy Corinth: A History of the City to 338 B.C.* Oxford.

Sanders, L. J. (1987) *Dionysius I of Syracuse and Greek Tyranny*. Kent.

Schuhl, P.-M. (1946) "Platon et l'activité politique de l'Académie." *Revue des études grecques* 59: 46–53.

Schmid, B. (1947) "Studien zur griechischen Ktisissagen." Diss., University of Freiburg i.d. Schweiz.

Schneider, O. (1856) *Nicander*. Leipzig.

Scodel, R. (1980) *The Trojan Trilogy of Euripides*. Göttingen.

Sealey, R. (1976) *A History of the Greek City States, 700–338 B.C.* Berkeley.

Segal, C. (1981) *Tragedy and Civilization: An Interpretation of Sophocles*. Cambridge, Mass.

Seibert, J. (1979) *Die politischen Flüchtlinge und Verbannten in der griechischen Geschichte*. Darmstadt.

Seidensticker, B. (1978) "Archilochus and Odysseus." *Greek, Roman, and Byzantine Studies* 19: 5–22.

Sergent, B. (1984) *L'homosexualité dans la mythologie grecque*. Paris.

Servais, J. (1969) "Herodote et la chronologie des Cypselids." *L'antiquité classique* 38: 28–81.

Shapiro, H. A. (1989) *Art and Cult under the Tyrants at Athens*. Mainz.

———. (1976) "Personification of Abstract Concepts in Greek Art and Literature to the End of the Fifth Century B.C." Diss., New York University.

Shipley, G. (1987) *History of Samos, 800–188 B.C.* Oxford.

Spahn, P. (1977) *Mittelschicht und Polisbildung*. Frankfurt.

Stahl, M. (1987) *Aristokraten und Tyrannen im archaischen Athen*. Stuttgart.

Starr, C. (1977) *The Economic and Social Growth of Early Greece, 800–500 B.C.* New York.

Bibliography

Stauffenberg, A. von. (1963) *Trinakria: Sizilien und Grossgriechenland in archaischer und frühklassischer Zeit*. Munich.

——. (1960) "Dorieus." *Historia* 9: 181–215.

Stein-Hölkeskamp, E. (1989) *Adelskultur und Polisgesellschaft*. Stuttgart.

Stoneman, R. (1991) "Lyric and Society." *Classical Review* n.s. 41: 351–54.

——. (1984) "The Ideal Courtier: Pindar and Hieron in *Pythian* 2." *Classical Quarterly* 34: 43–49.

Strosetzki, N. (1954) "Motive in Gründungslegende." Diss., University of Leipzig.

Szegedy-Maszak, A. (1978) "Legends of the Greek Lawgivers." *Greek, Roman, and Byzantine Studies* 19: 199–209.

Taylor, M. (1981) *The Tyrant Slayers*. New York.

Thalmann, W. G. (1988) "Thersites: Comedy, Scapegoats, and Heroic Ideology in the *Iliad*." *Transactions of the American Philological Association* 118: 1–28.

Thomas, R. (1989) *Oral Tradition and Written Record in Classical Athens*. Cambridge.

Toher, M. (1989) "On the Use of Nicolaus's Historical Fragments." *Classical Antiquity* 8: 159–72.

Tozzi, P. (1978) *La rivolta ionica*. Pisa.

Ure, P. N. (1922) *The Origin of Tyranny*. Cambridge.

Vallet, G. (1958) *Rhégion et Zankle*. Paris.

Vernant, J.-P. (1982) "From Oedipus to Periander: Lameness, Tyranny, Incest in Legend and History." *Arethusa* 15: 19–38.

——. (1978) *Mythe et pensée chez les Grecs*. Paris.

——. (1974) "Le mariage." In *Mythe et société en Grèce ancienne*, 57–81. Paris.

Veyne, P. (1988) *Did the Greeks Believe Their Myths: An Essay on the Constitutive Imagination*. Translated by P. Wissing. Chicago.

Vidal-Naquet, P. (1978) "Plato's Myth of the Statesman: The Ambiguities of the Golden Age and of History." *Journal of Hellenic Studies* 98: 132–41.

Vlastos, G. (1970) "Equality and Justice in Early Greek Cosmologies." In *Studies in Presocratic Philosophy*, 56–91. London.

——. (1946) "Solonian Justice." *Classical Philology* 41: 65–83.

Walcot, P. (1978) *Envy and the Greeks: A Study of Human Behavior*. Warminster.

Wallace, R. (1985) *The Areopagus Council to 307 B.C.* Baltimore.

——. (1983) "The Date of Solon's Reforms." *American Journal of Ancient History* 8: 81–95.

Wallinga, H. T. (1984) "The Ionian Revolt." *Mnemosyne* 37: 401–37.

Waurick, G. (1975) "Kunstraub der Römer: Untersuchungen zu seinen Anfänge anhang der Inschriften." *Jahrbuch des Römisch-germanistischen Zentralmuseums Mainz* 22: 2.1–46.

Werner, R. (1971) "Probleme der Rechtsbeziehungen zwischen Metropolis und Apoikie." *Chiron* 1: 19–73.

West, M. L. (1974) *Studies in Greek Elegy and Iambus*. New York.

Bibliography

Westlake, H. D. (1969) "Dion: A Study in Liberation." In *Essays on Greek Historians and Greek History*. Manchester.

Wilamowitz, U. von. (1922) *Pindaros*. Berlin.

Wilde, O. (1965) *The Importance of Being Earnest*. New York.

Will, E. (1955) *Korinthiaka: Recherches sur l'histoire et la civilisation de Corinthe des origines aux Guerres Médiques*. Paris.

Will, F. (1958) "Solon's Consciousness of Himself." *Transactions of the American Philological Association* 89: 301–11.

Woolf, V. (1929) *A Room of One's Own*. New York.

Young, D. (1968) *Three Odes of Pindar: A Literary Study of Pythian 11, Pythian 3, and Olympian 7*. Leiden.

Zeitlin, F. L. (1986) "Thebes: Theater of Self and Society in Athenian Drama." In *Greek Tragedy and Political Theory*, edited by J. P. Euben, 101–41. Berkeley.

———. (1984) "The Dynamics of Misogyny in the *Oresteia*." In *Women in the Ancient World*, edited by J. Peradotto and J. P. Sullivan, 159–94. Albany, N.Y.

Ziegler, K. (1948) "Tyche." In *Paulys Realencyclopädie der classischen Altertumswissenschaft*, 2nd. ser., 7B: 1689–96.

Zörner, G. (1971) "Kypselos und Pheidon: Untersuchungen zur frühen griechischen Tyrannis." Diss., University of Marburg.

Züchner, W. (1942) *Griechische Klappspiegel*. Berlin.

Index

Index

Index

Index

Library of Congress Cataloging-in-Publication Data

McGlew, James F., b. 1955
   Tyranny and political culture in ancient Greece / James F. McGlew.
     p. cm.
   Includes bibliographical references and index.
   ISBN 0-8014-2787-8
   1. Despotism—Greece—History.   2. Greece—Politics and government—To
146 B.C.   3. Greece—History—Age of Tyrants, 7th–6th centuries, B.C.   I. Title.
JC75.D4M38   1993
321'.6'0938—dc20   93-15653